Listen with the Ear of the Heart

Eastman/Rochester Studies in Ethnomusicology

Ellen Koskoff, Senior Editor
Eastman School of Music
(ISSN: 2161-0290)

*Burma's Pop Music Industry:
Creators, Distributors, Censors*
Heather MacLachlan

*Yorùbá Music in the Twentieth Century:
Identity, Agency and Performance Practice*
Bode Omojola

Javanese Gamelan and the West
Sumarsam

Gender in Chinese Music
Edited by Rachel Harris, Rowan Pease, and Shzr Ee Tan

*Performing Gender, Place, and Emotion in Music:
Global Perspectives*
Edited by Fiona Magowan and Louise Wrazen

Music, Indigeneity, Digital Media
Edited by Thomas R. Hilder, Henry Stobart, and Shzr Ee Tan

*Listen with the Ear of the Heart:
Music and Monastery Life at Weston Priory*
Maria S. Guarino

Listen with the Ear of the Heart

Music and Monastery Life at Weston Priory

Maria S. Guarino

UNIVERSITY OF ROCHESTER PRESS

Support for this publication was provided by the Howard Hanson Institute for American Music of the Eastman School of Music at the University of Rochester and by a grant from the H. Earle Johnson Fund of the Society for American Music.

Copyright © 2018 by Maria S. Guarino

All Rights Reserved. Except as permitted under current legislation, no part of this work may be photocopied, stored in a retrieval system, published, performed in public, adapted, broadcast, transmitted, recorded, or reproduced in any form or by any means, without the prior permission of the copyright owner.

First published 2018
Transferred to digital printing and reprinted in paperback 2020

University of Rochester Press
668 Mt. Hope Avenue, Rochester, NY 14620, USA
www.urpress.com
and Boydell & Brewer Limited
PO Box 9, Woodbridge, Suffolk IP12 3DF, UK
www.boydellandbrewer.com

Hardcover ISBN: 978-1-58046-910-4
Paperback ISBN: 978-1-58046-992-0
ISSN: 2161-0290

Library of Congress Cataloging-in-Publication Data

Names: Guarino, Maria S., author.
Title: Listen with the ear of the heart : music and monastery life at Weston Priory / Maria S. Guarino.
Other titles: Eastman/Rochester studies in ethnomusicology ; v. 7.
Description: Rochester : University of Rochester Press, 2018. | Series: Eastman/Rochester studies in ethnomusicology, ISSN 2161-0290 ; v. 7
Identifiers: LCCN 2017057637 | ISBN 9781580469104 (hardcover : alk. paper)
Subjects: LCSH: Church music—Vermont—Weston. | Music in monasteries—Vermont—Weston. | Benedictines—Vermont—Weston. | Weston Priory (Weston, Vt.)
Classification: LCC ML3011.8.W37 G83 2018 | DDC 781.71/200974365—dc23 LC record available at https://lccn.loc.gov/2017057637

A catalogue record for this title is available from the British Library.

For my Mom and Dad, who took me to the library, taught me to search for God, and let me quit hockey to become a musician. This book, and the journey described in its pages, would be nothing without them.

Contents

Preface	ix
Acknowledgments	xiii
Introduction	1
1 Ethnography in a Monastery	21
2 Singing like Benedictines: A Visit with Gregorian Chant	43
3 Singing like Weston Monks	61
4 My Novitiate: Understanding Craft	91
5 Music as Craft: Creating a Tradition	111
6 Monastic Spirituality: Learning to Listen with the Ear of the Heart	142
Notes	165
Bibliography	173
Index	179

Photographs follow p. 90.

Preface

Resonance: Music in Catholicism

It was an unseasonably cool April morning when I walked up the steep hill from Morningside guesthouse as I had done countless times before. Over the years, brother John and I had often talked about our various writing projects.[1] That morning, we discussed my progress with the present book and his own work to share some of their founder's writings with a new group of oblates. I was helping him with that project, so he handed me a pile of papers. On one of the sheets he had written: "This is the sign of the novice: always to return to the beginning." I had heard him talk in this way before, about how we are always standing on the threshold of a new beginning, always novices in a perpetual experience of learning and relearning. It was serendipitous. I was struggling through manuscript revisions, trying to establish a sense of direction, and here was brother John telling me: return to the beginning.

That is exactly what I did. I went back to the guesthouse to reflect on the experiences that sparked my interest in my research area. As the chapters that follow attest, I had spent years thinking about issues of ethnography and field research in a monastery. But that morning, I considered that it was not ethnography that pointed me toward Weston Priory. It was music. I knew the brothers' music well from my Catholic upbringing. The folk-inspired liturgical music of Weston Priory became an important part of the soundscape for generations of Catholics throughout the latter half of the twentieth century as guitars replaced organs and communal singing became the new normal in the post–Vatican II American Church. I wanted to see, hear, and understand the music in its home context. But more than that, I wanted to understand how and why people use music—any kind of music—in their religious practices and what their choices and discourses tell us about why that matters.

During the first year of my graduate work, I did a brief ethnographic research project with musicians in a local Catholic parish with three different Masses featuring either a Gregorian chant ensemble, a choir with organ accompaniment, or a praise band consisting of drum set, electric guitar, bass, and vocalists. I found that the members of the chant ensemble espoused the strictest definition of permissible liturgical music. For them, Gregorian chant was the true music of the Church even though it was rarely heard outside of monasteries. One member experienced the organ as appropriate for church, but under no circumstances did she think guitars were acceptable. Most members of the chant ensemble shared her opinion, which is not uncommon in Catholicism: instruments reminiscent of popular music do not belong in church.

I chose that field site anticipating that it would engage exactly this type of conflict over liturgical music, and my experience there played an important role in shaping my early approach to my work with the Weston monks. I thought in terms of simple binaries: chant versus folk music, sacred versus popular styles, Latin versus vernacular language. The Weston monks were famous for their vernacular liturgical music accompanied on guitars, and I wanted to know why and how they replaced Gregorian chant and Latin—the traditional liturgical style of Benedictines—with music resulting from their own creativity, reflective of the popular culture of mid-twentieth-century America. I hoped that this kind of investigation would speak broadly to the sociocultural significance of communal singing while uncovering the deep significance of music in liturgy as it allows participants to navigate their identities, relationships to one another, and ideas about community, tradition, spirituality, and belief.

My early approach was founded not only on my own experience but also on scholarly discourses, which mirror those of musicians, liturgists, clergy, and parishioners. Since the sweeping reforms of the Second Vatican Council, the debates have been contentious. One side celebrates the reforms and the resulting musical creativity, the other decries both as a "crisis" of the liturgy.[2] Certain kinds of music are either appropriate or inappropriate, good or bad, authentic or inauthentic, effective or ineffective in worship. On one side, folk music is positioned as the root of the crisis. On the other, Gregorian chant is the enemy of reform.[3]

When I spoke with the members of the chant ensemble during that early field research project, these issues emerged strongly within a familiar tension wherein newer worship styles are positioned against those that have come to be seen, over the course of time, as properly sacred and traditional. These issues are not limited to Catholicism. Liturgical music is often a site of tense debate illustrating a perennial question that has confronted religious communities and institutions for, presumably, as long as there has been religion: what are the rules of worship? A worship community uses music, actively and consciously, to create ritual by creating the communal bonds that make an authoritative, powerful, and effective religious experience. The issues are many, and the stakes are high. What is and is not acceptable? What sorts of words and actions are appropriate? Which best reflect the religious beliefs in question? What language do we use to address the divine? Is it the work of all the faithful, or only a select few?

These questions apply broadly across the rituals of everyday life. What we do and how we do it participate in the most basic aspects of who we are. This is what I wanted to understand when I first knocked on the door of Weston Priory. Mine is not a theological or historical study aimed at determining what sorts of music are best or most appropriate for liturgy. It is not a defense of one style over another. It is instead about how musical performance becomes a rich, dynamic, complex context within which participants shape, enact, and lend meaning to their lives. It is about navigating the dynamic spaces between individuality and collectivity, self and other, creativity and tradition, historical consciousness and local authenticity.

Considering these questions from an anthropological perspective within a Christian context is relatively uncommon. Fanella Cannell points out that Christianity has been underrepresented in ethnography for a variety of reasons related to the way the humanities developed relative to Christianity. She suggests that anthropology's approach to—and avoidance of—Christianity has potentially limited its development.[4] Her work prompts a question: what might we learn as a discipline by engaging more deeply and thoroughly with Christianity? Or, in my case: by taking seriously, from an ethnographic perspective, the epistemologies and ontologies of a community of Benedictines, might I learn as much about humanistic inquiry as I learn about music, liturgy, and monks? The answer is a resounding Yes.

Extending Cannell's questions to my own discipline further explores what ethnomusicology might gain by engaging thoroughly with Christianity. The study of music in religion has long been an important field for ethnomusicologists, with a growing subset of scholars studying Christian contexts. Jeff Titon's *Powerhouse for God*, Melvin Butler's work on Caribbean music and religion, Timothy Rommen's "*Mek Some Noise*," Glenn Hinson's *Fire in My Bones*, and Deidre Sklar's *Dancing with the Virgin* are all important precursors to the present study as each approaches the problems and possibilities of the ethnographic study of Christian practices and beliefs. Similarly, the volume edited by Monique Ingalls, Carolyn Landau, and Tom Wagner, *Christian Congregational Music*, and the important collection edited by Philip Bohlman and others, *Music in American Religious Experience*, speak broadly to a seemingly basic—but in fact deeply complex—question: Why do we sing in church? The practice is so common as to seem universal. If we try to understand it in all its variety and complexity, across various articulations and in many traditions, what might we better understand about what it means to be human?

Engaging these ideas in a living Benedictine monastery is about far more than Latin or vernacular, chant or folk, guitars or organs. Instead, it is about uncovering the deeply held values, ontological and epistemological questions, and the very real and often terribly mundane demands of living in a community. And so this book is a study of liturgical music, the creation of tradition, and the Benedictine way of being, but it is also an interrogation of the very processes of research and writing. It is ethnography in pursuit of ethnography, a project that constantly turns back on itself in the contemplative model of monastic *conversatio*.

Both Vatican II and the call toward reflexive ethnography seem as if they are far behind in the rearview mirror where we leave the things we used to argue about. But questions of Latin or not Latin, guitars or not guitars, participating people or silent people are as divisive now as they were fifty years ago. Similarly, in the humanities, we may never reach consensus on the best way to conduct research, the appropriate balance between the subjective and objective, or the ideal writing style. In what follows, I contribute my voice to these ever-evolving, dynamic dialogues about human life, musical performance, religious experience, and the perennial question: how do we know what we know?

Acknowledgments

Gratitude and the importance of community were among the most important lessons I learned from the Benedictines. I am forever grateful to my Weston community. The Weston Monks said "yes" when I first knocked at their door and again every time I returned. Their hospitality and openness, as well as the gift of their time, conversation, encouragement, and friendship, not only made this book possible, it pushed my work in exciting directions as they offered me a unique glimpse into the monastic way of life. I am grateful to all of them: brother Alvaro, brother Augustine, brother Columba, brother Daniel, brother Elias, brother John, brother Mark, brother Michael, brother Peter, brother Philip, brother Placid, brother Richard, and brother Robert. I am especially grateful to brother John, who believed in me and in this project before I even knew what it would become. His gentle guidance and wisdom run throughout these pages.

My thanks are also due to my intellectual community, the professors who inspired and instructed me on my way. Michelle Kisliuk has been a constant source of support and encouragement. Her own work was an early inspiration as I first encountered ethnomusicology and ethnography. Her wisdom, experience, and critiques guided me in my journey from student to scholar as she encouraged me to find my own voice. Bruce Holsinger introduced me to the long history of monastic life and offered consistent support of my work to study living Benedictines. Kevin Hart introduced me to phenomenology and gently guided my study of Christian mysticism. He helped me to appreciate the poetry and the mystery. I am also grateful to my other professors at the University of Virginia, especially Richard Will and Melvin Butler; my professors at Tufts University, especially Rabbi Jeffrey Summit and David Locke; and my professors at the University of Vermont, especially D. Thomas Toner and Wayne Schneider. Each has contributed time, thought, energy, and support along the way.

I am deeply grateful to my family for their unconditional love and support. To my mother, for instilling in me a love of learning, for seeing a future scholar in a curious and verbose child, and for always encouraging me to realize my highest potential and pursue my goals. To my father, for showing me what it means to live with wisdom, faith, compassion, and kindness. To my brother and sister, for their love, laughter, and constant encouragement. To my husband, for believing in me and for never failing to support my dreams. To my children, Benedict and Zoe, who are the light and joy of my heart. And to Lily, my constant canine companion.

I also owe a great deal of thanks to the University of Rochester press. To Julia Cook and Ellen Koskoff, for their support of my vision for this book. I am especially grateful to Julia, whose comments, suggestions, and friendship have been invaluable. I am also grateful to the anonymous reviewers who gave their time to read my early manuscript and revisions; their reflections and insights have been extremely helpful. I similarly owe my thanks to colleagues at the 2014 National Endowment for the Humanities Summer Institute on the Study of Religion. They challenged and inspired me to engage more deeply with various aspects of my work.

In addition to all of these many people, my research was made possible by generous funding support: a field research grant from the Wenner-Gren Foundation, a monastic studies grant from the American Benedictine Academy, and a graduate summer research grant from the Buckner W. Clay Endowment for the Humanities.

Introduction

Contemplation is the highest expression of man's intellectual and spiritual life. It is that life itself, fully awake, fully active, fully aware that it is alive. It is spiritual wonder. It is spontaneous awe at the sacredness of life, of being.
—Thomas Merton, *New Seeds of Contemplation*

On Being Present

It was a brisk May morning when I stepped out of the guesthouse into the predawn darkness in what had become the daily ritual of my ethnomusicological field research with the Benedictine monks of Weston Priory in the rural Vermont mountains. The monastery bells echoed in the distance as I walked along the dirt road connecting the guesthouse to the chapel. The sound of gravel crunching beneath my feet seemed an affront to the intense stillness of the night forest around me. I thought about the archive of bulletins brother John handed me earlier in the week—a pile of letters and pamphlets saved over the course of nearly sixty years. Having read through the earliest bulletins before Compline—the last prayer of the day—the previous evening, I smiled as I recalled a 1961 bulletin with the brothers' humorous description of gathering for the first Divine Office prayer of the day: "Getting up at that hour is distinctly not among the pleasures in life. Yet there is always competition among the brethren to reach the chapel first."[1] I knew that no matter how fast I walked, brother Columba would already be in the dark chapel. He always beat me there, regardless of how early I arrived. But seeing him each morning sitting in quiet repose had become a kind of comfort. I knew he would be there. It may be a simple statement, but this realization allowed me to begin to understand the complex experience of presence—the presence of selves and others—in a monastic community and in field research. I was alone with my thoughts in the dark forest. I would sit in the quiet stillness of the nearly empty chapel for the long Vigil prayer. I would speak to no one until at least late morning that day, if not later. But the brothers would be there. They would be present. I could depend on that.

I was certainly not the first ethnographer to feel more or less on my own in relatively unfamiliar surroundings. Even those not working in monasteries confront feelings of isolation as they encounter the intensity of the personal, emotional, social, and intellectual demands of immersive field research. During the Vigil that morning, I thought about this in terms of the idea of presence, and the concept of "full presence" that the brothers often discussed. As I watched them sing the morning psalms, meditatively chanting in collective unison, I considered what it meant for them to be present at that daily ritual, and for me to be present as a participating-thinking-writing-inquiring observer. Brother John—who had been a Weston monk for more than fifty years—had recently spoken with me about the importance of the communal element of their Divine Office liturgies. He explained that the prayer could only be fully experienced if the brothers collectively transcended their everyday discourses. Aside from the obvious implication that the prayer would not happen if the brothers did not show up or if they were distracted, I was not yet sure I understood what brother John meant. However, I was beginning to see that the collectivity of monastic life—the presence of selves and others—was more complex and important than I had anticipated. And it would be critical to my gaining any kind of meaningful understanding of the unfamiliar way of life around me.

I had failed to anticipate this in part because monastics spend a great deal of time in silence and solitude.[2] Fostering internal and external space while learning to dwell in that space is a central part of their way of life. The term "monk" comes from the Greek, *monachos*, meaning single or solitary, and while the Benedictines are founded on Saint Benedict's "cenobitic turn" toward a communal instead of hermitical way of life, monasticism emphasizes separateness and solitude for monks and visiting researchers alike.[3] I needed to understand the relationship and possible tensions between these two dimensions—the communal and the individual—in order to understand the brothers' concept of presence, and what it had to do with their music, their lives, and my work to understand both.

To this end, I considered the role of silence while the brothers sang their Morning Vigil prayer. Granted, it is difficult *not* to think about silence when living in a monastery. Benedictines have no strict vow of silence, but they do observe periods of silence each day, and they strive to foster what they call a "spirit of silence." The sixth-century Rule of Benedict—the primary normative document of Benedictine monasticism—cautions that words should be chosen with care and used sparingly. In his chapter on "Restraint of Speech," Saint Benedict says that "evil" speech must obviously be avoided, but sometimes even "good words are to be left unsaid out of esteem for silence" (6:2).[4] This is intended, among other things, to foster a quietness of mind that minimizes the internal chatter and distractible tendencies of the human consciousness. Without this internal stillness, it is difficult to be fully present to self and others. I wrote in my field notes after Morning Vigil that day: "I think I might be incapable of full presence. My mind is ever filled with chatter."

In his book on Benedictine spirituality, Michael Casey says that compulsive communicators might not be the best candidates for a monastic vocation.[5] When I read that during my field research I recognized my own personality, and I also recognized academia. What is the scholar's vocation but one of compulsive communication, both written and oral? Ethnography in particular seemed to me to rest on a foundation of nearly incessant communicating: conversations, interviews, meetings, oral histories, music-making, and writing, writing, writing. It is perhaps surprising then that silence became a key not only to understanding the role of music in the life of the monastery but also to understanding ethnographic research and writing, as well as the nature and potential of humanistic inquiry. In monastic silence it is both a challenge and a gift to be relieved from the constant chatter of everyday life. It is an invitation to enter into deeper ways of knowing by seeking understanding and embracing unknowing. According to Benedictine philosophy, if I can dedicate myself to this silence, my words will come from a place of deeper stillness, reflection, and understanding.[6] A monk will not be the isolated monachos but a vital part of a collective consciousness. Likewise, I will cease to be the isolated ethnographer and instead become engaged in the dynamic interpersonal space of sociocultural research. It is the foundation of an inward-turned contemplative disposition that looks outward toward the presence of others.

In this Introduction, I explore that disposition as I describe some of the experiences that challenged me, and, in so doing, became central to my research with the monks of Weston Priory. I describe how I came to understand and apply a research method I think of as contemplative ethnography. This positions my work in wider academic narratives, and it acquaints readers with my approach to long-term immersive field research with a community of monks. It also establishes a foundation for the narrative that follows in the rest of the book, which is intended to evoke my own process and recreate the rhythms of learning among Benedictines. This process was a years-long experience of gradually gaining understanding of both the monastic and ethnographic vocations, and the role of musical performance therein. It was the work of letting each experience open up to and build upon the next in the unexpected and unexpectable spaces of field research. Allowing my narrative to unfold similarly is intended not only to mimic this process steeped in monastic dialogue and discourse but also to make readers "present" in this process in the hope that it will spark further ideas and points for contemplation and conversation. This does not require agreement. While I do hope that my work resonates with readers, I learned from the Benedictines that opening up a dialogue creates space for contrary viewpoints, differing interpretations, and counteropinions. But this is what makes conversations worthwhile and productive. It is my hope that my study of a small Benedictine community in rural Vermont prompts and contributes meaningfully to such conversations about music, monasticism, and sociocultural research.

To this end, this Introduction does the usual work of describing my research context and goals, but with a focus on some of the problems and possibilities I encountered. This allows me to discuss the research methods that emerge within and inform and support my work. These methods are inclined toward sensibilities I encountered in the monastery: listening, presence, and a focus on the complex interpersonal spaces and shared experiences of knowledge and being. Familiar to ethnographers, these topics form a perspective that I find meaningful not just for researching monasticism or even religion generally, but as a broader ethnographic sensibility for humanistic inquiry. It offers a way to account for and push beyond necessary but tired discussions of reflexivity in sociocultural research. Never hyper-self-conscious and yet never losing sight of the role of the self in complex self-other dynamics, a contemplative ethnographic disposition maintains the vital assertion of reflexivity—that we as researchers are a presence in the field, a positioned subject among subjects—but it reframes the discussion. Even when thoroughly positioned and reflexive, ethnography is not a self-centered pursuit. Rather, it is a complex interpersonal dialogue founded on the researcher's ability to interrogate the complexities of presence by turning toward the self and, in so doing, turning toward others in the rich exchanges that unfold over time and reward our patient waiting, our careful preparation, and our mindful attention with knowledge and understanding.

Understanding the Unfamiliar

The monks of Weston Priory live a contemplative monastic life in a small Benedictine monastery in the mountains of southern Vermont. They gather for prayer five times per day: Vigil in the early morning, Terce at mid-morning, None in the early afternoon, Vespers in the evening, and Compline at night. They add a late morning Eucharist service to the schedule on Saturdays and Sundays. This daily round of prayers is called the Divine Office, or *opus dei*, meaning, "work of God." The brothers are not cloistered; their prayers are open to the public, and their guests, who stay in the monastery guesthouses, join them for prayer, meals, and work throughout the day.

Benedictine prayers are primarily sung. Unlike many Benedictines, the Weston monks do not use Gregorian chant; instead, they use music of their own composition featuring a style that blends monastic practices with the guitars, poetic lyrics, narrative style, and simple, memorable melodies typical of mid-twentieth-century popular American folk music. They began recording and publishing their music in the early 1970s as part of a wider movement toward new liturgical practices following Vatican II, and their songs became popular in Catholic parishes. Alongside groups like the Saint Louis Jesuits and singer/songwriters like John Michael Talbot, the Weston monks were part of a liturgical movement that acted as both a catalyst for and a reflection of the sweeping changes that resonated throughout Catholicism during the 1970s and 1980s. The Priory gained a reputation as the home of the famous "singing monks." This reputation draws thousands of visitors to Weston each year.

When I arrived at the Priory, I followed the ethnographer's mantra of participant-observation by immersing myself in the rhythms of monasticism. This turned out to be easier said than done. After driving picturesque winding back roads at the beginning of my first visit, I finally turned up Priory Hill Road and saw the monastery: an old brown farmhouse tucked into the rolling hills of the Green Mountains. A small stone chapel extended from one end of the house with a wooden bell tower at the corner. A long gray building extended from the other end of the house. Small outbuildings lined a gravel driveway. There was a large pond surrounded by gardens and rolling fields. A few people sat in lawn chairs around the pond. Two men worked in the gardens. A sheep bleated in a field somewhere behind the monastery. Others bleated in response.

When they confirmed my visit, the brothers told me to go to the Gallery Shop upon my arrival so that someone could let them know I had arrived. A small sign on a building at the back of the property indicated that it was the shop. I entered to see a tall woman with dark hair and a cheerful smile standing behind the counter. I introduced myself. She told me the brothers were expecting me and directed me to wait in the parlor inside the monastery. Following her instructions, I walked back outside, across the courtyard, and into the monastery. The heavy door closed with a soft *whoosh*, and I stepped into a sitting room. The familiar activity of a summer afternoon faded behind me. I hoped I was in the right place. After several minutes, a man came through a side door. He wore plain khaki pants and a pale orange, short-sleeved, button-down shirt. He made eye contact with me, smiled broadly, extended his hand, and nodded as he spoke in a gentle tone, "Welcome. I'm brother Philip."

I stood, shook his hand, and said, "hello" and "thank you." I was unsure what else to say. I had never met a monk before, but this middle-aged man in a simple shirt and pants hardly fit the usual image of an austere holy man hidden away in a mountain monastery. His smile put me at ease, but it also surprised me. When I reflected on my response later, I realized that I had expected him to be more severe and unapproachable, perhaps intimidating or foreboding.

Brother Philip handed me an envelope with, "Welcome, Maria! Morningside," written across the front in large, loopy handwriting. Inside was a key to the women's guesthouse along with information about prayer times and meals. He told me about the bells: they would ring a few minutes before each prayer throughout the day, at mealtime, at the end of the work period, and before evening recreation. I tried to commit these instructions to memory as we walked down the cloister walk hallway, but I was already forgetting the details—did the bells ring on the hour? At noon? Before prayer?

When we reached the refectory, brother Philip pointed out the long wooden table set against the wall and explained that meals would be served buffet-style and eaten in silence while one brother read aloud from a book, usually nonfiction. He showed me my place at the table, arranged in a U-shape with room for the thirteen brothers and several guests. All of the seats at the table faced inward toward the middle of the room. At dinner several hours later, after misinterpreting the bells and nearly missing Vespers, I would disturb the silent monastic mealtime by sending a cherry tomato rocketing off of my plate into the middle of the room when I tried, noisily, to stab it with my fork. I would fail to finish my supper by the end of the meal, gracelessly shoveling soup into my mouth while the brothers cleaned up the refectory around me. I would sit in the chapel for more than forty-five minutes before Compline after again misinterpreting the bells. I had no idea how thoroughly bewildering my first day in monastery life would be as brother Philip walked me back to the parlor. We parted with a smile and a nod, and the Priory door closed with a soft *whoosh* behind me as I returned to the warm sunshine and relaxed activity of a summer afternoon.

During my initial interactions with the brothers, I struggled to get my bearings in the rhythms of monasticism, and I was unsure how to engage with the people around me. This was perhaps evidence of the romanticized image of monasticism that has, in the words of Katherine Bergeron, enchanted the modern world.[7] Yet monastery life is filled with the daily realities and social interactions that are part of any home. The Weston monks spend as much time singing the Divine Office as they do reading, cleaning the kitchen, weeding the gardens, shoveling snow, caring for animals, beekeeping, washing laundry, chopping wood, and other work. As one of the brothers once pointed out, in an effort to describe his experience of the mundane realities of monasticism: there is a time for prayer and meditation, but there is also a time to change the filters on the septic tank.

These are indeed ordinary realities that help to temper a romanticized image of monks, but monastery life was far from familiar. I had embarked on field research in my own backyard—I was hardly more than sixty miles from the town where I grew up. I had spent months preparing, and years studying. Nevertheless, I was struck by the intensity of ethnographic research. This came roaring to my attention late one night very early in my field research when a shriek came from the room at the other end of the hallway in Morningside, the women's guesthouse: "Aiyeeee!!"

Hearing the shriek from the warmth of my bed, I felt certain that one of my fellow guests had seen a mouse. I did not want to deal with a mouse; I am not fond of them. But as a voice called to me in thickly accented English: "Maria! Are you awake?" I reluctantly got out of my bed, put on a brave face, and opened the door. Brother Daniel's mother, Lupita, stood in the dark hallway. She had come from Mexico City to visit her son. She was in a white nightgown with long sleeves, a high neckline, and a lacy collar. She held a flashlight in one hand, and a Spanish-English dictionary in the other. Looking horrified, she said, "I see—a—mouse!" She said the words carefully, pointing to the entry for "mouse" (*el ratòn*) in her dictionary.

I followed Lupita to her room, where she stood outside the bathroom door and pointed, looking at me with a stricken expression. I looked into the bathroom but did not see a mouse. Between Lupita's limited English and my nonexistent Spanish, we communicated with gestures and single words. "Gone," I said, shaking my head, shrugging my shoulders, and smiling to show that everything would be okay. "Outside," I motioned with my hands and arms to indicate a scurrying mouse headed for the door. "No," she said shaking her head. "In—bathroom." She then began to motion with her arms as though she were sweeping the floor. "Do we have—sweep?" she asked, continuing to motion with her arms. She repeated the phrase and gesture, and, after several awkward moments of mutual misunderstanding, I finally realized she was asking for a broom.

I found two brooms. Lupita took one, and I held the other, more as a show of solidarity than for any practical purpose. I did not have the fortitude to squash a little mouse. We must have been quite a sight standing there in our pajamas, holding brooms, staring at the tiny bathroom while Lupita pointed her flashlight into the dark corners. Our language barrier being what it was, we communicated with gestures, primarily encouraging smiles and shrugging shoulders.

We spent more than thirty minutes in our vigil outside the bathroom door, but no little creatures scurried across the floor. I finally retired to bed and encouraged Lupita to do the same. The bells at the monastery rang at 4:45 a.m. for the Morning Vigil prayer, and I wanted to get some sleep. I sensed that Lupita would not sleep soundly or even go back into her room until someone found the mouse and got rid of it. As I watched her settle in on the living room couch to sleep with her broom propped up next to her, I hoped that she would be able to rest. I also hoped that the mouse was not making a nest in the warm, fluffy down of my sleeping bag.

In my research proposals, I had made claims about what I would do in the field and how I would gather and interpret data; but when I arrived at the monastery, field recorder and notebooks in hand, that process was no longer theoretical. It involved real people whose lives and experiences were not my own, and whose perspectives I could not presume to understand. This was obviously true of a group of men living a relatively secluded religious life, but my experience with Lupita brought me to a deeper level of understanding about the space between self and other and the complex processes of gaining understanding. Standing guard with brooms and flashlights outside her bathroom door, we established a bond of friendship and interpersonal understanding, but we were not suddenly of one mind. Our language barriers illustrate this only too well. I could not then, and I cannot now, represent Lupita's feelings about that night. However thoroughly I can describe what she said and did, I can only tell the story from my own perspective, based on my own experience. Ethnographers had made this kind of observation long before I stood outside that bathroom, but by removing a shared language from our interaction, I gained a very immediate, practical awareness of the critical role of interpersonal experience, empathy, and close observation of gesture and behavior—that of others as well as my own—in generating understanding and creating ethnographic knowledge.

During a later field research visit, I again encountered the difficulties of understanding the unfamiliar in the interpersonal spaces of ethnography when I drove the back road between the guesthouses and the monastery on my way to Morning Vigil. It was November, and a thunderstorm had rolled into Weston during the night causing a fallen tree to block the road. Encountering it, I got out of my car to find that the long-dead tree was rotted through and had snapped in half when it fell. As I tried to move the tree, the glow of headlights down the road told me that a car was approaching from the men's guesthouse. The car sloshed to a stop in the deep mud. I breathed a sigh of relief as I waited for the man to help with the tree. And I waited. Standing in the driving rain, I realized with disbelief that the man was not getting out of his car. Frustrated, I bent down, picked up the smaller half of the broken tree, and flung it out of the way. As I decided how to manage the larger half, the man suddenly got out of his car, ran to where I was standing, and helped me toss the tree into the woods.

I thanked him and started back to my car, but he stopped me. He hollered against the storm: "I was sitting there thinking, what is that girl doing? I thought you must be having some sort of religious experience. It seems like a strange time to be doing that, but whatever." He shrugged his shoulders and raised his eyebrows as he said "whatever." I hardly knew how to react. Perhaps he wanted to excuse his lack of chivalry, but I felt rather offended, as if I had been forced into a stereotype of women and spirituality. And his statement suggested that he was unconvinced that I *wasn't* having some sort of religious experience. We each got into our respective cars and continued on our way to the chapel for Morning Vigil, but I could not stop thinking about our brief exchange. After spending much of the day reflecting on it, I realized that it raised an immediate ethnographic research issue: how would I ever come to understand an unfamiliar way of life when my experiences and expectations might lead me to very different conclusions than those of the people around me? A car stopped on a back road might indicate a moose, a fallen tree, or a woman having a religious experience in the rain. When there seems to be one obvious, reasonable conclusion—in this case, "tree"—and my preconceptions might cause me to be dismissive, even judgmental, of other perspectives—the "religious experience" suggestion—how do I remain open to many ways of knowing, especially in a religious setting? How do I learn to understand the world from another person's perspective? And how do I bring to consciousness the otherwise unconscious responses that might cause me to be dismissive or judgmental? Maybe I was having a religious experience.

This is perhaps the relationship of any two people: I see things one way, someone else sees things another way, and the interpersonal space of shared experience allows each of us to find our own kind of meaning while sharing some dimensions of that meaning. But in field research, I felt that I had created a space where the stakes of understanding—and the potential problems of misunderstanding—were higher. My experience in the rain helped me to realize the extent to which this could hinder my ability to engage in conversation with the brothers. Not only did I not know how to talk to monks, I feared that I lacked enough shared knowledge and experience to understand them in any meaningful way.

This calls to mind Clifford Geertz's famous example, from Gilbert Ryle, of the problem of understanding the meaning of a wink. How is one to know if a wink is a wink, a twitch, a parody of a wink, conspiracy, ridicule, satire, or something else? This supports Geertz's argument that thoroughly detailed—"thick"—description is essential in understanding meaning.[8] C. W. Watson pushes these ideas further in his discussion of anthropological fieldwork. He calls my experiences with the mouse and the tree "point[s] of departure" that are crucial to anthropological research. Instead of talking about the meaning of a wink, he talks about the meaning of a smile. He points out that a smile can mean many things, and we may miss that meaning even among people and circumstances very familiar to us. This becomes much more difficult in the "alien culture" of field research.[9]

How much murkier, then, must the experience, knowledge, and subjectivities of the ethnographer make these waters? Since the reflexive turn in anthropology, ethnographers generally recognize that we cannot—and would fail in trying to—become fly-on-the-wall observers accessing objective truth unknown to the people with whom we work.[10] My role in the field was not to understand the world from someone else's perspective *instead of* my own; it was not to shed myself of my subjectivities in order to capture objective truth and facts. Even though I had read a wide variety of reflexive, thoroughly positioned, subjective ethnographic writing, it took the immediacy of embedded field research to make me realize this. As I did, I also realized how much more straightforward, and less murky, "capturing facts" can seem. Watson discusses this as he defines field research as a process of "making ourselves inward with a culture to the point where we feel as comfortable with it as we do with our own." He finds that this leads to understanding as we realize, "even if we do not know the meaning of this one particular smile of the moment, we know at least the range it can encompass—we know how many types of ambiguity there are in the text."[11]

On the one hand, I wonder if this is really what field research is about. It suggests that if I can only become immersed enough, I will not get things wrong. Or, perhaps, I will know all of the possible ways that I can get things right. This seems like a variation on the theme of capturing facts, I am just capturing more possible facts. On the other hand, it also suggests that field research is not only a process of *knowing*, but a process of learning the extent of what we do not know. It is not about capturing facts but gradually seeing the vastness of the landscape, gradually knowing our not-knowing.

One of the virtues of this approach to the problem of (mis)understanding is that its focus is not primarily on the ethnographer and her ability to see, hear, know, understand, and thickly describe enough to totally comprehend the social and cultural realities around her. It instead opens up a focus on the interpersonal nature of ethnography and the reality that there will never be a point at which one's knowledge is complete. There is no single, final answer, only a dynamic, ever-changing context where a "me" and at least one "not-me" share words, gestures, and experiences. This speaks to the importance of an approach to research and writing that does more than simply bring the problems of understanding to consciousness. The researcher must learn to attend intentionally and critically to many layers of experience as she works to understand the extent of what she does not know.

Reflexivity, Dialogues, *Conversatio*

I found that this was not my default mode when I began my field research. I made a conscious effort to position myself within the monastery community as a researcher. I felt that I was not on retreat, as were the many guests who visited the Priory, and I endeavored to make that clear. I told myself that I was being honest with the people around me about my intentions. Looking back, however, I think I did this in order to claim a space as an observer. The moment I stepped into the field I adopted, like a reflex, the usual scholarly gaze that seeks to capture and represent an aspect of human life. I had not intended to be the objective scholar—in fact, I had intended just the opposite—but I tried to position myself that way nonetheless.

The reflexive turn in ethnography was old news by the time I started my field research, but still I read recent ethnographic scholarship that was built on the objective remove of the researcher, and I encountered studies that continued to question the omniscient scholarly voice. Clearly, the reflexive turn was still turning, and I was beginning to see why. In the moment of field research, I struggled to position myself. And while I knew that reflexivity was supposed to help me recognize the knowledge, worldviews, and experiences I brought with me into the field, it could not then become a means of reclaiming an objective space as an observer who had recognized, and thus conquered, her own subjectivities.

Part of the problem was that I expected to notice everything, write it all down in rich detail, and then figure out how to interpret it. I thought that the work was all on me, and the brothers and their guests would just do what they do so that I could observe and interpret. While I knew the ethnographer's mantra of participant-observation well, I had not yet discovered its real value, nor did I anticipate all that I would learn through participation in the everyday life and music of the monastery.

Turning this into a lived reality required a shift on my part as I adjusted to the Benedictine sensibilities around me. This became a long-term process of learning how to learn. That is perhaps an unusual phrase for a scholar—did I not know how to learn after many years of graduate school? I thought that I did, but, by immersing myself in the monastic way of life, I very quickly realized that my research would unfold in ways I could neither anticipate nor control.

My interactions with brother John were especially instructive in this process. For example, after supper in the evenings, I often helped him move the leftover food from the buffet table to the kitchen. One evening, I moved large pots of soup onto a rolling cart while brother John gathered up cutting boards, knives, and blocks of cheese. Other guests cleared and wiped the dining tables. Two brothers set out silverware for breakfast. The sounds of dishes being washed and put away intermingled with quiet conversations as everyone worked around the kitchen and refectory. As I moved down the table to gather the salad bowls, brother John asked if I had a pleasant afternoon. I told him that I had been working on writing some material on the early development of their music, and I was struggling to describe their daily prayers in a way that adequately captured the experience. I had only managed a kind of play-by-play that did not evoke the lived reality of the Divine Office. He stood behind the full cart, ready to roll it into the kitchen, and said that sometimes discourse is not equal to the task of capturing the ideas we want to convey. He suggested that we find new words when the old ones no longer work. With that, he rolled the cart into the kitchen, concluding the conversation without telling me what these "new words" might be, or giving any more concrete suggestion as to how to describe their music if discourse was not equal to the task. The dishes would not wash themselves while we stood around chatting about music, and brother John had said all that he needed to say. He was content to leave things open-ended by posing an idea for further thought. He opened up a dialogue by questioning my basic assumption: that words *could* describe experience.

This brief exchange was one of my earliest introductions to a monastic style of discourse, and it is illustrative both of the way my research unfolded and of my approach to organizing and presenting it in this book. In preparing to conduct interviews and engage in conversations in the field, I focused primarily on questions and answers. The researcher asks, the researched answers. The researcher analyzes the answers, then asks more questions. My conversations with Benedictines did not follow this pattern. The brothers welcomed me into long, gradually unfolding dialogues without clear answers, but where meaning(s) would emerge in the process, where I would gain insight by patiently attending to the experiences, relationships, and rich conversations that unfold over time.

When I started my research, I wanted to get it all very quickly. I wanted a sparkling revelation to jump out at me. What I found is that it is easy to be taken in by the novelty of monastic life. It is very unusual and striking, especially at first glance. But, to really understand it, I had to get under the surface and uncover the foundations, the little everyday moments and deep-rooted characteristics that define it and give it meaning. It can be easier, or at least more straightforward, to consume the unfamiliar as an outsider by taking in whatever one finds most appealing and accessible. I found it far more difficult to commit my time, presence, and mental energies to the long-term process of understanding and writing about a way of being that is not my own. Even as publication deadlines mean we must commit our thoughts and ideas to writing, seeking this kind of knowing is a lifetime pursuit that deeply engages, emerges from, and reflects the humanity toward which it is directed.

Benedictines have a term that speaks to this process: *conversatio*. The Rule of Benedict uses the phrase "coversatio morum" in chapter fifty-eight. It is often translated as fidelity to the monastic life, and is one of the promises—typically called vows—made by a novice monk. In practice, conversatio names the lifelong process of conversion to and through the monastic way of life. It is a fluid, dynamic concept rooted in the balance of talking and listening—conversation and silence, learning and reflecting—that becomes the heart of the monastic profession. Conversatio is about process and change in pursuit of and supported by the stability of the monastic family.

Directing my research sensibilities—and my writing—toward monastic conversatio meant focusing on rich, nuanced dialogues rooted in the long-term unfolding of questions and answers.[12] For me, conversatio as a research and writing method became a process of learning paradox and contradiction, mystery and uncertainty. While conversatio is arguably the oldest process through which to gain a thorough, deep understanding of Benedictine life, its paradox is that the knowledge and understanding it gives lead always and already to increasingly complex questions and uncertainties within which the monastic person, and the scholar of monasticism, dwell for a lifetime. When the scholar practices her professional craft and commits her interpretations to writing, she can only represent the state of the questions and understandings as they exist in that moment, and invite readers into the rich, complex dialogues.

Initially, I struggled with this shift in my research sensibilities, from question-and-answer to lived dialogue steeped in uncertainty. My goal was to write about monastic life, and so to contain it in a way that the printed word cannot help but do. I wanted to access something that felt final and concrete enough to be so captured and contained. But it is the work of finding my own path through the ebb and flow of disparate parts, my own understanding formed in the context of a communal mentality, that in the long run marked my work as distinctly monastic and decidedly ethnographic.

By living this process, I gradually became a part of the knowledge and understandings I wanted to access. I became part of the story I wanted to write. But this does not mean that I became an independent expert. My knowledge was and is bound up in the cyclical processes and interpersonal connections of research. I am not the first to experience this; an awareness of the effect we have on the field is the foundation of the reflexive turn in anthropology and ethnomusicology. Interpersonal spaces are not only where learning happens and knowledge is created, these research spaces are themselves a way of knowing. Ethnomusicologists in particular have long understood that musical performance is an especially rich context in which to experience and engage these realities. In my own research, the Weston monks subtly encouraged me to find this way of knowing, to let go of my need for concrete answers by instead finding meaning in the questions and dialogues that meet my inquiries and the living processes that result in understanding.

Contemplative Ethnography

For Benedictines, conversatio is part of a contemplative sensibility rooted in the Rule of Benedict, and a living expression of that Rule. The Rule is a normative document; its prologue and seventy-three short chapters cover the practical, spiritual, and ritual elements of monastic life, from the kind of clothes to wear, to the times and texts for daily prayer, to the kind of food to eat, when to eat it, who cooks it, who cleans up, and who keeps track of the pots and pans. The opening line of the Rule advises monastics, "Listen . . . with the ear of your heart" (Prologue:1).[13] This phrase establishes a foundation of the monastic way of being. On the one hand, it is outward turned. Listening is directed toward and requires attention to other people in order to hear them, literally and metaphorically, and thus create a stable community life. At the same time, the "ear of your heart" suggests an inward turn supporting a disposition of reflection, focus, and thoughtfulness. It implies love, compassion, and empathy. This becomes a contemplative way of being founded on a two-part turn at once toward self and other. The monastic life is one of patient attention that waits to see what will unfold through the hours, the days, the seasons, the years. It is highly personal and individual, and yet it cannot exist without or outside of the community of sisters or brothers.

This is one of the many foundational tensions of monastic life: turning inward upon the self to seek and understand that which is outside of the self, moving closer to others by moving closer to self. With one word, "listen," Benedict establishes this complex foundation. He sets up the monastic contemplative disposition. It occurred to me gradually over the course of my field research, as I started to recognize how thoroughly this disposition had shaped my research methods, that ethnographers would do well to take Benedict's advice. Were there a Rule for Field Research, "listen" ought to be its opening word.[14]

That is one of the conclusions that unfolds through the course of this book: the monastic epistemology and ontology are remarkably, even surprisingly, similar to the kinds of questions ethnographers like to ask, and the ways of knowing that ethnomusicologists tend to pursue. I went into the field hoping to learn about the monastic, thinking that I was an ethnographer already. But instead, the monastic taught me about the work of humanistic inquiry. By learning to listen to Benedictine monks, I came to understand the dynamic interplay of personal and interpersonal experience, individual and collective knowledge, and the shared spaces of mutual inquiry. I understand such research methods as "contemplative ethnography," after the monastic sensibilities that inspired them. More than a reflexive turn toward the self, humanistic inquiry requires a deep understanding of the interactional, personal, ethical, social, and political relationships of research and writing. It requires a thorough examination of the processes through which knowledge is created.[15] It requires scholars to understand not only how they encounter and interpret their research context but also how the act of writing participates in these meaning-making processes.

Often, this kind of positioned, reflexive approach is criticized as narcissistic or hyper-self-conscious. But rather than an excessive focus on the self, a contemplative ethnographic sensibility pays careful attention to personal *and* interpersonal experience, as well as the mindful, observant, reflective space of self-other encounter. Like monastic conversatio, a contemplative disposition is inclined toward experience and presence. But, however foundational they are, these categories can be problematic and difficult to define. As Erazim Kohák points out, "as humans, we experience before we theorize, and what we theorize about is primordially given as lived experience."[16] He suggests that intersubjective understandings—the presence of selves and others—keep us from being locked in our own private worlds, and that this intersubjectivity allows us to understand the experience of another person.[17] This recalls my stories of the fallen tree and the mouse in Morningside. I cannot take on the perspective of another, and I cannot become objective, but I can access layers of intersubjectivity that allow me to understand, on some level, the experience of someone else.[18]

In suggesting a contemplative approach to ethnography, I draw on an understanding of contemplation grounded in Western monastic history, thought, and contemporary lived practice.[19] Drawing on this tradition, as well as Kevin Hart's discussion of the history of *contemplatio* and Bernard McGinn's work on the history of Christian mysticism, I define contemplation broadly as an intentional attention to self and other in the pursuit of knowledge and understanding.[20] I think of the contemplative as a sensibility, or way of being, directed toward wisdom, human experience, presence, and the dynamic relationship between interiority and exteriority. It is open to and supports many ways of knowing, while recognizing the effect of the subject on the processes of knowing. It looks toward both the actual and the possible.[21] This relates to my previous discussion of winks and smiles, and the work of understanding many possible answers—and the extent of what we do not know—rather than pursuing a single truth or reality. Rather than depending upon ever more detailed descriptions to understand the extent of possibility, the ethnographer can focus more intensely on a contemplative sensibility that is firmly grounded in listening in order to *hear* and *understand*. This kind of deep listening is distinct from a usual approach to conversation, for example, in which we typically listen in order to respond. Such an approach is self-centered: it focuses on how someone's words relate to me. In deep listening, the goal is instead to be fully present to another person in order to really hear them and work toward shared understanding. This is a dynamic, active listening that looks for deeper layers of meaning in human interaction and, where ethnomusicology is concerned, musical performance. It supports creative, improvisatory, even playful discourse.[22] It is an attention steeped in silence and conversatio, grounded in and supporting a two-part turn toward self and other.

Using "contemplative" as a description of ethnographic methods may seem to suggest a return to the detached stance of the objective observer, or, worse still, an overly intellectualized revival of armchair anthropology. Kevin Dwyer specifically warns against the dangers of a "contemplative stance" when he suggests that contemplative language in anthropology separates subject from object, resulting in interpretations that are divided from the social interactions that generated them.[23] He argues for a focus on dialogues to maintain firm grounding in "concrete, mutual experience."[24] For Dwyer, dialogues are an alternative to contemplative language because they focus on interaction and process.[25] He and I share a similar emphasis on self-other encounter, process, and the role of the subject as a participant in both the human experience under consideration and the knowledge created from that experience. Where we differ is in our understanding of contemplation. He treats contemplation as the opposite of action in the social interactions of anthropological research.

Robert Ulin treats contemplation similarly, but to question rather than support dialogic ethnography: he argues that dialogic anthropology "comes dangerously close . . . to a contemplative stance by disregarding praxis and the plurality of subjects that negotiate the historical and political process."[26] For Ulin, dialogues are contemplation instead of praxis; for Dwyer, dialogues are the solution to the dangers of a contemplative stance. Though they disagree on the problems and solutions, they share a use of "contemplative" that is indicative of philosophy. It is evident, for example, in Ludwig Feuerbach's "contemplative materialism," which assumes that consciousness has direct access to the world, and Edmund Husserl's argument that we are both contemplative and active beings at once consciously aware of our place in the world and active in constituting that world.[27]

This dual existence, as Brian Morris describes it in his discussion of human agency in anthropology, treats contemplation as distinct from action.[28] Such a usage suggests that ethnography can be understood as consisting of discreet activities: thinking and doing. The danger, in Dwyer's warning, is that the anthropologist will be too much in her own head, too much removed from social interactions. Geertz echoes this caution in his well-known warnings against the narcissistic pitfalls of "I-Witnessing" or "Diary Disease" reflexivity.[29] The caution is well-taken. But the contemplative approach to ethnography that I advocate is not theorizing instead of, or in favor of, active, engaged work—observation without participation, theory without grounding in experience, thinking instead of doing, self instead of other. Rather, it is a thoroughly engaged sensibility deeply grounded in social interaction. This is not to reject the dualism suggested by Husserl.[30] Indeed, the methods of contemplative ethnography are firmly grounded in phenomenology. It is also not to ignore that contemplation suggests deep thought, reflection, even meditation. It is, however, to point out that a simplistic binary of contemplative-or-active does not account for the nuanced, varied dynamics of contemplation as a lived reality steeped in the complex interiority and exteriority of self-other encounter, interaction, and experience.

Presence and Performance in Constructing the Field

In the Author's Note at the beginning of his *New Seeds of Contemplation*, American Trappist monk Thomas Merton reflects that his work on spirituality and the interior life is "the kind of book that writes itself almost automatically in a monastery."[31] No two monasteries are quite alike, even within the same order, but there are common threads that link monastic practices across geographic, cultural, and religious divides. Contemplation is primary among these threads, and it becomes both a means for navigating the many tensions and contradictions of monasticism and a source of those very same tensions. Being in a monastic context means confronting the challenge of a thorough, unapologetic, unself-conscious inward turn, and attempting to understand how such an interior focus on the self shapes the exterior: behaviors, awareness of others, interpersonal relationships.

Like Merton, I have found that the ethnographic methods I discuss emerged almost automatically in a monastery. They not only reflect this context, they are a manifestation of the very ways of being and knowing that they seek to understand. This is a foundational tension of field research: the ethnographer cannot know how to know a given context until she begins to study the context, and, in the end, what she knows is bound up in the processes by which she came to know it. The methods I discuss, and my approach to the written narrative of my research, are thus highly specific to the context that inspired them, but I do think they have wider-reaching implications for ethnographic research and writing. As a contemplative sensibility allows monastics to navigate the paradoxes of their vocation, so can it allow ethnographers to navigate the tensions and contradictions, interiority and exteriority, personal and interpersonal dimensions at the heart of what it means to be human.

This becomes in some ways a question of locating—and constructing—"the field." With whom does the researcher enter into dialogue? With what knowledge? Whose? Located where? How far can we push the boundaries of the field, and the boundaries of evidence, to consider what constitutes field research "data?" Who participates in creating and interpreting the data? To what, and to whose, ends?

This returns to the idea of presence with which I began my discussion of the challenges and possibilities of field research in a Benedictine monastery. Presence is of particular importance in anthropology and its sister discipline, ethnomusicology. "Being there" is a methodological foundation that distinguishes ethnographic research, and the knowledge it generates, from that of other disciplines.[32] Simon Coleman and Peter Collins point to the importance of "a metaphysics of presence" in ethnography, and the role of "face-to-face, *in situ* encounters" in obtaining cultural knowledge. But they caution, "'presence' cannot be taken for granted as a concept or technique, and in practice has contained within its rubric a huge range of activities and degrees of success in gaining access to social groupings."[33] Simply "being there" is not enough. The ethnographer brings a certain kind of attention and intention to ethnography, and in doing so, she critically engages the presence of selves and others in the research and writing process. How might that presence be better understood and brought to consciousness? Reflexivity is not, ultimately, narcissistic or solipsistic—it is the practice of turning the consciousness toward the spaces where knowledge is created and understanding is built. It is not self-consciousness, but self-other-consciousness.

As I learned time and again as I experienced the highly regulated life of the monastery, the problem of presence is at once philosophical and deeply practical. It is not just a question of where I am physically, but where my head is, where and how my focus is directed. Reflexivity teaches me not to leave this unexamined or unstated. This is likely a familiar experience for anyone who has engaged in intensive field research. Just showing up is not enough to turn a traveler into an ethnographer, a musician into an ethnomusicologist. Attention and intention define being-in-the-field. It may be subtle, but the researcher's way-of-being-present turns "hanging out" into field research.[34] This pushes beyond primarily geographic, spatial, or temporal notions of the field. Rather, the boundaries of the field are flexible; one thing that binds them temporally and spatially is the presence of the researcher, a specific contemplative presence of intentional attention.

This positions the field as a dynamic, creative, playful space of presence, experience, listening, reflecting, and participating. It is not unlike Coleman and Collins's discussion of "performing the field." They use performance as a metaphor to point to what they call the "play of social relationships" between researchers and the people with whom they work.[35] These relationships are not limited to a single physical site, and they include embodied, verbal, visual, and, I would add, musical interactions. Performance further takes account of the way that fields shift over time, are always in the process of becoming, and can be created and re-created as a process.

Having said all of this, my field research occurred in a very specific, bounded spatial and geographic place: a monastery. I know when I am at the monastery and when I am not at the monastery. Much of my writing attempts to evoke that sense of place because so much of my knowledge is bound up in the monastery as a destination that is not only not-at-home but is intentionally set apart in order to foster the life of the monachos. The processes by which the Weston monks create "monastery" as an experience and form of life are the very processes I worked to understand and in which I tried to immerse myself. And so while I suggest a critical rethinking that would push these traditional notions of the field, I do not advocate rejecting or resisting the fact that there often is a bounded place where the social interactions and contemplative work of our ethnographer selves and our research others primarily take place.[36] But one of the virtues of this way of thinking about the field as performance and presence, and our work therein as contemplative, is that it is not limited to or even primarily focused on a strictly bounded "field." Instead, it opens up the discussion to focus on dynamic interactions and processes.[37]

Applying this approach to my own research meant looking toward—and learning to participate in—ethnographic, monastic, and musical practices that are at once deeply personal and thoroughly interpersonal. It was about learning to listen in an effort to understand and participate in a collective voice. I needed to develop an awareness of the lived sociocultural and musical realities I had entered into. This was a contemplative approach to ethnography: an experience steeped in silence and presence, the two-part turn of listening with the ear of the heart, and the dynamic personal and interpersonal tensions of stability and transformation in monastic conversatio; it was active, participatory, and deeply engaged in social interactions, while at the same time recognizing the individual intensity, personal processes, and intellectual work of field research.

This is what I have tried to capture in the narrative of music and monastery life that follows, but it took me quite a while to understand and articulate it. On a midsummer afternoon early in my field research, I sat in the parlor of Weston Priory waiting for the lunchtime bell to ring. Eight monastery guests were in the room with me: five women and three men who were staying in the guesthouses for the week. Two of the brothers joined us. The sound of vibrant conversation filled the room as I chatted with the woman next to me. She appeared to be in her fifties and described herself as a stay-at-home mother preparing to enter the Episcopal seminary for a later-in-life career change. She had arrived at Weston that day, and, after telling me that she was on what she described as a "discernment retreat," she asked what brought me to the monastery. When I told her about my field research, she asked what ethnographers do. Her tone and emphasis were friendly, but she was sincere in explaining that ethnography did not fit her understanding of research work.

I had yet to thoroughly interrogate all that I have discussed in the preceding pages. I probably should have said that I was still unsure what I was "doing" at the monastery. Instead, I told her that I would participate in monastic life as much as possible, converse with the brothers and their guests, and write about my experiences and observations in an effort to understand some specific dimensions of life at the Priory. The clanging monastery bells called us to dinner before we could continue our conversation, but I made note of our chat in my little pocket notebook—doing the participating, observing, conversing, and writing I had just described to her—as I traversed the long cloister walk hallway to the refectory. Because, as important as all of the critical, philosophical discussions of ethnography are, field research happens in the practical, unpredictable, serendipitous, surprising, sometimes frustrating encounters and experiences of everyday life. It happens while we are still working to understand what is happening. It is the work of being present, and asking others to share their ways of knowing and being with us, even if we are not always sure how to navigate our presence and pursuit of understanding in the field.

Chapter Outline

The narrative begins in chapter 1, where I explore the history of Weston Priory and aspects of day-to-day life while engaging the dynamic tensions that animate ethnographic research. Chapters 2 and 3 look at Benedictine music and prayer with a focus on understanding the Weston monks' musical and liturgical style. Chapter 2 describes my visit to Saint-Benoît-du-Lac, comparing what I experienced of Latin liturgy and Gregorian chant to my emerging understanding of the Weston monks' practices. This develops a broader understanding of Benedictine practices, and it shows how I developed a more nuanced approach to the study of language and music in monasticism. Chapter 3 then focuses on the development of the Weston monks' musical and liturgical style, especially the processes through which they replaced Latin and Gregorian chant with vernacular language and music accompanied on guitars. This chapter becomes a history of the early development of the brothers' music, one that has yet to be formally written and represents an important moment in the history and practices of American Catholicism. However, this history is set in the context of their present experiences and their work to confront the question: what is the vernacular, really, and what does prayer, music, indeed the whole of life, in one's own authentic voice look and sound like? It is about what it means to sing like Benedictines and sing like Weston monks.

Chapter 4 takes up the topic of learning how to learn, and then applies that to the deeply practical and yet thoroughly philosophical ideas the brothers shared with me and I worked to understand. More a series of dialogues than the pursuit of questions and answers, this chapter focuses on my efforts to learn about the brothers' epistemology and ontology, their ways of being and knowing, both by sharing in everyday experience and by recognizing that I would become part of the understandings I sought to gain. This section begins my discussion of "music as craft" by examining what craft means to the Weston monks in theory and in practice.

In chapter 5, I draw the focus from craft to music as craft. I discuss the active work of creating a tradition, telling the local story in musical and liturgical performance, and the brothers' approach to collective composition. I begin to understand the brothers' collective consciousness by participating in their music and working with them as they record a new album. This leads to chapter 6, where my focus turns to the spiritual dimensions of these experiences. From the sheep pens to the recording studio, I discuss the brothers' spirituality in terms of turning toward the self, toward one's brothers or sisters, and toward the created world in a spirit of wonder and awe. Returning the discussion to music, I suggest "musical *metanoia*" as a means of understanding the spiritual dimensions of musical performance from the perspective of the monastic musician. I conclude the story of my work with the Weston monks by bringing the discussion full circle as I realize that ethnography is itself a kind of metanoia, a way of being and knowing that is not, in the end, all that dissimilar from the monastic form of life.

Chapter One

Ethnography in a Monastery

> The Prophet says: Seven times a day I have praised you (Ps 118:164). We will fulfill this sacred number seven if we satisfy our obligations of service at Lauds, Prime, Terce, Sext, None, Vespers, and Compline. . . . Concerning Vigils, the same Prophet says: At midnight I arose to give you praise (Ps 118:62).
>
> —Rule of Benedict, 16:1–5

Morning Vigil

Finger-picked guitar strings broke the silence of night: a simple tune followed by a chord plucked out gently, one string at a time. No light except for the faintest blue glow of the coming dawn filtered in through the high windows. A single candle flickered in the center of the chapel. A collective breath from the schola, a small group of brothers who lead the singing, then a slow Alleluia sung on the tune the guitar had just given. A gentle, three-note movement on -*lu* and an upward step on -*ia* brought a sense of uplift, lightness, and subtle energy. A carefully picked guitar chord marked the syllables but did not establish a regular beat.

They sang the next line: This is the day our God has made. The rest of the brothers responded: Alleluia.[1] It was more like a chant than a song. They articulated each word on the same pitch until the final four words stepped down in a simple cadence. This time the Alleluia also stepped down, mimicking the cadence. The schola brothers sang the next line: Jesus our hope is risen. This time the cadence stepped up, mirroring the meaning of the words. The response again, Alleluia, was similarly uplifted: vowels and syllables extended by more ornate melismatic movement. The opening chant continued through several phrases, each with a responding, Alleluia.

There was no steady beat. Only a subtle suggestion of meter created by the emphasis of the syllables of each word, marked by the plucking chords of the guitar. It at once evoked the natural rhythms of the spoken word, the carefully crafted meters of poetry, and the regulated pulse of song. The brothers sang in unison, breathed in unison. Except for the slight movement required of the guitar player, they sat essentially motionless in their semicircle.

The chapel was no echoing, reverberant cathedral. It was once a small barn, home to livestock instead of monastic chants. The dark wood beams and widows set high along the roofline suggested its former identity. The slight acoustic warmth of the space lent a richness to the chanted words that at once seemed to wrap the brothers—and those of us listening to them—in gentle sound while also absorbing that sound back into the monastic silence from which it softly emerged, silence that seemed to dwell in the very walls around us.

Another chant followed the opening Alleluia. This time, it was strictly syllabic: a single pitch for each syllable of the text. Collectively, the brothers sang the first phrase in unison: Come ring out our joy to our God; hail the rock who saves us; we come before you giving thanks; with songs we sing out your praise.[2] The pitches of the first line stepped upward, evoking the joy of which the lyrics spoke. Each successive line stepped gradually downward, leading to a slight pause and collective breath before the next phrase. Again, the guitar marked the emphasized syllables suggesting poetic meter without creating a steady beat. The brothers continued in this way through the end of the chant, Psalm 94, which praises God for the gifts of the natural world, then takes on the first-person voice of God to caution the people to listen to God's voice without hardening their hearts.

This was the beginning of the Morning Vigil nearly two weeks into my first field research visit, and I had very little understanding of what I was hearing liturgically or, really, musically speaking. I had expected to come to Weston and find a group of guitar-strumming, antiestablishment, countercultural monks playing the folk-inspired songs I remembered from my upbringing in the Catholic Church. It took one of the daily Divine Office prayers for me to recognize that, while these preconceptions were not incorrect, the music of Weston Priory was quite different, and far more complex, than I anticipated. While the folk choir in my church, and, I assumed, many others, strummed along and sang out loud when they played the music of the Weston monks, the brothers themselves had quite a different approach to liturgy and music. It was quieter, gentler, and steeped in centuries-old monastic traditions that were related to, but ultimately quite different from, anything I would have experienced in a parish church.

Although they sang their own songs frequently when the liturgical rubrics called for a hymn, they never strummed their guitars or sang with the big, hearty, full-voiced approach of a parish choir. The guitar was finger-picked, giving a gentle movement to the chord progressions. Their voices were equally gentle, with a timbre reminiscent of each brother's own speaking voice. Not only did I quickly realize that my field research had placed me in very unfamiliar and unexpected surroundings, I also recognized that I had entered into a kind of musical and liturgical puzzle. Each piece seemed simple enough: basic tunes, clear lyrics, formulas repeated each day. But they added up to a more complex whole.

It was still too early in my work for me to make sense of the finer points of what I was hearing, so I tended to focus on the lyrics. Articulated as they were, slowly and clearly in each chant, it seemed that the words mattered very much and I would do well to pay attention to them. That morning, I considered that the sung words of Morning Vigil broke the silence of night for the brothers in an important way. It was a collective utterance calling to mind themes that seemed fitting for the start of a new day: a community of Christian monks reminding themselves and one another to appreciate the gifts of creation, to recognize their divine source, and to maintain a focus on listening for that source.

I wondered how starting each day with that kind of intention and attention affected their way of being. I wondered how it might affect my own if I started each morning by quietly noticing everything around me and being grateful for the gifts and mysteries of the day ahead. It was something I managed to do easily in the monastery, when I began every morning alongside the brothers in Morning Vigil. But I had yet to notice or take account of the many subtle shifts in my consciousness that were beginning to form after only two weeks in the rhythms of monastic life. The daily round of Divine Office prayers, the periods of work and study, the emphasis on silence. I was as yet unaware, but all were beginning to influence how I experienced and engaged with the world around me.

My alarm had beeped dutifully that morning at 4:30 a.m. I swatted around the nightstand seeking the snooze button. After being at the Priory for so many days, I had, until that morning, adjusted well to the early start of the monastic day. But it was the morning after my experience with Lupita and the mouse, and I had slept fitfully, convinced—as only one exercising the reduced logic of the nighttime can be—that every noise was an uninvited critter seeking a warm snuggle in my sleeping bag. Finding the snooze button, but knowing I needed to get myself up and out the door for Morning Vigil, I decided I had better get up. Walking quietly around the house so as not to wake Lupita, who was sound asleep on the couch, broom still propped up next to her, I quickly got myself dressed and ready.

By 4:45, I was on my way out the door of the Morningside guesthouse. It was raining, as it had been on and off for the past few days, so I popped open my umbrella. It was late spring. The gentle blue glow of dawn was just illuminating the dense forest around me. Accompanied by the chirping birds and gentle pitter-patter of the rain falling on the trees, I made my way up the hill to the Priory. I tried to move intentionally, but mindfully and slowly, taking in my surroundings as I walked. I recalled a line from one of the brothers' songs I had seen in a book in their Gallery Shop: "Live fully this moment." I tried to notice and appreciate the sound of the rain: the rhythm of individual raindrops on my umbrella, the muffled wash of sound as tiny droplets hit the leaves overhead, the crunch and squish of my shoes on the damp road. I noticed how the rainwater ran in miniature rivers down the hill. The monastery bells began to ring ahead of me, and the rain seemed to dampen their reverberant echo. I was beginning to learn that, while a sense of direction and purpose is important, monastery life resists the tendency to rush through our lives and experiences. Mindfulness. Patience. Humility. After less than two weeks at the Priory, I had already seen that these values were embodied even in the literal steps one takes to get from point A to point B, from sleep to Morning Vigil, from nighttime to dawn.

Suddenly, a noise in the woods snapped me out of my intentional pondering of raindrops and rivulets. Something moved about in the woods, breaking twigs and rustling leaves. Walking through the Weston woods at any dark or nearly dark hour always made me just a bit uneasy. The Priory was tucked into the wilderness of the Green Mountain National Forest, alive with critters big and small. I turned toward the woods. I saw nothing but trees. I scanned the thick carpet of undergrowth as far back as I could see. Still, I saw nothing but forest. I inhaled deeply, trying to discern the scent of a bear. I am no great outdoorswoman, but my maternal grandfather once told me that bears have a distinctive odor sort of like the smell of a wet dog. Like so many grandparents, he enjoyed passing along bits of information that are potentially useful, but really say: This is who I am. This is who you are. This is what it means to be part of our family. Growing up, it never felt useful to me to know what a bear smelled like, but when I walked in the Weston woods I was grateful for the wisdom of my grandfather. That morning, I smelled nothing but the cold, crisp mountain air. I breathed a little sigh of relief.

Never one to be left behind when the boys went hunting, and certainly not one to let men dominate the tales of life in the north country, my grandmother also passed along her own wisdom. She liked to say that when God was all done with creation, he took the parts he had leftover and made the moose. She warned that they are dangerous; they are huge, but surprisingly difficult to see from close range because their skinny legs are so tall that by the time you know you are near one, you are probably underneath it. This is particularly terrifying in a car, but as I walked it occurred to me that it would be unfortunate to bump into a moose on foot. However unlikely that scenario, it seemed reasonable to me at 4:45 a.m., so I looked up to make sure there was no moose towering over my head. I saw nothing but a cloudy sky. The noise I heard was likely a small animal startled by my presence as I passed by. Whatever it was had startled me right back, and I was suddenly wide-awake in spite of the early hour. I looked straight ahead and walked a little faster toward the chapel, forgetting my monastic pursuit of unhurried movement.

Several minutes later, I approached the monastery and finally relaxed. I realized I was breathing hard from nearly jogging down the road. I made a conscious effort to walk a little more slowly and breathe a little more calmly. A car drove up Priory Hill Road, shining bright headlights on the dim landscape. The male driver and his female passenger walked along the stone pathways toward the chapel. I approached the door just as it closed behind them. A single iron lantern set the large chapel door in a soft yellowish glow. I closed my umbrella, and, grabbing the large, curved iron handle, gently pulled the chapel door toward me. Though large and very substantial, the door made little noise, only the soft whoosh of heavy wood sliding across the rug beneath my shoes. Everything in the monastery seemed to take on a quiet affect.

I entered the dark space of the chapel. The narrow windows and cloudy gray skies meant that little light had yet made its way in. As we approached the long days of summer, the chapel would become a bit brighter for Vigil each day, then gradually darker again as the summer waned into autumn. But dark as it was that morning, the light that spilled in through the open doorway as I entered felt like an affront to the space within. With a *whoosh* the door closed behind me.

My eyes took a moment to adjust to the darkness. Eight people were already there, scattered around the seats in the visitor's gallery. To my right, the couple who had entered ahead of me were just sitting down. To my left, I saw a young woman I recognized as a guest staying with me in the women's guesthouse. Ahead of me, an entire row of four chairs was occupied by a group of older women sitting straight up, feet flat on the floor, heads upright and alert. I had seen the same group at the evening Vespers service the night before. Further up on the left an older man sat with a cane leaning against the chair next to him. He held his forehead in his hands, rested his elbows on his knees, leaned forward, and looked down. Deep in prayer? Meditating? Falling asleep? These were sometimes difficult to distinguish at Morning Vigil, in myself and those around me. I vacillated between mental chatter, prayer, meditation, and drowsiness almost every morning.

I sat down in a chair at the front of the visitors' area—traditionally called the "nave." I took off my jacket as quietly as possible, wishing I had remembered to unzip it outside so as to avoid disrupting the silent chapel with the clamor of a zipper. Even a very brief experience of monasticism had increased my awareness of small details that would often go unnoticed in my typical everyday life: raindrops, walking, small sounds, the changing light of the gradually shifting seasons. As far as I was concerned, this had little to do with the music I was there to study—oh, how wrong I was—and so I had yet to really attend to these layers of awareness and experience.

I sat straight up in my chair with both feet on the floor. I rested my hands on my knees, closed my eyes, breathed deeply, and tried to quiet my mind. I was no great contemplative. A quiet mind often eluded me. My thoughts raced as I pondered the notes I wanted to make in my little pocket notebook when the Vigil ended; there was much I wanted to remember about my experience with Lupita and the mouse the night before. I wondered what the day would bring, and if I would be working with brother Daniel and the sheep. This got me thinking about work, which made me think about my own work, which made me start worrying about my research. Was I using my time effectively? Was I making the most of each day? Was I asking the right questions? Taking enough notes? Should I have written down more details from Vespers the previous evening? Was my recorder turned on? Had I changed the batteries? And so on.

My mind seemed to be whirring out of control. I thought to myself, "Stop thinking!" But that only made me think about not thinking. I wondered what the other visitors in the chapel were thinking. Were they able to quiet their minds? Were they deep in thought? Deep in prayer? Fighting sleep? Pondering breakfast? I tried to regain some sense of focus by breathing deeply and slowly. This seemed to quiet my mind, but it also threatened to allow my latent drowsiness to surface. I thought of the story of one of the Desert Fathers, Abba Poeman. He was once asked if monks who fall asleep during prayer should be woken. He said that if he saw his brother sleeping, he would put his head on his knees and let him rest.[3]

I decided to open my eyes and try to attend to what was going on around me. Brother Columba sat in what looked like silent prayer in the brothers' area at the front of the chapel, traditionally called the choir. Nicknamed "Nonus" by his confreres—a name roughly translated as "big brother" and traditionally given to someone who strictly enforces the rules in an effort to keep younger brothers in line—brother Columba sat in a simple cross-legged position on a prayer mat on the floor, propped up on two round prayer cushions. His hands rested on his knees, his head was bent slightly forward, his eyes were closed. He had a gentle smile on his face. As he did every morning, he wore a white tunic, blue sweatpants, and thick wool socks.

Not surprisingly, when I stopped thinking so much about not thinking, my mind became much quieter. I finally began to settle into the silence of the Vigil just as brother John entered the chapel from the monastic enclosure at the back of the choir. He wore a white tunic and dark blue pants. He carried a faded red prayer cushion and a round frame drum. His stocking feet made a soft swishing noise as he walked to his seat at the front of the chapel. With care and a little difficulty, he dropped to one knee on his prayer mat, turned around, sat on the stacked cushions, and pulled his feet under him in a gentle lotus pose. Immediately, he settled into what looked to me like meditative prayer: he sat straight up with his head forward, eyes closed, and hands resting on his knees. His small stature, sturdy build, and careworn hands gave him the look of a farmer-turned-Buddha.

Brother Peter and brother Elias entered the chapel and quietly walked to their places—brother Peter to a padded wooden chair, brother Elias to the monastic bench on the far end of the brothers' semicircle. Brother Peter sat with his hands folded in his lap, brother Elias with his hands on his knees. Both closed their eyes. Meanwhile, brother Augustine entered the chapel, guitar in hand, stocking feet swishing on the floor. He sat on a chair and laid the guitar down gently beside him.

The monastery bells rang—the "five-minute warning" bell. The metallic clanging reverberated as more tunic-clad monks filed in silently from the sacristy door at the back of the choir. They all seemed so quiet, mentally and physically, that their presence changed the atmosphere in the chapel. They brought a calm energy and sense of anticipation to what was, moments earlier, just a silent, nearly empty space. Brother Placid walked in, barefoot, carrying a large red lectionary, glasses hanging on a chord around his neck. He sat on his prayer cushion and pulled his feet up on top of his knees in a full lotus pose. Brother Alvaro sat in a chair next to him. Brother Mark kneeled on a mat and placed a small bench over his lower legs to support his kneeling position. Brother Daniel sat in a chair near the top of the semicircle. Brother Robert sat on one of the benches that lined the choir. Brother Michael, carrying a guitar and prayer bench, knelt in front of a music stand between brother Elias and brother Augustine.

With eleven brothers thus assembled around the chapel, sitting still and silent, brother Richard walked into the chapel and took his place at the top of the semicircle near the sacristy door. Sitting down on his prayer cushion and crossing his legs under him, he completed the semicircle of monks. Brother Michael picked up his guitar. I felt the energy in the room shift from individual, internal quiet to the collective space of Morning Vigil. With gently picked notes on a guitar and quietly chanted words, a new day was about to begin.

Breakfast

> There are times when good words are to be left unsaid out of esteem for silence. . . . Indeed, so important is silence that permission to speak should seldom be granted even to mature disciples, no matter how good or holy or constructive their talk, because it is written: "In a flood of words you will not avoid sin" (Prov 10:19); and elsewhere, "The tongue holds the key to life and death" (Prov 18:21).
>
> —Rule of Benedict, 6:2–6

> Monks should diligently cultivate silence at all times, but especially at night.
>
> —Rule of Benedict, 42:1

Just over half an hour later, Morning Vigil concluded as quietly as it began. The last guitar chords and chanted words reverberated away as silence returned to the chapel. I felt the collective energy dissipate, but I noticed that I felt awake and far more focused than I had been at the beginning of the Vigil. At some point, my mind had stopped racing. The brothers remained seated and motionless in their semicircle. The guests and visitors likewise did not move. I sat in my chair, quietly waiting. After several moments, brother Richard stood, picked up his prayer mat, and walked out through the sacristy door at the back of the choir. One by one, the brothers followed, carrying their own mats, cushions, lectionaries, music stands, and guitars out with them. The only sound was the quiet shuffling of stocking feet on the wood floor. Brother Daniel was the last to leave. As he did, he walked to the center of the choir and blew out the candle that had burned throughout the Vigil. With the candle extinguished and all of the brothers returned to the monastic enclosure, the guests and visitors began to stand up one by one and walk out of the chapel.

I turned off my handheld digital recorder and tucked it into the small canvas bag I had stashed at my feet. I gathered up my coat and left the chapel, but instead of continuing through the large wooden doors to go back outside, I turned down the hallway that runs alongside the chapel and leads to the parlor and monastic enclosure beyond. Stillness and silence are a way of life in the monastery. Seldom was this more apparent than in the dark early morning hours when the very walls seemed to be steeped in quiet and calm because of Grand Silence, maintained from the end of Compline in the evening until the brothers' daily morning prayer and community meeting, called Chapter.

When I tell friends and acquaintances about my field research in monasteries, many of them recoil at the notion of required periods of silence. Indeed, my own initial encounters with monastic silence were unexpectedly intense. On the first day of my first visit to Weston, I sat at a picnic table writing in my field journal. I had only just arrived, but already I felt immersed in the most impressive quiet and stillness. Any sound cut through the air and seemed to reverberate around the entire grounds. A bullfrog alongside the pond began to croak, and the sound was jarring. Cars drove up Priory Hill Road for the evening Eucharist, and they were like a jet engine against the quiet. I sat at the table astonished: my life had given me little occasion to really know what silence sounds like, what it feels like. I was initially unsure how to behave in its presence.

In time, I came to understand that silence in the monastic context is not necessarily treated as a regulation in the restrictive sense, and thus is not intended to be experienced as limiting or stifling. It is meant to be freeing, to allow a monastic person to reposition himself or herself toward a different way of being in the world and with other people. A favorite story around the Weston kitchen tells of brother Columba answering the phone many, many years ago. The caller was a neighbor, and in a frantic voice she told him that her house was on fire and she needed help. As the story goes, brother Columba responded, in all seriousness: "Can you call back after Grand Silence, please?" Upon hearing the conversation, another brother picked up the phone and quickly mobilized to help the neighbor.

The story is always accompanied by uproarious laughter—indeed, monasticism is all about balance, so silence must have its counter in the moments of collective joy that turn a monastic house into a home, monks into brothers, guests into friends. While the tale is usually told as a way to poke a little good-natured fun at brother Columba by revealing him as not only a stickler for the rules, but something of a big brother in the Weston family, it also speaks to the nature of Grand Silence. This story at once demonstrates the serious attention required to uphold the rules of the monastery and also the flexibility and humor necessary for the rules to remain practical in everyday life. Silence for the sake of silence is not sustainable. For Benedictines, silence cultivates a spirit of listening and stillness that offers space and relief from constant chatter and idle conversation. This does not entail ignoring one another; it is an active, attentive silence in which one can gain a heightened awareness of one's individual presence in the communal space.

This was particularly the case in the refectory; in addition to breakfast occurring during Grand Silence, lunch and supper were eaten in silence while one brother read aloud. My early experiences of this traditional monastic practice left me reeling in the rituals of monastery life. I paid little attention to the brother reading as I found that eating in silence was an entirely new experience requiring all of my attention. I struggled to cut my food without making loud scraping noises. I occasionally slammed my knife with a loud *crack* when I cut my tomatoes, determined as I was to keep them on my plate. I sometimes set my water glass down a little too hard, making a soft *bang* against the wooden table. I felt like I may as well have been banging a gong.

I had spent several days since those early meals observing and participating in the choreography of communal dining in a contemplative monastic setting. At breakfast, I noticed that the brothers did not hesitate or waste time. Each had a more or less regular routine. Some sat at the table eating bowls of cereal or plates of toast immediately after Vigil. Others brought their breakfast into the monastic enclosure. Still others grabbed a cup of coffee on their way into the enclosure, perhaps having eaten already or preferring to eat later.

In my efforts to align myself with the monastic ethos, I tried to mirror this affect of regular ritual without hesitation or any hint of morning laziness, in spite of the early hour. That morning, I nearly bumped into brother Placid in the doorway as I walked through the refectory and into the kitchen. We both smiled and nodded a silent gesture of "excuse me." Brother Placid stepped aside and motioned for me to pass through the door first. I nodded a silent "thank you," and walked by. In his blue sweatpants and red hooded sweatshirt, coffee in hand, he passed behind me and through the door to the monastic enclosure. I nodded a morning greeting to brother Elias as he stirred a pot of oatmeal and I poured myself a cup of tea. He smiled, nodded back, and silently indicated that I could help myself to the oatmeal.

I passed on the oatmeal, preferring toast made from the brothers' whole-wheat raisin bread. In the refectory, I cut a thick slice of the hearty homemade bread and popped it into a toaster. A guest stood next to another toaster waiting for his English muffin to pop. We smiled at one another. While I waited for my toast, I brought my tea to my seat at the end of the dining table. A male guest was seated at a table on the far side of the room. He sipped a cup of coffee and looked out the windows at the pond, gardens, and mountains. Two female guests entered the refectory from the cloister walk. They were Sisters of Saint Joseph staying in the guesthouse for the week on their annual joint retreat. They went into the kitchen and I heard the quiet rustle of cereal being poured into bowls.

As had become my routine, I buttered my toast and slathered it with honey from the brothers' apiary. The golden honey dripped over the edges and onto the plate. I returned to my seat, next to another female guest who was painstakingly deconstructing a grapefruit. She moved slowly and intentionally. I wondered if this was her usual habit for eating grapefruit, or if she was trying not to make unnecessary noise, or if her unhurried approach was a result of her time in the calm, meditative space of the monastery. We smiled at one another. While all of my fellow guests were kind and friendly, I appreciated that conversation was not an option in the silence of the refectory. We did not ignore one another, but instead took our cues from the brothers as we gently, quietly offered space. I used mine to look out the large windows. The sun was rising over the mountains, casting the mist rising off of the pond in a light blue glow and revealing the dark outlines of trees, fences, and hills. I laid my napkin across my lap, crossed my legs, sat back in my chair, and enjoyed the view with my toast, dripping with sweet golden honey.

The Morning Study Period

By 6:30 a.m. I was back in the guesthouse sitting at the dining room table with my laptop open in front of me. I had just finished writing down the events of the night before, and I was beginning to reflect on some reading I had been doing during my visit: *Knowing How to Know*, a collection of essays on field research. I was particularly inspired that morning by Judith Okely's essay, "Knowing without Notes." It discusses how knowledge gained in the field is contained in the mind and memory of the researcher, and so ethnographic knowledge becomes embodied as the field becomes part of the researcher's way of being. Okely talks about how she herself changed and adapted in the field. It inspired me to begin to pay attention to how I changed within and as a result of my time in the monastery. I started taking notes on my early morning spent watching rivulets of rain and trying to quiet my mind in Morning Vigil. I looked up from my computer and gazed out the windows for a while at the woods surrounding the little guesthouse. I decided I needed to spend more time paying attention to small moments and seemingly mundane experiences.

As I thought along these lines, I began to realize that my experiences with Lupita—and our language barriers—were illustrative of my own attempts to understand and engage in field research. I decided I needed to spend more time thinking about that, too, when Lupita emerged from her room holding a bag of fudge. She had purchased it the day before in the country store in the village, and I could see that a mouse had been snacking on it. She was very disappointed. We decided that all food should be tightly closed in the refrigerator. We also decided to name the mouse Hershey, both for his dark brown color and his love of chocolate fudge. It added a bit of levity to the problem, and, I hoped, helped Lupita to relax a little. She was still very upset about the presence of the mouse. Cute name or no, Lupita wanted it gone.

She fixed herself some toast in the kitchen, then sat down at the table with me. I was a little unsure what to do. Should we maintain the silence of the house? Or should we engage in friendly conversation? I did not want to ignore her or be rude, but I also wanted to make the most of the quiet of monastery life, and offer Lupita the same. The silent morning study period had set me on a productive train of thought, and I was hoping to follow it. Lupita seemed to understand, and we settled into a companionable silence. Lupita munched on her toast while I typed. We both drank mugs of hot tea that I had prepared in the kitchen. The inspirational quote on my tea bag read, "Experience brings wisdom." My tea bag, it seemed, knew more about monastic life and field research than I did.

While pondering this, I interrupted our quiet with a sudden sneeze. "Jesus help you!" Lupita said, loudly and a bit abruptly. I was startled both by the phrase and the intensity with which Lupita uttered it. I smiled and chuckled a little. "What is the translation in English?" Lupita asked, also smiling. "We usually say, 'God bless you,'" I responded, realizing it was as unusual a thing to say after a sneeze as, "Jesus help you." Lupita repeated, "God—bless—you." "Yes," I said, "but your phrase works, too!" She explained, using her knowledge of English and her pocket dictionary, that there was an influenza epidemic in Mexico at the beginning of the twentieth century. She then mimed through gesture that people who sneezed were likely to die—she pretended to sneeze, then leaned over limply with her eyes closed and tongue hanging out. People said, "Jesus help you," whenever someone sneezed because they probably could use the divine assistance. We both laughed. Later, I wrote about the conversation in my journal and noted that meaning, which relies so heavily on context and shared cultural knowledge, is often lost in translation.

As we chatted, a local neighbor who is a friend of Lupita's arrived. Lupita had called her about the mouse, and she had brought supplies: cotton balls soaked in mint oil to deter the pest, a plastic bucket to trap the mouse alive and release it outdoors, and airtight baggies for the fudge that had not yet been nibbled on. They sat down to chat in the living room—Lupita's friend spoke Spanish quite fluently—and I went to my room to get ready for the day's work period. When I emerged, another neighbor who helped keep up the guesthouses had arrived to set traps. I was as eager as Lupita for the mouse to be gone, but I wondered how that fit in with my attempts, inspired by my early morning walk and the words of Morning Vigil, to recognize and appreciate the world around me. Surely that mouse had as much need of a warm, cozy house as did I. But still, I did not want to share my sleeping bag, or Lupita's fudge, with it.

The Morning Work Period

> Idleness is the enemy of the soul. Therefore, the brothers should have specified periods for manual labor as well as for prayerful reading.
> —Rule of Benedict, 48:1

Just after 9:00 a.m. I made my way back up to the Priory. I sat in the parlor and marveled that I had already attended Vigil, eaten breakfast, and spent two hours taking notes, making a new friend in Lupita, and finding some inspirations for my ongoing attempts to figure out how to be a field researcher in a monastery. Grand Silence was ending for the brothers, and the day's labor was about to begin. I waited to see which of the brothers might have work for me to do, and what that might entail.

It was late spring and still quite chilly in the morning—I needed a scarf, hat, and gloves when walking to Vigil—but by 9:00 a.m. the sun was shining, the air was warm, and the bright cloudless sky promised a beautiful day. The rain had stopped, and the trees rustled in a gentle spring breeze that brought warm air up into the Weston hills. Brother Peter stood in the chapel plaza with his camera around his neck when I entered the monastery. He wished me a good morning and said, with a smile, that he was taking advantage of the clear skies and morning light to take a few photos around the grounds. I told him I was getting ready to help with the morning work, and he said, with a smirk, "I hope they give you something pleasant to do!" I thought I sensed a little sarcasm in his voice. He emphasized "pleasant" in a subtly foreboding way. I smiled and replied, "Yes, I hope so, too!" He laughed and said, "Well, you'll have to learn sooner or later that monastery life isn't all meditating and singing."

I sat in the parlor reading a book while I waited. After a little while, brother Daniel came around the corner. He wished me a good morning and said that I could work with him with the animals and the bees if I wanted to. I stood up, eagerly accepting his offer. Brother Daniel grew up in Mexico City, and he spoke with a deep voice and Spanish accent. He was one of the youngest brothers in the community; at the time, he was in his late forties. Standing in the parlor in brown pants and a button-down shirt, he asked for my shoe size. I said seven-and-a-half, unsure why it mattered. He replied that he thought I might be able to wear a six in men's sizes. I must have looked confused, because he went on to explain that my shoes looked nice, and I probably would not want to be mucking around in manure with nice shoes. My chat with brother Peter came to mind. Pleasant tasks, indeed. Morning Vigil came to mind. Appreciating the gifts and mysteries of creation, indeed. But I had worn my old trail shoes intentionally, assuming I might get dirty, so I told him I would be just fine without muck boots.

Brother Daniel then spent several silent moments thinking intently about something. I was not sure what, but he seemed to be considering my clothing. I wondered: Had I dressed inappropriately? I wore jeans and a long-sleeved purple shirt that was not particularly nice. Brother Daniel said simply, "We'll have to get you something white to wear." I gathered we were no longer talking about manure issues. Brother Daniel said that purple would not be an ideal color to wear around bees. He then said that he had to change his shoes, and he would meet me in the plaza outside the chapel.

I went outside and sat on a stone wall watching the sheep and llama. The sheep huddled together near a small barn on the edge of the pasture. The llama stood by himself off to the side. Brother Daniel emerged from the monastery in well-worn tan work pants and an old blue sweatshirt with a small Weston logo. He carried two pairs of work gloves. He smiled and gestured for me to join him.

We walked down into the pastures toward the small barn. I felt as if I was taking two hurried steps for each of brother Daniel's long strides. We were in the fields behind the monastery, which I could see was built into a slight hill and so was two stories tall on the back side. The main building had a series of sliding glass doors that marked the brothers' rooms, each overlooking the pond, pastures, and rolling hills beyond. A larger set of windows in the center lent a similar view to the community meeting room. The building continued toward the woods, and brother Daniel pointed out that beyond the brothers' rooms was the library and the laundry room. The kitchen, refectory, and chapel were all on the front side of the building.

Brother Daniel and I entered the pasture and were immediately greeted by happy sheep. They bleated loudly, butted their heads against us, and chased each other around. "Hola," brother Daniel greeted them, then continued to speak to them in a flurry of Spanish. We opened the door between the two pastures and herded the sheep from one into the other. I had never herded sheep, and had no idea what to do, but it did not take much effort on my part. Once they saw that the door was open and one or two sheep had gone through, the rest stampeded after them with a heavy clopping of hooves.

Enter Noël, the llama. From the far side of the pasture he noticed the movement of the sheep and he wanted to be a part of whatever they were doing. He came running. Galloping, really. But brother Daniel wanted him to stay put, so he quickly ushered the last of the sheep through the gate and shut it just as Noël reached him. I was on the sheep's side of the gate and Noël looked at me, making soft little whining noises while batting his long llama eyelashes. I had never been so close to a llama, and I felt a sense of awe at the beautiful, strong animal before me. He looked gentle and kind with his big black eyes and black-and-white face, but I sensed that he was keenly aware that brother Daniel had some sort of plans for him.

Noël was a new addition to the Weston family. He had only recently moved to his new home at the top of Priory Hill Road. Brother Daniel spoke to him in Spanish with a gentle tone of voice. He patted Noël's head while saying to me, "Noël knows that I will be his friend, but we are not friends yet. You'll see that." He was right. I did.

Becoming friends involved putting Noël into a harness that fit around his nose and then hooked up to a leash to allow brother Daniel to walk him around the pasture. Brother Daniel wanted to put Noël into his harness. Noël wanted no part of it. He saw the harness and ran. Brother Daniel chased after him. In the open pasture, there was a lot of room to run and Noël was quick on his feet. Brother Daniel eventually chased him into an enclosed pen where he could be easily cornered. He finally got a hold of Noël only to lose his grip. The chase resumed. I stood among the sheep, unsure what to do. Seemingly out of nowhere, a large ram suddenly slammed into my legs with his full weight. I fell over. Brother Daniel and I must have been quite a sight, one chasing a llama and the other sitting in a sheep pen.

Standing up and keeping an eye out for the ram, I watched brother Daniel try again and again to harness Noël. I was surprised that he seemed never to become frustrated. He did not raise his voice. He remained calm. He was never hurried, never flustered. He spoke gentle words to the crafty llama and waited until Noël was ready to be caught. He spoke lovingly: "Good boy, Noël, good boy." Finally, he got a hold of the llama and called to me to fetch a bucket of grain from inside the barn. I snuck out of the sheep pasture, managed not to let the insistent ram out behind me, found the grain, and ran to brother Daniel. He held the llama gently around his neck and asked me to hold the grain to his nose. As Noël leaned in for the grain, his nose went through the harness, and I allowed him to eat the grain as a reward. Training a llama was not something I ever imagined myself doing, but every time Noël shoved his muzzle into the harness and got a few nibbles of grain I did feel that we were all becoming friends.

With Noël successfully harnessed, brother Daniel walked him around the pasture. As they walked, I moved a water bucket from one pasture to another. Happy sheep galloped at me whenever I came near. "Look at those crazy characters," brother Daniel said as they trotted en masse around the pasture. Noël even got into the act, chasing a sheep here and there, galloping after them when they ran in another direction.

As this went on, brother Daniel and I mucked out the sheep stalls with pitchforks and wheelbarrows. The mess was not too bad, and as we scooped we chatted pleasantly. I asked about his mother, Lupita, and he said, with a grin, that he heard we had become good friends because I protected her from the mouse. I explained that I did not actually see the mouse, which was probably best for everyone involved, but I was happy to stand guard with his mother outside the bathroom door. Brother Daniel explained that his mother lived in Mexico City, so country life was not very familiar to her. He went on to tell me that she was a musician, a retired teacher, and a very active grandmother. He spoke of his siblings and his nieces and nephews.

With such a large, loving family back home, I wondered why he decided to move to Vermont to become a monk. He told me the following story: He met the brothers in Mexico City when they visited a community of Benedictine sisters there. Those sisters were brother Daniel's grammar school teachers, so he knew them well. He visited them once while the Weston brothers were also visiting. At the time, he had just finished university and he thought he would be a runner. He wanted to run in the Olympic games, and had been training for years to do so, but his times were not fast enough. This sense of disappointment was compounded as he began noticing the poverty, pollution, and injustice around him. Where once he could see to the eternal snows on the mountains from his home, now he could not see to the end of his neighborhood.

In 1985 a devastating earthquake hit Mexico City. Brother Daniel felt that he did nothing special to survive, but was simply lucky. He remembers digging with his hands in the rubble alongside another man trying desperately to help those buried underneath. The experience prompted him to examine his life.

He decided that he wanted to live a different kind of life, something that felt more meaningful than spending hours every day training to run.

He considered the priesthood, and met a priest who greatly inspired him. Brother Daniel described him as a tremendously loving, giving man, but also a man who seemed lonely. He knew that the isolated life of the priesthood was not the life for him. He remembered the Weston monks, but he had two friends who had tried the monastic life in America and could not bear the winters. He decided to visit Weston, going in the winter in order to see if he could stand it. Within a few years, he became a Weston monk.

After telling me his story, he said that what brought him to Weston is not as important as why he has stayed: living in community. He explained that in a monastic family he gives the gift of himself and brings all that he can to the community. He then receives the gifts offered by all of the others. It is an experience of deep friendship and the bonds of the common life.

This conversation surprised me. At no point did brother Daniel mention feeling called to a religious vocation, a common discourse in Catholicism. Instead, he spoke of paying attention to a series of life experiences and feeling that he must make a choice. Surely many people would interpret this as being "called" by God, and I suspect brother Daniel would not deny such an interpretation. But when he described his vocation, I did not feel as though he was preaching to me about living a life for God. He spoke of brotherhood, family, and an alternative to a life that increasingly felt devoid of meaning. I forgot, for a moment, that I was speaking with a monk. A monk wearing muck boots and shoveling manure into a wheelbarrow.

After finishing our cleaning duties, we moved the sheep to their new pasture and headed up the hill behind the Priory where I saw several beehives enclosed in an electric fence. Bears love honey, as I learned from Winnie the Pooh, and when I asked brother Daniel about the fence he confirmed that it was there to keep the bears away. He turned it off, lest we get a shock, and produced his beekeeper outfit from the barn alongside the hives. He said I should wear the suit. I agreed wholeheartedly.

I went into the barn and pulled the heavy white canvas suit on over my jeans and T-shirt. Brother Daniel is at least a foot taller than me. I looked rather silly in his white coveralls, but neither an apiary nor a monastery are places for vanity. I put long white gloves over my arms and a hat and veil over my head. Dressed and ready, we headed into the bees' enclosure set into a small hill on the edge of the forest. I held the smoker, which brother Daniel had painstakingly filled, fueled, lighted, and tended. He explained that bees have an extraordinary sense of smell, and the smoke disorients that. But if the smoke is too hot it burns them, so it has to be cool smoke. As I compressed the bellows to keep the smoke going, brother Daniel opened the first hive. "Hola, hola," he said to the bees. He talked to them in Spanish as he disassembled the hive to add a second level. We loaded new honeycomb-laden layers into a second level to encourage the queen to lay more eggs, and then we reassembled the hive. We repeated this at several of the other hives while thousands of bees flew around us creating a constant, buzzing din.

I could hardly believe I was beekeeping, and I wondered how surprised brother Daniel's younger self would have been if he knew he would become a beekeeper/shepherd/monk at a monastery in Vermont instead of an Olympic runner. It was quite a morning—far from anything I thought I might do when brother Alvaro asked if I would like to join in the day's labor. As the bells rang to mark the end of the work period, we had to rush to put everything away and clean up in time for dinner. But as I sat in the parlor, hungry and tired from a morning in the pastures and apiary, I felt as if I was beginning to participate in the rhythm of monastic life. I felt less like an interloper or out-of-place researcher among retreatants and more as though I would become a friend. Like Noël the llama.

A Brief History of Weston

How I felt after the morning work period is perhaps how each new member of the community has felt as he has tried to figure out how he fit—or not—into the Weston family and the monastic vocation. While some people are perhaps naturally inclined to thrive in a monastery context, ready-made monks or nuns do not arrive at the Priory door. And those who do arrive at the door must spend a great deal of time getting to know the specific way of life of the monastic community around them, and the community must spend time getting to know each newcomer. Both must determine whether it is a good fit. This does not mean everyone must be the same, or fit some kind of strict mold, even if this kind of regularity reflects the usual popular image of monastic life.

After eating lunch with the brothers and their guests, attending the short None prayer, and commiserating with Lupita who had already found a mouse in the trap in her bathroom but insisted it was not Hershey, I spent the afternoon sitting at a picnic table taking notes on my experiences that day. I focused on the rhythms of monastic life, and how they seemed to come together in a complex dance. I wrote: "The brothers live a carefully choreographed life that is at once simple and yet enormously intricate and complex, like pieces of wool carefully woven into a solid fabric, the design of which at once reveals and obscures the many strands that make it and the regular, predictable structure that holds it together. It is a reflection of its individual parts, and yet it is greater than the sum of those parts. The monastery is a kind of living fabric rich with human experience and the pursuit of unity but not sameness."

In a conversation with brother Elias very early in my research, he mentioned brother Leo as an important inspiration for these dimensions of life at Weston. We sat in the living room of the original monastery building which was once a small farmhouse. Brother Elias smiled brightly as we spoke, and he told me about his early experiences as a Weston brother. He explained that as a young man in the early 1960s he was working in a store, getting up every day, eating, going to work, coming home, eating, then going to bed. He saw the same people on the same days buying the same foods. The same truck brought the same food on the same day. It all felt very rote and predictable. He felt it was not a route to happiness for himself. He said, "And one day, I remember, I was standing in front of the aisles of the store saying: What is this? Is this what life is about? There has to be more."

It was a question that started his process of seeking the "more." He found it, in part, in a recording of Gregorian chant. He recalled listening to the record and thinking it was really marvelous. He wanted to know where that kind of music lived, and so he started to look into different kinds of monastic communities. He began with Trappists in Genesee, New York, but found their way of life too limiting. Strict silence and a very enclosed community were not for him. However, he thought the life itself was very beautiful and, in his words, felt that the "monastic bug" had bitten him. A friend suggested the Benedictines and told him about two relatively new communities in New York and Vermont. He said, laughing, "Now I grew up in New Jersey, and I thought New Jersey was the center of the world, so Vermont meant nothing to me. I thought, *Vermont??*" We both laughed.

He visited Mount Saviour in Elmira, New York, first. But, as he explained it, "No bells went off." So he drove to Vermont and up the hill to Weston Priory. His heart sank when he saw the small farmhouse—in which we were then sitting—the attached barn serving as a chapel, dilapidated outbuildings housing various livestock, and land covered in brush and scrub. But when he knocked on the door and was welcomed inside, he felt an overwhelming sense of having arrived at home.

He went on to talk about how things do not always necessarily run smoothly and it is not always easy. He said, "If I had to choose twelve people to live with, I do not think I would have chosen these particular twelve. Now that's the mystery of community. *I* came up the hill, I *drove* three hundred miles to get here, to find this community, but in a way the community found me." He said that the people who have each given their word and given their life to creating the Weston monastic family welcomed him when he knocked on the door and continue to welcome him each day. He explained that, as in any family, there is no option to say, "You bug me, please leave," even when the brothers might grate on each other's nerves. But, he said, "there is an overriding blessing that we all experience however each of us came here, for whatever reasons. This is a daily thing."

He went on to explain that what brought each of them to Weston matters, but what is more important is what keeps them there. For him, he said it is, "Love. Respect for my person. An acknowledgment that who I am is good. I don't have to measure up. I don't have to be someone else." I was grateful to him for his honesty, and I recognized that I had felt a similar sense of welcome when brother Philip first greeted me at the door. Brother Elias went on to explain, "There is something beautiful in being the person that each of us are as gifts of God. And that's even more work than trying to blend yourself in with so many others, or only living with people you think are best for you."

Before this discussion, it had not occurred to me that flexibility and variety would be defining features of monasticism. It was in his discussion of these traits that brother Elias mentioned brother Leo. He said that he always thinks of brother Leo and his approach to the Rule of Benedict when he reflects on the distinctive characteristics that he found at Weston: openness, welcome, and flexibility. It was the first time I had heard one of the brothers mention their founder, Abbot Leo Rudloff, who became brother Leo when he retired and lived out his later years at the Priory. As brother Elias rooted his experience of monasticism in the vision and inspiration of their founder, I realized that, for the brothers, the history of the Priory and the story of its founding were an important part of the everyday life I was trying to understand.

Traditionally, monasteries have founding narratives that tell the story of the local community. When visiting a monastery, it is not uncommon for the founding narrative to be printed in a booklet or presented on plaques or posters. Like hagiography, folk tales, or legends, founding narratives are at once historical, creative, and instructive. The Weston story begins with Abbot Leo Rudloff, a Benedictine monk of Gerleve Abbey in Germany. He came to the United States as a young monk who, during World War II, was sent by his abbot to seek out possible means of refuge should religious houses be suppressed by the Nazis.[4] He settled in the United States, began teaching in a seminary, and looked for a possible refuge for his brothers back home. During this time, he also gained a reputation among his pupils and friends as an inspiring voice for the emerging liturgical movement that would usher in the Second Vatican Council and the many changes that followed in its wake.

The Gerleve monks were indeed forced to seek refuge as the Nazis turned them out of their Abbey to convert it into a home for unwed mothers. But the monks found help elsewhere and did not join brother Leo. After spending several years in the United States, and increasingly feeling that he was unlikely to ever return to Gerleve, brother Leo felt inspired to found a new community that would reflect his vision for a return to a simpler monastic observance based on scripture and the Rule of Benedict instead of the lengthy constitutions that had become commonplace. He shared this vision with his friend, Damasus Winzen, who fled Maria Laach Abbey to seek refuge for his confreres and later founded Mount Saviour in Elmira, New York. The two young Benedictines envisioned communities where all brothers would be equal instead of being divided into the social hierarchy that positioned ordained priest-monks above nonordained lay brothers. But before he could realize his vision, brother Leo was called back to Gerleve, which was reclaimed after the war. He was given a new assignment: to become abbot of Dormition Abbey, a German Benedictine monastery on Mount Zion in Jerusalem. The assignment was fraught with difficulty, but it was as abbot of Dormition that he was able to found a dependent Priory in the United States and finally begin to realize his vision for monastic renewal.[5]

While Benedictines had been around more or less continuously for fifteen centuries, many periods of decline and subsequent periods of revival found Abbot Leo on a mountain in Vermont ready to start a new community. After Saint Benedict founded his first monasteries in the sixth century, the Benedictines experienced several centuries of growth. By the Middle Ages, abbeys were often at the center of church and civic life. Many amassed extensive wealth and power. Medieval monks would likely have been surprised that, at the turn of the nineteenth century, most European monasteries were gone and only a handful of Benedictines remained. This decline occurred gradually through a series of social and political changes that reshaped European life, often violently: Reformation, French Revolution, Napoleonic Wars, Inquisition.

Around the middle of the nineteenth century, young priests and lay people, especially in Germany and France, looked at the abandoned or ruined abbeys around them and recalled the monastics who once called them home. These young men and women not only wanted to revive the monasteries in order to pursue the religious life, they also wanted to reform the Church by returning monasteries to the center of liturgical practices.[6] Their vision became an active revival of a monastic life inspired by the austerity, scriptural devotion, rich liturgical traditions, clerical work, and institutional structures of the Middle Ages.

Benedictine houses began to flourish again. The newly reestablished monasteries quickly expanded by founding smaller dependent communities in a hierarchical congregational system. Each congregation followed the founding abbey's model, often relying on extensive constitutions to regulate and maintain their monastic observance. But congregations differed, sometimes greatly, in their interpretation of the Rules and traditions of monastic life and their ideals for how that life should be lived.

Reflecting the colonialist spirit that dominated Western Europe at the time, this revival also featured a missionary drive that sparked the beginning of American Benedictine monasticism.[7] In 1846, a German monk named Boniface Wimmer brought a group of monastic recruits to rural Pennsylvania. They founded Saint Vincent, the first Benedictine monastery in the United States, based on an active, clerical, missionary way of life. The community thrived.

By the end of the nineteenth century, American Benedictine monks and nuns had a widespread network of monasteries, but not all of the new monasteries embraced Wimmer's active pastoral vision. Swiss monks founded communities based on a more contemplative, prayer-centered life. They created the Swiss-American congregation as an alternative to the missionary spirit of the American-Cassinese. This split between active and contemplative had been familiar in monastic life for centuries. Such disparate approaches were common even though Benedictine houses adhere to the same basic Rule. Yet, even with their differences, both types of communities depended on the same centuries-old monastic class system: ordained priest-monks as distinct from nonordained lay brothers. Ordained monks spent their time either in active ministry or near-constant prayer and study, so they did not participate in the physical labor necessary to maintain the monastery. Nonordained lay brothers did all the manual work and were separated from their ordained confreres: they did not have voting rights in the Chapter, were not allowed to enter into solemn vows, did not participate fully in the Office prayers, and had separate living accommodations. Strict separations developed between priests, addressed as "Father," and lay monks, addressed as "Brother."

This social hierarchy was standard practice in European monasteries for centuries, but, by the end of World War II, American Catholic populations were well established and the missionary focus and pastoral system that the lay brothers supported began to fade. During this turning point in the history of the Benedictines, Abbot Leo purchased a run-down farmhouse and founded Weston Priory with a monastic observance centered on prayer, a brotherhood based on equality, and a renewed focus on the Rule of Benedict.

American culture made a tremendous shift during these postwar years, creating the fertile ground for a community like Weston Priory. Young people in the 1950s began to anticipate the counterculture that would mark the 1960s.[8] Meanwhile, American Trappist monk Thomas Merton was writing extensively on his own monastic journey, inspiring a new generation of young men and women to seek out the spiritual life. Brother Augustine is an excellent example: in one of our earliest conversations he recalled reading Thomas Merton and French existentialists as a teenager, reading the Bible from cover to cover to ease his boredom in school, and seeking an alternative way of life that would break away from what he experienced as the tedium of a nine-to-five job. In 1959, his search led him to Weston where there were eighteen other aspiring monks ready to build a new way of life that would run counter to the social norms of the time. The land was rough, the roads were impassable in winter, and the hard manual labor of the farm took its toll on the brothers' spirits and bodies. In spite of these challenges, or perhaps because of them, Weston thrived, and brother Augustine was among those who welcomed brother Elias when he knocked at the door.

They also welcomed me when I arrived. As I retired to bed that night after checking in with Lupita and making sure the mousetraps were in order, I felt that my own efforts to participate in the daily realities of monastic life, and my work to get to know the brothers and allow them to get to know me, would allow me to find my own way into understanding the religious, musical, and human context into which I had entered. I also sensed that it would be a long, gradual process. But like brother Elias, I drove up the hill. I knocked on the door. I thought I had found the community. But really, the community would find me, and only then would I begin to learn what I had come to the monastery to learn.

Chapter Two

Singing like Benedictines

A Visit with Gregorian Chant

> We felt that we could partake of the meditation, that we could be borne up in the mystic ascent to eternity, to serenity.
>
> —Richard Crocker, *Introduction to Gregorian Chant*

> But the cold stones of the Abbey church ring with a chant that glows with living flame, with a clean, profound desire. It is an austere warmth, the warmth of Gregorian chant. It is deep beyond ordinary emotion, and that is one reason why you never get tired of it. It never wears you out by making a lot of cheap demands on your sensibilities . . . it draws you within, where you are lulled in peace and recollection and where you find God.
>
> —Thomas Merton, *Seven Storey Mountain*

Rooted in Gregorian Chant

I had my first formal interview with brother John during an early November visit to Weston. I was still getting my bearings in the monastic life around me and my role as ethnographer. My discomfort showed as I haltingly began the conversation, "I thought maybe we could start . . . I'm curious about . . . Could you tell me about what brought you here? To become a monk?"

Brother John smiled kindly, likely recognizing both my nervousness and a familiar question. He chuckled lightly as he said, "Of course. Well, it might not have a lot to do with music!" We were all still navigating my self-identification as an ethnomusicologist studying the brothers' music. "Actually," he went on, his facial expression becoming just a bit more thoughtful, "when I was a parish priest up in the Hardwick area, I was quite close to the Trapp family. I got a lot of feeling for good folk music with them." He referred to the Von Trapp family of *Sound of Music* fame. They made their home in Vermont after their flight from the Nazis, made legend in film. "But before that," brother John continued, "I was in the seminary and we had a lot of Gregorian chant. At that time, it was the 1940s, and the chant was pretty strong in the seminaries." He explained that the seminary piqued his interest in liturgical chant, while the Trapp family singers introduced him to a wider variety of folk, popular, and religious music.

He paused for a moment, seeming to collect his thoughts, and I actively suppressed my tendency to jump in to fill a momentary lull in conversation. Brother John folded his hands in his lap as he went on to describe the rugged farm life he encountered when he first came to the Priory in 1957. He laughed as he recalled chanting the Divine Office in Latin for hours every day even though few of the novice monks had studied either Latin or Gregorian chant. "The poor fellows didn't have a clue what they were saying! But even there, there was something to the music that added a simple, harmonious value to the life. It kind of took the edge off from a very harsh life, I would say, because in those days we had a lot of manual labor." He gestured around himself as if to indicate the fields around the monastery, explaining that the Priory was a working farm in the early days and it was very rough work. He smiled as he recalled that coming in and out of the house six times during the day to sing prayer helped to root the early community in the spiritual life of monasticism. Even though their prayer was really just the psalms at the time, brother John recalled that the experience of chanting with others encouraged them in what he described as "the search for God, the search for deep meaning in life, the search for harmony with who you're living with and what you're living with."

Perhaps because I still associated men in vocations with the Catholic priests of my childhood, this was not the way I expected a Benedictine monk to talk about music in the monastery. I anticipated a discourse on rules and regulations for liturgy, and perhaps a discussion of beauty and aesthetics. I had defended research proposals that assumed the centrality of such discourse. I wanted to know about Gregorian chant versus folk music. I imagined it like a battle between the old and the new, the traditional and the innovative, oppressive Latin and liberating vernacular. With these preconceptions swirling in my head, I was glad when the conversation began to turn naturally back toward Gregorian chant. Still new to field research, I was waiting for that golden moment when an informant would say exactly what I wanted to hear to confirm all that I assumed with such confidence to be going on around me.

Brother John became quietly thoughtful again. I shifted awkwardly in my seat. I had yet to grow comfortable with the gradual pace of conversation in the monastery. He smiled as he explained that chanting the Office was a very important part of being at the Priory: "I would say it even helped a lot with our relationships with one another. We would make mistakes of course in choir, and that would give us a little sense of humor to work with, but it also gave a sense of, um, almost sensitivity to one another." He explained that because the Chant had a single, simple melody, they had to develop an awareness of each other. This differed from their other work: "We had to become aware of one another in a more gentle way from our working on the farm or doing the house chores, where we would rub elbows in a harder way." He ended by saying he was unsure if he was addressing my question, and I realized I had forgotten what I had asked him in the first place. This was a good thing. It meant he was directing our conversation. But it did not help my discomfort in adjusting to my role as researcher/interviewer. I haltingly told him that I thought we were talking about what originally brought him to Weston, but I added that all of his thoughts were wonderful and he should continue talking about anything he felt important. This is when he first mentioned Saint-Benoît-du-Lac, a large Benedictine abbey just over the Vermont-Quebec border.

I asked if he was originally from Vermont. With a broad smile and animated face, he said, "I'm a native Vermonter! I never want to leave this!" He said that he grew up in Burlington before becoming a parish priest in the rural northeast corner of the state, not far from the Canadian border. He said that he visited Saint-Benoît with seminary friends. On one occasion, they took a boat up Lake Memphremagog, which is bisected by the Vermont-Quebec border. They paddled from Newport, Vermont, to the abbey, which sits on the lake. They had packed camping gear, expecting to set up their tents somewhere in the woods along the lake. He recalled his surprise when they paddled into the monastic enclosure without realizing it and saw monks jumping in the lake, clearly enjoying themselves on a hot summer day. It seems I was not the only one to be surprised when encountering the less-than-expected aspects of monastic life. The monks invited the young seminarians to join them for dinner and set up their tents along the shore near the abbey.

Brother John recalled sensing a deep joy and fraternal love in the monks. In a later conversation, he would point to this as one of the earliest moments in his own monastic journey. But that day, our conversation inclined toward music, and brother John returned to the narrative of his early experiences as a Weston monk:

> In the early days, we took the Gregorian and the chant very seriously. We were fortunate to have generous teachers. In fact, we had wonderful teachers from Saint-Benoît-du-Lac. They sent their choirmaster down here to give us choir lessons. Then there was a European master liturgist from Quarr Abbey, and he was really top man in Gregorian chant in the congregation of Solesmes at the time. He loved coming here because we were just starting and we weren't far enough along yet to be prejudiced!

He explained that they continued with the chant for close to ten years. He talked about the accents, the cadences, the modes, and the flow of Latin phrases. I asked if any of their current music was related to Gregorian chant, and he talked about their chanted psalms and their continued use of Gregorian modes. He then explained a bit about how the chanted psalms work: "We use *recto tono*, mostly. But there's a certain thing at the mediant, you go like that." He made a hand gesture to indicate "that." His hand started low, around his abdomen, then swooped up gently and did a little loop at the level of his shoulder. It was then that I realized that Gregorian chant was much more than the traditional music of the church that scholars, musicians, and liturgists discussed, and often argued over. More than the music in medieval books filled with neumes and intricately illuminated capitals, it was a lived, embodied music for a very present form of life, passed from one generation of monastics to the next in a process both written and oral. Brother John went on, "Gregorian is very nice from that point of view. It has set forms. You could pick it up in two or three days, although it seems really complicated." He chuckled a bit, seeming to enjoy this characterization of chant.

I felt my research proposals unraveling in bits around me. I was trying to hold it all together, clinging to my original notions of the Weston monks turning away from chant in an antiestablishment resistance to oppressive Church structures. I never expected brother John to speak so fondly about chant, nor did I think it would have anything to do with their present practices. I realized then that it was rather important for me to experience Gregorian chant as a current, living practice in a monastic context. I needed to understand the Weston monks' roots in the traditional music of the Benedictines. I decided that I needed to visit Saint-Benoît-du-Lac.

Être Present à la Presence

It was a bright, sunny summer afternoon many months later when I knocked on the door of Villa Saint-Scholastique, the women's guesthouse at L'Abbaye Saint-Benoît-du-Lac. The white, two-story farmhouse was tucked into a small patch of woods on the abbey grounds. The trees concealed the sweeping views of the mountains around the abbey and Lake Memphremagog below, but they also offered the guesthouse a sense of quiet seclusion in relatively busy surroundings: At least two dozen cars in the abbey parking lot, several people wandering the grounds, a few couples scattered around the fields having picnics, a family with three small children playing along the edges of an apple orchard, and a group of five men conversing animatedly as they stood around their motorcycles. A monk in a blue union suit drove a large tractor along the parking lot and into the orchard. Another monk dressed similarly drove a tractor along a side road and into the monastic enclosure toward what appeared to be a dairy farm. A third monk in a black tunic and hooded scapular—the habit traditionally associated with the Benedictines—walked through one of the fields, across the parking lot, and into the front doors of the large abbey. Several people walked in and out of the main entrance doors, some carrying plastic bags that appeared to have come from the abbey shop within.

I was surprised to see so many people and so much activity. I had not anticipated that the abbey would be such a popular regional tourist destination. When I made my way across the Vermont-Quebec border and drove along Lake Memphremagog that morning, I experienced a definite sense of transition from the outside world to the sensibility I had come to associate both with my research and with my monastery self. The towns around the lake were busy with the almost frenzied excitement and activity of a hot day in the always-too-short summer season. Families crowded the beaches as boats of all kinds dotted the lake. But when I rounded the north end of Memphremagog and began to drive along the western side of the lake, I began my transition to the pastoral calm of monasticism. Bustling lakeside towns turned to a rural landscape of farms and rolling hills. Driving along a ridge high above the lake, I turned onto Chémin des Pères—the road of the fathers—and took in sweeping views of the lake and surrounding mountains. As the winding road became the monastery driveway, I was aware of a sense of anticipation of the quiet calm and physical remove of monasticism.

Instead, I felt a bit intimidated when I pulled into a very large, moderately full parking lot and saw the vast stone abbey. Constructed of light gray stone, it looked almost white in the bright summer sunshine. The long building evoked the simplicity of monasticism in its straight lines and largely unadorned exterior, but it also suggested a heritage in gothic church architecture with a tall bell tower and decorative brickwork. A high, solid wooden fence enclosed the land around the abbey, leaving the main entrance accessible but preventing the public from accessing any of the land beyond the monastery. Signs on the fence read "Privé" and "Clôture Monastique: merci respecter notre solitude." The enclosure included the entire hillside down to the deep blue of the lake below, and it contained the brothers' dairy farm from which they produced exceptional French-style cheeses. The land in the areas accessible to the public was largely covered by trees and vast apple orchards, the fruit of which went into the brothers' hard ciders and other apple products.

When I made my reservation, the francophone woman on the phone told me to go to the Villa Saint-Scholastique when I arrived. The women's guesthouse was aptly named for Saint Benedict's twin sister, Scholastica, who is traditionally revered as an important founder of women's monasticism. It took a few minutes for me to spot the house tucked among the trees. Walking through the parking lot toward the house, I found a gravel path. An old piece of poured concrete at the head of the path had the phrase "Ave Maria" carved into it. Knowing this was Latin for "Hail Mary," I took it as a personal note of welcome nonetheless and began to feel the sense of Benedictine hospitality with which I was becoming familiar.

With the activity of the abbey now quietly behind me, I walked up to a side door on a small porch marked with an entrance sign. I knocked on the door unsure what to expect. I waited for several moments wondering at what point I could knock again without being rudely impatient. Just as I was about to rap on the door, a nun in a simple blue habit opened it. She greeted me softly in French and asked my name. I responded in my best French, quiet and a bit halting, but with a friendly smile that I hoped made up for what I lacked in fluency. She immediately switched to English, with a friendly smile of her own. Her English was far from fluent, and as we did our best to communicate in a blend of our respective native languages, I was reminded of my experiences with Lupita. I wished that I had learned from her and carried a pocket dictionary to help with communication. But we did well enough, and the gentle nun told me some of what I needed to know about the house before introducing me to the sister who would be in charge of showing me to my room.

During our conversation, we managed to talk a bit about my experiences with Benedictines. She had heard of the Weston monks and was very surprised to hear that I took my meals with them and was allowed to converse openly with them. She said, in a frank tone, that I would have no such contact with the Saint-Benoît monks. I had anticipated this, but it was the first time during my field research that I was uncomfortably aware of my status as a female researcher among monks. I sensed that, from her perspective, it was unusual both because I am female and because the monastic way of life perhaps should not include personal interactions with anyone outside the community. She explained that at Saint-Benoît, men stayed in guest quarters within the main abbey building and could take some of their meals with the brothers, but were largely excluded from contact or interactions.

I knew that my visit to Saint-Benoît would be vastly different from my work with the Weston monks; it was not extensive or embedded, I could not have open interactions, and I had a very specific, comparative perspective in mind. I wanted to observe a more institutional style of monasticism with a rich Gregorian chant practice. I wanted to see—and hear—chant as a living tradition. My limited engagement and narrowly defined gaze influenced my way of being at Saint-Benoît and shaped what I learned as a result of my time there. However, the experience turned out to be hugely valuable in ways I had not anticipated: it opened up my understanding not just of the Benedictine way of life and the role of music and language therein, but of my entire approach to my research.

Another nun entered the parlor in which we were standing. She greeted me, but in her rapid French I missed her name. I introduced myself, attempting to do so in what I thought was clear French. She nodded and began to speak in halting English. Her manner was direct, almost abrupt, compared to the quiet gentleness of the first sister. She was clearly the Guestmistress, and she took charge of welcoming me for my visit by running through the rules of the house: maintain silence at all times, no talking, no slamming doors, no loud shoes. She paused to be sure I understood what she said. I nodded and she brought me up the stairs to room #21 on the second floor. Upon opening the door and handing me my keys, she explained that meals would be served promptly after prayers, I must do my dishes, and I must not bring dishes to my room. She firmly instructed me to always make the bed, turn off the lights, and close the front door tightly without slamming it. She checked again to make sure I understood all that she said. She then said, "fumez-vous?" I looked puzzled. She repeated herself sharply while miming smoking a cigarette. "Oh! Smoke? Do I smoke? No. I don't smoke," I said, shaking my head. "Bon." She replied. She continued with the dress code for the chapel: nothing sleeveless, nothing low-cut, no shorts. Her demeanor was stern and no-nonsense. I was too intimidated to even consider talking in the house or failing to make my bed. At first, I found it all very alienating; hardly the blissful peace and calm I associated with a monastic retreat. But as I realized that I was sharing the house with more than a dozen other women, I appreciated the stern sister's efforts to maintain peace, quiet, and tidiness.

After showing me how to get to the dining room in the basement of the house, the sister told me about the brothers' cheeses and apple products. She told me that she loves them, and she encouraged me to buy some but not to forget them in the refrigerator. She opened the refrigerator door to reveal a bag of cheese left behind by a prior guest. Before walking back upstairs, she told me that it was nearly time for Vespers, and she would see me promptly afterward for dinner. I smiled, thanked her in English and French, and returned to my room to get settled.

As I walked up the stairs from the dining room, I saw a sign reading, Être présent à la presence (To be present to the presence). I recognized this concept of presence from my time at Weston, where I had been thinking about the challenge to be "fully" present with all that this suggested about the complexities of the monastic life, as well as my role therein as a researcher and visitor. Now here was the concept of presence, greeting me in the far less familiar territory of the Villa Saint-Scholastique. How, I wondered, would my presence in these surroundings be different? And what would I learn from it? I recalled a phrase from a poster I had seen in the Villa parlor. It advertised the opportunity to stay at Saint-Benoît and live "paix et silence." The poster did not say that you could live *in* peace and silence, but that you could *live* peace and silence. I sensed that there was an important difference, related not only to the concept of being present to presence but also to the monastic life I was trying to understand. With all of these thoughts making their way into my first entry in my field notes, my visit to Saint-Benoît had begun.

Understanding Language

When the bells tolled for Vespers that evening, I was already halfway across the parking lot headed toward the abbey, walking with perhaps a dozen other people. The sound of the bells made me quicken my pace. The abbey was clearly designed to receive many visitors and tourists. The main doors opened to a large lobby. Signs pointed to an information desk, a check-in area for male guests, the entrance to the men's guest rooms, and the stairs that led down to the abbey gift shop. A wide hallway extending from the far end of the lobby naturally guided visitors toward the abbey church. I walked down the hallway with around a dozen other people, some of whom carried cameras in spite of signs requesting no photos. Similar signs at the entrance to the church requested silence. One lengthier sign pointed out that in the house of God, modest dress is befitting: "Maison de dieu une tenue modest est de mise."

With their impressive chanted liturgies, and their equally impressive cheeses, I quickly understood why Saint-Benoît drew so many visitors. Large crowds meant that the monks had to work hard to maintain their privacy. It was rare for me to see any of them outside of the public prayer hours, or outside of their walled enclosure. To this end, they found ways to inform their visitors about the monastery without needing to be in contact with them. The long hallway with high vaulted ceilings had a series of large posters lining the walls. These displays, in French and English, contributed a museum-like quality to the public spaces in the abbey as they shared the local founding narrative and created a kind of historical archive. The posters explained that in 1901 anticlerical laws forced the monks of the French monastery of Saint-Wandrille into exile in Belgium. Unsure of their future in France, they eventually looked to transfer their foundation to Canada. Many European congregations were already well established in North America at the beginning of the twentieth century, but the Solesmes congregation, of which Saint-Wandrille was a part, had yet to found a community there.

I found the story of Saint-Benoît remarkably similar to that of brother Leo and Weston Priory. In 1912, Dom Paul Vannier was sent to Quebec to look into possible locations for the monastery and prepare for the arrival of his brother monks. He purchased a farm, and several postulants and professed Saint-Wandrille monks were sent to the new monastery. However, the events of World War I cut off all communication with the founding abbey. By the end of the war, Saint-Wandrille had found refuge in Belgium and the monks decided not to come to Canada. The young Saint-Benoît community continued nonetheless, and it began to thrive in the strongly Catholic province of Quebec.

Additional posters discussed the Rule of Benedict and showed the brothers at work and prayer. They also mentioned the style of Benedictine prayer and the Gregorian chant tradition for which the Saint-Benoît monks had become famous. This is exactly what I anticipated hearing as the hallway opened up into a vast, high-ceilinged narthex leading to the abbey church.

I opened a heavy door and entered the back of the nave. The chapel was very large and felt quite empty even though around forty people were in it. Wide rows of pews flanked a center aisle. I guessed they could hold several hundred visitors. The unadorned walls, columns, and vaulted ceilings were all constructed of light bricks the color of pale sand. The floors were a shiny off-white marble, just lighter than the walls. The monks' seats filled the area between the nave and the altar—called the "choir"—and their black wood created a sharp contrast against the light, almost ethereal background of marble and brick. The pews were made of a similarly dark wood, and I chose one near the front, just behind the low wooden barrier separating the public area of the chapel from the brothers' area.

As I walked down the long aisle to choose a seat, a monk in a black tunic and scapular sat down at the organ on the left side of the choir. He began to play as his brother monks gradually filtered in. The organ sang grandly, filling the vast church. It was clearly built for the space; it somehow seemed to belong there. I felt engulfed in the reverberant sound, surrounded by the distinctive resonance of a massive organ with pipes reaching up into the high vaults of the ceiling. The organist swayed gently back and forth as he played a light contrapuntal melody. Everything about the experience communicated "church" to my sensibilities: organ, resonance, the solid seat of a wooden pew. The surroundings also communicated "institutional church" in exactly the way I had anticipated when I decided to visit Saint-Benoît. In fact, I found myself a little alienated by the organ for exactly that reason, and, thus, I felt distanced from whatever the monks were about to do. I was still working to plumb the depths of all the baggage I brought with me into my field research. Having been raised in a post-Vatican II Catholic Church where guitars were the soundtrack for our preferred mode of anti-institutional populism, the organ prompted a resistant reflex in my subconscious. With my mind inclined as it was toward comparison, I assumed that Saint-Benoît would be completely different from any Divine Office prayers I had experienced at Weston Priory. It would be the negatively valued, institutional style that the Weston monks had tossed out in favor of their own music. Or so I thought.

The organ stopped and the brothers began their evening Vespers. They chanted the opening call to prayer in Latin, and I was a bit startled to realize that

I understood it. Not only that, I recognized that it was a variation on a similar call to prayer used by the Weston monks. I knew what they were doing, and all of a sudden the surroundings became familiar and my organ-prompted alienation subsided. I sat in the church a bit astounded. For the first time, I had the experience of appreciating Latin in a Church context. I had always positioned it as the language of oppression, keeping the people from understanding the priestly rituals of liturgy. But there I was, finding it comprehensible and familiar.

As Vespers continued, I noticed that some of the prayers were chanted in French and some in Latin. Because I did not readily follow the rapidly chanted French, I was further surprised to find that in a setting where I was given a choice between two foreign and variously unfamiliar languages, the Latin portions of the prayers emerged as more familiar and, thus, preferable to the local vernacular. I began to understand what brother John was talking about when we discussed the brothers' early efforts to learn Gregorian chant. The experience set the seeds of a thorough shift in my thinking about my research. I realized that I had created an overly simplistic understanding of language, inspired as much by my own experience as by the literature on liturgical music. I would not be looking at Latin versus vernacular, chant versus folk, nor even a straightforward comparison of the new and innovative versus the old and traditional. This kind of thinking would cause me to miss the deeper meanings of both tradition and innovation, as well as the problems and possibilities of music, language, and performance in monastery life and liturgy.

With my wheels turning, I set to scribbling notes in my pocket journal as Vespers concluded. I looked up to see the stern Guestmistress sister walk by my pew. She looked at me and, giving an ever so slight smile and raise of the eyebrows, looked at my journal before moving on down the aisle. I glanced around hastily, wondering if this kind of activity in the abbey church seemed inappropriate to her. I feared a reprimand upon my return to the house. I rushed out of Vespers eager not to be late for dinner.

Compline at St-Benoît-du-Lac

Compline is limited to three Psalms without refrain. After the psalmody comes the hymn for this hour, followed by a reading, a versicle, "Lord, have mercy," a blessing, and the dismissal. Each of the day hours begins with the verse, God, come to my assistance; Lord, make haste to help me, followed by "Glory be to the Father" and the appropriate hymn . . . The same Psalms—4, 90, and 133—are said each day at Compline. . . . Let us consider, then, how we ought to behave in the presence of God and his angels, and let us stand to sing the Psalms in such a way that our minds are in harmony with our voices.

—Rule of Benedict, 17.9–11, 18.19, 19.6–7

By the final night of my stay at Saint-Benoît, I had adjusted well to the rhythms of monasticism and was more than ready for the peaceful calm of one last Compline. A week of seven-a-day Divine Office prayers, and a good deal of time spent with the brothers' prayer books, had rendered the liturgies far more comprehensible than they had been on the evening of my first Vespers. From the Latin *completorium*, meaning complete, Compline signifies the end of the day and is the last of the daily prayers in the monastic Divine Office. Benedict focuses on the psalms in determining the texts for prayer, and his system can become rather complicated. For example, some psalms have themes that are suited to certain times of day, so these are assigned to their appropriate prayer hour. Psalms 4, 90, and 133 are sung nightly at Compline. Other psalms are specified for particular hours, but change from day to day. In the chapter on the order of psalmody, Benedict suggests the psalms for Prime, a morning prayer hour: "On Monday, three psalms are said at Prime: Psalms 1, 2, and 6. At Prime each day thereafter until Sunday, three psalms are said in consecutive order as far as Psalm 19. Psalms 9 and 17 are divided into two sections. In this way, Sunday Vigils can always begin with Psalm 20" (18.4–6). Psalms are similarly assigned to Vigils, Lauds, Terce, Sext, and None. Omitting those that are assigned elsewhere, four psalms are recited each evening at Vespers in numerical order. According to this system, the entire psalter is chanted in the course of a week.

Benedict then adds scripture readings, responses, hymns, prayers, verses, and canticles. The resulting formula establishes a clear set of prayer texts, but at the same time leaves a surprising amount of room for interpretation. Even in the division of the psalms, the part of the Divine Office to which Benedict devotes the most attention, he shows flexibility: "Above all else we urge that if anyone find the distribution of the psalms unsatisfactory, he should arrange whatever he judges better" (18.22). Ultimately, it is not the order of the liturgy that is most important in the Rule; it is the act of gathering for communal prayer throughout the day, with a focus on singing the psalms: "Let us consider, then, how we ought to behave in the presence of God and his angels, and let us stand to sing the psalms in such a way that our minds are in harmony with our voices" (19.6–7).

As the sun set behind Lake Memphremagog, and the abbey bells rang for Compline, I was still certain that the institutional, more strictly hierarchical abbey was obviously different from the small, egalitarian Weston Priory. But the more time I spent at Saint-Benoît, the less certain I became about the exact nature or importance of those differences. The monks spent their days moving between periods of work, prayer, and study. They cared for animals, worked the land, chanted prayers, maintained silence, hosted guests, and revered Saint Benedict. They wore black habits, lived behind high walls, and distinguished ordained from nonordained brothers, but the defining characteristics of their day-to-day lives felt familiar in ways that I would come to see as distinctively Benedictine.

In the chapel, there was just enough daylight and candlelight to allow me to find my way to a seat. All the lights were off except for one small spotlight illuminating a simple wooden statue of the Virgin Mary. I sat in what had become my usual pew at the front of the nearly empty chapel. Compline drew few visitors, but it quickly became my favorite of the Divine Office prayers, largely for its simplicity, brevity, and sensibility of calm, quiet darkness. Gradually, in the silence of the dark chapel, the monks entered. They gathered with neither urgency nor delay, making their way to their seats along the sides of the choir. They wore traditional Benedictine habits: long tunic, scapular, and hood, all in black, tied at the waist with a black cord. They wore black rubber-soled shoes that made no sound as they moved about the church.

The monastic benches that lined the sides of the choir reminded me of the ones at Weston, except that each seat had a partition separating it from the seats on either side. Not an armrest, these partitions turned the benches into long rows of individual stalls. This style of monastic bench is common in Christian monasteries. Each monk had several liturgical books shelved in front of him, a folding wooden seat, and a kneeler. When the seats were folded up, a small, shelf-like protrusion nicknamed the "mercy seat" gave the brothers a place to lean during lengthier standing prayers. The community seemed to have at least fifty monks, but the number of choir stalls in the large abbey church suggested that it could house more than twice that number.

As they entered for Compline, the monks seemed like a grouping of individual men moving about in ways unrelated to those around them. However, when all had gathered, the abbot knocked on the arm of his chair and they became a cohesive whole. In unison they stood and turned, the rustle of fifty black scapulars breaking the silence.

While most of the Saint-Benoît daily prayers featured a mix of Latin and French, Compline was primarily sung in French. Facing the altar, the monks chanted their call to prayer in unison. It was a simple chanted variation on the invocation specified in the Rule of Benedict: "God, come to my assistance. Lord, make haste to help me." A *Gloria Patri* doxology followed:

> Abbot: *Dieu, viens à mon aide!*
> Monks: *Seigneur, à notre secours.*[1]
> Everyone, bowing low at the waist: *Gloire au Père, et au Fils, et au Saint-Esprit, maintenant et à jamais; au Dieu qui est, qui était et qui vient, pour les siècles des siècles, Amen.*[2] *Alleluia.*

The simple chanted tones created a wash of sound as the words reverberated around the abbey church. The brothers' voices blended in a loose unison that lacked any strictness or formality. Still bowing low, they quietly chanted the Examination of Conscience on a single, almost mumbled tone:[3]

> *Je confesse à Dieu tout-puissant, je reconnais devant mes frères,*
> *que j'ai perché en pensée, en parole, par action et par omission;*
> *oui, j'ai vraiment péché.*
> *C'est pourquoi je supplie la Vierge Marie, les anges et tous les saints,*
> *et vous aussi, mes frères, de prier pour moi le Seigneur notre Dieu.*[4]

They then stood, turned to face one another, and began the psalms. They chanted Psalms 4, 90, and 133, all in French. The psalms were chanted in an antiphonal style with a faster recitative tempo and more complex tonality than I had heard at Weston. The Gregorian modes provided the melodic contours. Each mode has a main chanted tone, called the "tenor," a group of pitches called the "mediant" that occur around the middle of each phrase, and a concluding cadence at the end, called the "final." At Compline, they used the Eighth Mode with a mediant giving a gentle upward motion in the middle of each two-line verse and a final stepping down from the tenor, then upward away from it before returning to it on the final word of the verse.[5]

As the brothers on one side of the nave came to the end of their line, their rhythm slowed and their volume tapered. This heightened the sense of sighing or exhaling created by the falling melodic movement of the Eighth Mode, and it created an opening for the brothers on the opposite side—already taking a deep breath in anticipation—to begin the next phrase, resuming the quick tempo of the chanted lines at a fuller volume in the resonant space of the vast, empty church. They sang with a full, open timbre and steady, rich tone. Their sound was free of vibrato, and they hit each pitch exactly without wavering or sliding from note to note. There was a sense of practice and precision mixed with the relaxed calm of simple chanted lines.

When the psalms ended, they sang a brief Latin hymn, a brother read aloud a short selection from scripture, then another brother led the call-and-response of the *Kyrie*.[6] After a brief pause, one brother chanted the words "notre père" on a single tone. Silence followed, during which I assumed the monks were each praying a silent *Notre Père*. I wondered if they chanted the words to themselves on the tone given by the cantor, and, as I had heard this prayer—the Lord's Prayer, or Our Father—in both French and Latin during my visit, I further wondered if the monks chose one language or the other when praying silently to themselves, or if they always used the language prompted by the cantor, or if they used their own native language. I sat in the church in silence, considering issues of language instead of praying the Our Father—I would have chosen to think the words in English even though I had both the French and Latin translations in a prayer book in front of me—and I realized that the question of liturgical language is complex in part because language can be deeply personal and internal as well as communal and external. It can evoke and emerge from a sense of heritage, place, and the familiar as well as a sense of ritual, space, and the sacred. In a liturgical context, language moves among and between all of these categories at once.

After a lengthy silence, the abbot recited a blessing and a small group of monks moved to the center of the church. I had seen them do this throughout my visit. These ten monks were the Choir Monks who devoted much of their time to learning and performing Gregorian chant. They stood in a semicircle with one monk, called the choirmaster, facing the group. He raised his arms and they began to sing a long, florid *Ave*. The pitches gently moved downward then swept up to a bright *Regina Caelorum*, each syllable of *Caelorum* marked by a gradual movement back down.[7] The opening line, with its graceful motion up toward and then down from Regina, emphasized praise for the Queen of Heaven. She was the high point of the line. She was the object of devotion. As I recognized the Marian Hymn—a type of song with which monastics traditionally end their day—my gaze was automatically drawn to the only light in the room shining on the statue of the Virgin Mary.

The round, steady tones of the Compline hymn gently filled the abbey and seemed to wrap the monks, like their black habits, in the Benedictines' traditional mode of praise. In unison they sang: *Ave Domina Angelorum*. This time, the melodic and rhythmic emphasis landed on Domina, lady. They ended each day by honoring not God, not father, not son, but mother. In other words, not the usual male imagery that so saturates Christianity to the exclusion of women's knowledge, experience, voice, and power. While I instinctively wanted to resist Marian devotion and its perpetuation of problematic virginity-purity-holiness narratives, it seemed to me that the Compline hymn was about choosing to honor humanity.[8] But not just any humanity: a woman's humanity as deeply connected to and even the physical source and manifestation of divinity. A woman as the Mother of God. I smiled to myself as I thought that the Compline hymn was perhaps a centuries-old tradition of monks ending each day by saying goodnight to their mother. As they sang their final utterance of the day to their Domina, I appreciated the power and reverence that she claimed in that space. She was the only woman allowed behind the barrier, beyond the monastery walls.

The florid, melismatic melody typical of Gregorian chant made it difficult for me to follow the rest of the syllables and words, so I meditated on these ideas as I became absorbed in the sound. It was difficult not to; the vast emptiness of an abbey church gives Gregorian chant its characteristic resonance, as if the voices are coming not just from the men singing in the choir but from the walls, the vaulted ceilings, the very air in the room. I wondered how they learned to sing like that, to open their mouths and produced a wide open tone that was rich, steady, round, neither too warm nor too cool, neither bright nor dull. It was not that the sound was free of inflection or interpretation. Each line swelled gently toward its highest point, then relaxed. The tempo varied ever so slightly through each florid passage. A little faster here, then slowing again there. It reminded me of the give-and-take of the chanted psalms; each line seemed to move and flow from one to the next. It brought a quiet energy to the dark room as the full tenor voices seemed to achieve unity not only in the simplicity of their tone but also in collectively creating a characteristic style appropriate to the monastic prayer it was intended to support. To *be* a Benedictine is to *sing* like a Benedictine. It felt sacred, ancient, and ethereal. In the words of chant scholar Richard Crocker, "We felt that we could partake of the meditation, that we could be borne up in the mystic ascent to eternity, to serenity."[9]

As the hymn gradually wound down to its concluding phrase, *Et pro nobis Christum exora,* I noticed that my breathing was slow and regular, and the constant chatter of my inner monologue had ceased. I had partaken in the meditation. Perhaps this meant that I was fully present. I was unsure if I was present to the presence, as the guesthouse sign had encouraged, but I certainly felt that I had participated in Compline internally in an important way. I did not need to sing along with the monks—such participation was absolutely not appropriate at Saint-Benoît—to be included in the experience. I occupied some kind of in-between space that was effective for opening up a way of knowing and understanding monasticism.

Of course, as soon as I took a moment to notice my presentness, it faded as my thinking mind took over. The monks left the church and I pulled out my notebook. Squinting in the fading light, I scribbled: "not ancient, revived, don't forget." I wanted to resist, somehow, being absorbed in the cultural and historical references of chant. I wanted to resist the romanticism of becoming enchanted. But as I encountered the ethereal beauty of this revived medieval art form, I felt that I understood, in a very real and immediate way, why the Solesmes monks felt so strongly about its restoration.

Restoring Chant, Creating History

For many people, Gregorian chant is at once familiar and unfamiliar. Albums recorded in abbey churches by Benedictines have made headlines for their surprisingly wide popularity and strong sales, such as the album *Chant* by the Benedictine Monks of Santo Domingo de Silos in the early 1990s and, more recently, *Benedicta: Marian Chant from Norcia* by the Monks of Norcia. In her work on this phenomenon, Katherine Bergeron points out that, in spite of its apparent familiarity, defining chant is really very difficult. It is a form of sacred music, and thus wedded to its attendant ritual practices, but it is also a kind of exotic music that is appealing precisely for its otherness and sense of temporal and spatial distance.[10] For people like me—visitors who sit in the resonant chapels of monasteries—chant can become a kind of musical and spiritual tourism, a chance to experience this familiar-yet-distant Other.

Gregorian chant, as it is performed in this context, is the result of the revival and restoration of Benedictine life undertaken in the nineteenth century by French monks. And while the study and practice of Gregorian chant has long been a topic of debate for practitioners, scholars, and liturgists who discuss the formation and continuity of chant, the appropriate vocal technique, the correct execution of rhythm, and the place of chant in contemporary liturgical practices, the people who buy Gregorian chant albums and visit monasteries to hear chant recognize a performance style that has become the accepted, familiar style whether or not early music scholars and chant experts agree that it is the most accurate or authentic interpretation of the medieval manuscripts.[11]

In the anticlerical, anti-Church, postrevolution atmosphere of nineteenth-century France, once-thriving monasteries sat empty for more than a generation. When Prosper Guéranger, a French priest, looked at the priories and abbeys that were largely in ruins, he wanted to revive the Benedictine life in France, but Benedictines were unseen and unheard in his lifetime. As he went about restoring the priory of Saint-Pierre-de-Solesmes, he depended on the Rule of Benedict and surviving sources, especially medieval chant manuscripts, to help him understand how the monks lived, what they did, how they looked, and how they sounded. Bergeron describes this as the work of restoration not unlike that of restoring the many ruined medieval Cathedrals in France. She suggests that restoration is not a question of repair or rebuilding, but of reestablishing a state that may never have existed at any given time. It is not about returning a building to its original condition, but about returning it to history, which is itself a modern idea of imagining the past as an object of self-conscious study.[12]

This is perhaps counterintuitive to what is typically imagined as the work of restoration, but it is exactly the kind of project Guéranger undertook as he worked to restore the Benedictine life and monastic liturgy to Solesmes: he studied the layers of the past to imagine a present way of life. He looked at sources and ruins for evidence. In the process, he created something that may have never existed as such at any given time. This is not to suggest that the Benedictine life and musical practices that sprang from the Solesmes revival were or are inauthentic, but rather to position them in the context within which the past was reimagined in the present and for the future. It was the work of creating history in present performance.

This bears significantly on the music that resulted from the Solesmes revival: Guéranger did not simply want to return chant to the monastic liturgy, he believed that the music would restore the monastic life it was intended to support. For him, understanding the lyrics and melodies preserved in medieval notation was one thing, but figuring out how the chants should sound and how they should be performed was quite another. Phrasing, rhythm, and vocal style were not recorded in the manuscripts, so he and the choirmasters who followed him made a series of choices about how the music should be performed in a manner both authentic and beautiful. But more than this, they believed that through their diligent work to restore musical performance they would restore the foundational elements of monastic life. They believed that song exists in and calls up memory such that it could preserve and offer access to a past way of life that was lost to their present time. Song was the voice and echo of a way of being, and it had a unique capacity to bring it back to the present.[13]

That their work resulted in a musical style that is unlikely to have existed as such at any given time, and that is as much a reflection of nineteenth-century French ideas about song as medieval musical practices, does not seem to lessen its appeal or its reputation as an enchanting, mysterious echo of the past. To point out that Guéranger and the Solesmes choirmasters were the products of their place and time is not to discredit or devalue the Solesmes monks' ongoing work to maintain Gregorian chant practices. Indeed, chant restoration was an impressive undertaking of diligent, careful study that returned a rich monastic heritage to the Benedictines and those who visit them. But in experiencing the chant of an abbey in the Solesmes congregation while studying academic discourses on Gregorian chant, I became deeply aware that the distant, ancient, mysterious music of the Church that I expected to encounter was in fact a far richer and more complex reflection of the musical, religious, and cultural heritage of the monks who created it in a very specific, and not-so-distantly past, moment. It reflects the ideas, traditions, and creative imaginations of the monastics who restored it and of those who continued to perform it. But if my experience at Saint-Benoît—along with the enduring popularity of monasteries in the Solesmes congregation and their chant albums—is any evidence, Guéranger and his monks seem to have succeeded in their broader goal of creating liturgical music that would foster a particularly Benedictine way of life preserved in song.

This is what my visit to Saint-Benoît helped me to understand. Musical performance, and all of its attendant choices of language and style, has a far more complex relationship to the Benedictine life—and the monks who live it in specific places and times—than I had originally imagined. I expected Saint-Benoît to be a kind of counterpoint to Weston, but instead I learned that there are elements that make Benedictine liturgy and life distinct, elements that an insider would recognize: the Divine Office with its regulated rhythm of prayer; the chanted psalms, Gloria Patri, Kyrie, readings, blessings, and hymns; the physical choreography of standing, bowing, leaning back, and sitting; the rows of benches turned to face each other instead of a central altar, orienting the focus toward the community; the quiet, contemplative aesthetic; the emphasis on silence; the balance of daily work, study, and prayer; the blend of hospitality, community, and solitude. I went in search of difference, but instead found similarities that started to point me toward deeper, more enduring, more important aspects of the Benedictine way of being and the music that emerges from and sustains it.

Chapter Three

Singing like Weston Monks

Let us consider, then, how we ought to behave in the presence of God and his angels, and let us stand to sing the psalms in such a way that our minds are in harmony with our voices.

—Rule of Benedict, 19.6–7

We get up in the morning and we come together to sing. In the afternoon, we sing. In the evening, we sing. At night, the last thing we do is come together to sing.

—Brother John

It's all about the liturgy of the hours, returning each day to prayer.

—Brother Michael

The Kitchen and the Heart of the Monastery

The Weston kitchen was designed to sustain a large family. Stainless steel countertops, a high-speed sanitizing dishwasher, a deep restaurant-style sink, and a walk-in refrigerator lend something of an industrial look, while bright red countertops, pegboard-covered walls, rustic wood cabinets, and high windows lend warmth and a farmhouse style. Longer windows in the corner cast light on a built-in bookcase filled with cookbooks. In the opposite corner, a large walk-in pantry holds cooking equipment and various pantry staple foods.

On a warm July afternoon following an equally warm morning spent weeding and watering the garden with brother Columba, brother Daniel, brother Michael, brother Richard, and three fellow guests, I arrived in the refectory to find lamb on the buffet table. "Oh, I love lamb, what a treat," whispered the woman standing to my right. We could hear the sheep bleating outside as they sheltered from the July heat in whatever shade they could find. "Let's not tell *them* we're eating lamb," she said, with a little wry smile, cocking her head toward the sheep. I wondered if she knew that the lamb on the table was in fact from the brothers' own sheep. I decided not to mention it. Whereas the brothers preferred to eat meat that they themselves raised in a caring, sustainable environment, guests were often a bit squeamish when they realized that the cute sheep were destined to be their dinner.

This said, some of the brothers and many of their guests were vegetarian. Whenever meat was on the buffet table, a meatless option was also offered. Saint Benedict anticipated such scenarios, it seems, as the Rule states: "For the daily meals, whether at noon or in mid-afternoon, it is enough, we believe, to provide all tables with two kinds of cooked food" (39:1). Having two options accounts both for "individual weaknesses," and an inability to eat certain foods whether out of preference or necessity. Benedict suggests that fresh fruits and vegetables also be served, when available, along with a "generous pound of bread" (39:2–3). He supposes this to be sufficient for any meal, and indeed the Weston buffet table matched this description almost exactly. Feast days and times of excessive manual labor call for more food, and Benedict takes this into account. But he also cautions, "Above all, overindulgence is to be avoided, lest a monk experience indigestion. For nothing is so inconsistent with the religious life as overindulgence" (39:7–8). The Rule is nothing if not practical.

I tend not to eat red meat, and I had spent too much time with the sheep to feel that I had the wherewithal to have them for lunch. I continued down the table toward the vegetarian dish, an unfamiliar food that looked as if meatloaf and zucchini bread were squished together into one tightly packed, veggie-loaded mass. The little sign read "carrot and mushroom loaf." I had never eaten such a thing. It was not unappetizing, just unfamiliar. I took a modest slice, then added cucumber salad to my plate, along with broccoli leftover from Sunday dinner, and a thick slab of whole-wheat bread.

When all were served, brother Michael sang the dinnertime blessing prayer and we sat down. We ate in silence as brother Michael read from President Obama's autobiography, and brother Richard and brother Placid poured water or iced tea into waiting glasses. As I ate, I found that I quite enjoyed the carrot-mushroom loaf. It was entirely unfancy, unassuming, hearty home-cooked food. The carrots were sweet. The mushrooms were earthy. The whole thing clung together with the help of eggs and, I supposed, breadcrumbs, lending an almost quiche-like density and moistness. I enjoyed it so much, I had to have the recipe.

When everyone finished eating and brother Richard rang the bell to end the mealtime silence, I spent a few minutes in conversation with the woman sitting next to me, the one who had been so thrilled to see lamb on the table. She had enjoyed it tremendously. I wanted to catch brother Elias before he moved on to other tasks, so I picked up my plate and carried it into the kitchen. A brother stood at the sink rinsing dishes and loading the dishwasher. A guest emptied the dishwasher. Brother Placid stood at the sink on the other side of the room washing serving ware and baking dishes. Brothers dried and put away those dishes. Another brother cleaned up the leftovers. Brother John had two female guests helping him to clear the refectory. Two more female guests wiped down the tables while two male guests set out the glasses and silverware for supper. All jobs seemed to be covered, and while I would normally jump in to help with one of the tasks, I really wanted to chat with brother Elias. I spotted him across the kitchen stirring a huge stock pot filled with what I assumed would be the soup for supper that evening. I crossed the room, trying unsuccessfully to avoid getting in anyone's way, and asked brother Elias about the carrot-mushroom loaf.

He looked pleased, and said that he thought it was a really great recipe. He replaced the lid on the pot, put down the long spoon he had used to stir the soup, and began to walk toward the bookshelves in the corner. He explained that some of the brothers are vegetarian, and he was pretty sure the recipe was in the *Moosewood* cookbook. Brother Elias was to Weston what the cellarer would have been in Saint Benedict's monasteries. He ordered food, kept track of provisions, and organized meals. The kitchen was a place of pride for him; it was the heart of the home, and he did a lot of the work that kept it ticking. In search of the recipe, he scanned the built-in shelves. They contained a small library of home cookery. Most of the books seemed old and well loved. Many were vegetarian, including the *Moosewood* cookbooks, an early edition of *Laurel's Kitchen*, and a host of other vintage, seventies-era volumes. There were several classics from Betty Crocker and *Gourmet*. There were books on tofu, soup, organic foods, whole foods, and baking. There were holiday cookbooks and pasta cookbooks. Every book brother Elias pulled down seemed to overflow with margin notes, recipe cards, and bits of paper. Bookmarks indicated favorite recipes, each with handwritten details about how to double or triple the quantities. Crossed out sections showed where the recipes had been amended over the years. The collection stood in the bookshelves, a silent witness to the Weston family, and an archive of their everyday lives.

Brother Elias found the book he was looking for, and it was indeed the original *Moosewood*, a now-classic vegetarian cookbook created by the owners of Moosewood restaurant in Ithaca, New York, at a time when vegetarian foods were not easy to come by. Penciled-in margin notes explained how to triple the original recipe. Notes in the margins suggested possible substitutions for some of the ingredients. A fellow female guest noticed us looking at the cookbook, and, as she emptied a small bucket of water into a nearby sink, exclaimed, "That cookbook changed my life!" She went on to tell us that, when she became a vegetarian in the 1970s, it was not easy to get things like tofu and tempeh in the grocery store, and vegetable-based main courses did not appear in Betty Crocker. *Moosewood* allowed her to be a home cook and a vegetarian.

Brother Elias handed me a pen and a blank note card. "I also have a wonderful recipe for tofu rounds, if you'd like it," he said, and he went in search of it while I copied lists of ingredients and instructions.

While I was a Priory guest, much of my contact with the brothers occurred in these sorts of informal conversations in the kitchen. We frequently chatted while standing over sinks of dirty dishes, steaming dishwashers, and trays of leftovers. We discussed a wide variety of topics: my research, current events and politics, the weather, the Priory gardens and animals. Brother Augustine and I often exchanged book recommendations and talked about our favorite authors while packing up the leftovers. He suggested that I read Susan Brind Morrow's books that blend anthropology, archaeology, environmentalism, and memoir.[1] They influenced the way I thought about research and writing. Brother Columba always kept me up to date on the Red Sox during baseball season while he loaded the dishwasher and I put the clean dishes away. As a boy, he sold ice cream in the bleachers at Fenway Park and watched Ted Williams play. I never tired of his stories.

I was drying dishes one evening with brother Placid when I learned firsthand about the problems that arise in community life when no one calls the plumber because everyone thought someone else had already done it. The sink backed up and brother Placid turned to brother Richard, "I thought the plumber came to fix this. Did you talk to him?" Brother Richard had not, but was sure brother Elias had done so. Brother Elias, passing by the sink and hearing the conversation, said, "No, I'm sure it was brother Augustine who talked to the plumber." Brother Augustine assured them that he had not. And so the conversation continued around the kitchen as the sink backed up and brother Placid and I looked at the dirty dishes with dismay.

The kitchen may have been a place for conversation, but it was never a place to linger or meander. At least, not until the dishes were done. I had many conversations with brothers and guests in a clean, quiet kitchen between dinner and the bell for midday prayer. But until the kitchen was clean, each brother had his assigned task and completed it in a dedicated space. Guests joined in an effort to help the work move more quickly, even if we did sometimes clog up the works in spite of our best intentions. My favorite times in the kitchen occurred when a particularly attentive bunch of guests had been at the Priory for several days and had experience enough to make the kitchen run smoothly alongside the brothers. I suspect the brothers also appreciated these days as activity swirled in a careful choreography. Someone loaded a cart with the leftovers from the buffet table. Someone else helped to pack up the leftovers and put them in the fridge. Pots, pans, and serving dishes went to the sink to be hand-washed by one brother, dried and put away by another. Everyone brought his or her own plate into the kitchen, scraped it into a bucket destined for the pigs, and piled it next to the deep, stainless-steel sink. A brother stationed at this sink prewashed dishes in a bin of water before loading them into the dishwasher. Another person stood at the dishwasher, putting away the clean dishes. Someone else sorted silverware. Another group cleared the refectory tables, wiped them, and set them for the next meal. Everything was remarkably efficient as the kitchen buzzed with activity. Except for pleasant conversation, it could be done in silence as each person counted on the others to do their part and trusted that the system would work. It was like a daily post-meal metaphor for the entire monastic life.

The active domestic space of the kitchen and dining room are central to many homes, as had certainly been my experience growing up in a large extended family. Food is social history, and the kitchen becomes not only the heart of the home, but a place for people to perform their identities as part of a family or social group. In the kitchen, the interpersonal interactions that create relationships take shape and are manifest.[2] I created and performed my own identity as a guest of the Weston monks in this domestic space. In a gradual process, one meal after another, the brothers got to know me, and I got to know them. By learning where the serving spoons belonged, I learned where I belonged. By figuring out how to work with the brothers, I participated in the monastic life as thoroughly as in any Morning Vigil or evening Vespers. As we laughed at the jokes and humorous anecdotes that are part of Weston parlance, I became part of the conversation instead of just a passer-through or interloper temporarily checking out monastic life. The more I visited Weston, the more I became part of these tales and opportunities for laughter. For example, the story of the time I encountered a mama and baby black bear and ran terrified out of the Priory woods, very nearly running into the brothers' pickup truck as they drove up into the woods, is now a humorous part of the repertoire of kitchen conversation.

Not surprisingly, but entirely unexpectedly, the kitchen became the primary locus of my research. In a long series of informal conversations, the brothers and I joined in the mutual dialogues that became the foundation of my work. These are the unexpected moments that cannot be planned, but make field research exciting and invigorating. One September evening, for example, not long after my visit to Saint-Benoît, I talked with brother Michael as we washed dishes after supper. He loaded the dishwasher, the high-speed cycle ran its course, and I emptied the dishwasher when the cycle finished and the steam dissipated. We talked about liturgical music, particularly the processes of change that find older styles replaced by newer ones. We agreed that it is interesting how easily older styles are positioned as "traditional" and thus more authentic even though those styles were once new themselves.

In the Rule, the psalms are the foundation for daily prayer. Saint Benedict outlines a system through which monastics chant the entire book of psalms—all 150—in the course of a week. Most contemporary communities spread this out over two or more weeks, but the psalms remain the heart of Benedictine liturgy. Each community has a psalter—a book of psalms set to chant tones—and I had been working with a copy of the brothers' psalter to see what their translations were like. Brother Michael was interested in the similarities between it and Gregorian chant psalters, which got us onto the topic of Gregorian chant. As he put a steaming rack of clean plates on the counter, he told me that at one point several years ago he wanted to learn more about Gregorian chant. He is one of the youngest brothers in the community—he joined in the mid-1980s—so he did not experience the Latin liturgies of the 1950s and early 1960s. To aid his learning, he read a book on chant published by the Abbey of Regina Laudis, a community of Benedictine sisters in Connecticut who are well known for their chant tradition. He recalled being particularly impressed by the complexity of the chant systems, and marveled at the amount of time and effort required to learn and perform them well. I agreed, having spent countless hours reading about Gregorian chant just so I could understand the tradition, to say nothing about actually trying to sing the complex chant tones and florid hymns.

Brother Michael continued washing and loading dishes, and I stacked plates on the shelves above the dishwasher. I moved the empty rack from the counter, nearly bumping into another guest who was busy setting out bowls and cereal for the morning. As we continued to discuss the sisters at Regina Laudis and my visit to Saint-Benoît, brother Elias, who had walked across the kitchen to put a cookbook away on the shelves next to me, overheard us and joined the conversation. Brother Michael pulled a steaming rack of dishes out of the dishwasher and his glasses fogged over. I told the brothers that it seemed to me that Gregorian chant must be a primary focus of a choir monk's or choir nun's monastic vocation. They devote a great deal of time to practicing, preparing, and studying the chants, not to mention the time required to sing them in prayer.

Loading a new rack of dishes into the dishwasher while I put away clean plates, brother Michael agreed because, to him, Gregorian chant is an art form that requires a great deal of time and work. Brother Elias, who was setting out coffee and tea for the morning beside two female guests who were drying water pitchers, observed that it takes so much work to sing Gregorian chant really well that it could easily become the focus of work, prayer, and study. Knowing that balance is central to the Rule and Benedictine life, we wondered how the choir monks find balance, and whether or not the lay brothers in a community like Saint-Benoît wish that they, too, could participate in singing the chants. The divisions between ordained and nonordained monks was not part of life at Weston, and the idea felt foreign, even unappealing, to me as we stood together around the sink. I understood brother Leo's insistence on limiting the monastic social hierarchy, and I wondered how the communal nature of monastic prayer might be different in a more institutional, hierarchical community like the one I had seen at Saint-Benoît.

The Weston Musical-Liturgical Style in Compline

By the time brother Michael, brother Elias, and I were finished cleaning up, the bells began to ring for Compline. It occurred to me that with or without the rigors of Gregorian Chant, praying the Divine Office daily in its entirety can become extremely time consuming. Throughout the Middle Ages, the monastic social hierarchies assigned all physical labor to the lay brothers, allowing the ordained choir monks sufficient time to sing the entire Office every day. Some contemporary communities maintain this, but without these social divisions it is nearly impossible for the Weston monks to sing the psalter in one week or pause eight times during the day for prayer. This is primarily a matter of practicality—the pigs and sheep are not going to feed themselves while the monks chant psalms all day. But it is also about the pursuit of balance across the activities of each day.

As has become common among contemporary Benedictines, the Weston monks maintain chanted psalmody, but they spread the psalms out over multiple weeks. They also combine the eight daily prayers into five—Morning Vigil at daybreak; Terce during their daily community meeting, called Chapter; None after the noon meal; Vespers in the evening before supper; and Compline at night before bed. On the weekends, they add a late morning Eucharist service. The weekend Eucharist services are the most popular for visitors, drawing hundreds of people during the summer and fall months. Of these prayers, only the mid-morning Terce prayer is not open to the public.

Monastics tend to treat Benedict's Rule as a series of guidelines rather than inflexible standards. Because of this, and also because the Benedictines have no single presiding abbot or abbess responsible for all Benedictine monasteries, there is a great deal of local flexibility in monastic practices. Yet the daily rhythm of prayer, the centrality of the psalms, and the use of hymns, readings, verses, and responses mean that, however individual, the Divine Office is recognizable and familiar across Benedictine communities.

Brother Michael shut off the lights and set out empty dish racks for the morning, and the three of us walked out of the kitchen with brother Augustine and brother Placid, who had just finished hand-washing dishes on the other side of the room. We walked through the dark refectory and down the long cloister walk. Brother Michael and brother Augustine turned into the sacristy to get their guitars. Brother Elias and brother Placid took their places in the lines that had begun to form along the walls: brother Columba and brother Peter on one side; brother Alvaro, brother Daniel, and brother Robert on the opposite side. They were silent, focused, and solemn as they waited for their brothers to join them for the final prayer of the day.

I entered the chapel and found that several other guests had already gathered. The Stone Chapel was divided into two sections. The brothers' area, called the choir, was once a small barn attached to the side of the original farmhouse. The brothers entered it through the open doorway at the back of the chapel that connects the choir to the sacristy and the main house. A small partition stood in front of the doorway blocking any view of the sacristy beyond. A simple wooden cross hung on the partition. The Eucharist table sat in front of the partition—this table would traditionally be called an altar in Catholic churches. It was a simple but substantial four-legged table stained dark brown.

The walls were plain white, framed by dark brown hand-hewn beams. Monastic benches lined the walls on the left and right sides. The long benches, made from wood repurposed from the barns' cow stalls, folded up for standing prayers. Their hand-hewn look and dark brown color matched the beams and maintained the rustic simplicity of the barn-turned-chapel. Small green binders were tucked between the bench and wall. These were the brothers' psalters.

The brothers extended the chapel in the 1970s to accommodate the many visitors who began coming to the Priory. The visitors' gallery had a fieldstone floor, white walls, and brown beams. Padded wooden chairs sat in tidy rows with an aisle in the middle. There was a carved wooden portrait depicting Jesus holding a book and offering a sign of peace. Aside from this, the cross, a felt banner with seasonal pastoral imagery, tiny crosses in the nave representing the Stations of the Cross, and a potted plant, there were no other adornments or icons in the chapel.

When I entered the dark chapel that night, I went to my usual seat in the front of the visitors' gallery. It was silent except for the occasional cough or quiet shuffle of feet. As I sat down, I heard the telltale scratch and sizzle of a striking match. The area around the sacristy partition began to glow with the flicker of candlelight on the other side. The brothers entered, breaking into two lines around the partition. Brother Columba entered first, carrying a long wick with the flickering flame. He walked slowly, his shuffling gait and gently curved back were evidence of a long life and many years of labor in the monastery farm and gardens. He went to the center of the brothers' area to light a tall candle.

Meanwhile, the brothers positioned themselves along the sidewalls, six on one side and six on the other. Silence filled the chapel. Brother Richard, the prior, began to bow toward the center of the choir. The rest of the brothers followed his cue, bowing low at the waist. When they stood upright again, brother Michael strummed a chord very slowly on his guitar, picking each string individually and letting it ring. He took a deep breath and led the brothers in singing their call to worship.

The cantors—brother Michael, brother Augustine, and brother Elias—sang the opening line: "We are grateful for the fullness of this day." They sang slowly, with a melody similar to a chanted psalm: most of the phrase on a single pitch with a simple cadence on the final words. They articulated the words in a free rhythm that suggested simple duple meter. Brother Michael strummed his guitar on "grateful," "fullness," and "day," keeping everyone gently grounded by marking the natural rhythm suggested by the emphasis of each syllable in the lyrics but without creating a steady tempo or regular meter. It evoked gently flowing speech. The rest of the brothers joined in on the second line: "Creator, word, and spirit of new life." Again the melody remained spare: most words sung on a single pitch, stepping downward on "spirit" and "new life." Again, a simple guitar strum marked the emphasized syllables of "creator," "spirit," and "new life." These lyrics could easily be sung in a simple duple meter, but the periodic guitar strums coupled with moderate give-and-take in the very slow tempo interrupted the development of a strict meter or regular beat.

The brothers continued singing in this way with brother Michael strumming to mark the emphasized syllables at the beginning, middle, and end of each line: "We go to rest in your peace. We go to rest in your promise. Our hearts delight in the beauty of this day. Revealing your abundance; your abiding love." The melody of each line remained simple, but maintained the gentle downward steps to create an almost sigh-like effect as if each line was gently exhaling. As they sang, they emphasized this sense when they paused at the end of every phrase, taking a breath and creating a brief silent space before moving on. Taken together, the open meter, lengthy pauses, and simple melody created a sense of openness, silence, and patience as the call to prayer unfolded.

I had experienced many Compline prayers by that point in my research, but this was the first time I paid specific attention to the rhythm and meter, and I realized that the simple song lacked the sense of regulated anticipation that comes from a steady beat. When writing about the experience in my field notes later, I recalled reading Husserl's *Phenomenology of Internal Time Consciousness*. In it, he discusses how our consciousness of time defines our everyday experiences by allowing us to make sense of the world. He suggests that we are conscious of time because of retention and protention, meaning the memory of that which is immediately past and the anticipation of that which is to come. He offers the experience of music as an example: if we hear notes as individual "nows" then we cannot experience their relationships to one another and can therefore have no sense of a cohesive melody. Likewise, when we hear a series of notes, we do not store them simultaneously in our consciousness. This would result in a cacophony of sound with no cohesiveness. Rather, when we hear a series of notes we retain them in the order in which they occurred and we anticipate what might come next.

By playing subtly with beat and meter in their call to prayer, the brothers created a push and pull between retention and protention that heightened my awareness of the experience and helped to create the sensation of mentally and physically exhaling as each line gently flowed downward. Further, sitting in the gallery, my consciousness focused more intentionally on the words and the people around me because I could not rely on regulated musical time to get me from the beginning of the song to the end. In the extended pauses, open meter, and guitar strums that resisted and interrupted a regular pulse, my sense of anticipation was drawn out and awakened as my sense of retention lingered on the words I just heard.

Perhaps it is this experience that heightened my awareness of the words, "Creator, word, and spirit of new life" in the call to prayer. They are typical of the Weston version of the Gloria Patri doxology, a standard Trinitarian prayer in Catholic tradition and a fixture in Benedictine liturgy.[3] Early in my field research, I noticed that the Weston monks did not sing a standard Gloria Patri. I had seen this doxology in books on monastic liturgy, and I heard it chanted at Saint-Benoît, in Latin and French. It seemed to be such an important part of the Benedictine prayer hours, I began to wonder why the Weston monks did not use it. During one of our conversations over the dishwasher, I asked brother Michael about this. He explained that the community became increasingly aware of gender inequality during the 1970s and 1980s, specifically, the experience of women in a Church whose hierarchy is exclusively male. They began to use inclusive language in their new songs, and they rewrote the lyrics of existing music. At Weston, God is never referenced in the masculine; God is neither a "he" nor a "she" but simply "God." Further, references to "men" have become references to "people," and times when the liturgical prayers call for wording such as "all holy men and women" the Weston monks say, "all holy women and men."[4]

The brothers' interpretation of the Gloria Patri evolved as part of this awareness and the subtle resistance to institutional Church narratives that it fosters. Brother Michael explained that they noticed excessive talk of fathers and sons in the liturgy, and felt that this did not reflect openness to the experience of women. The subtext here—which was unspoken in our conversation—is that the Church has historically not been open to the experience of women or to their full participation in hierarchy and ritual. Brother Michael said that they tried to find different ways to express the same ideas without relying solely on masculine language.

Pausing only briefly after the call to prayer, the brothers began the chanted psalms. As is specified in the Rule of Benedict, they always chant Psalms 4, 90, and 133 at Compline. Acting as cantor, brother Michael chanted the opening line of Psalm 4 on a single tone, with a simple cadence at the end: "When I call, answer me, oh God of justice." He sang in a gentle tenor voice with a steady, clear, natural tone that lacked formality or the full, reverberating, open timbre of vocal training. It was very much like his spoken voice, but with the pitch and rhythm of chant. As he finished the line, the brothers on his side of the chapel joined him to complete the phrase on a single chanted tone: "From anguish you release me, have mercy and hear me." The way they leaned slightly on the emphasized syllables of some words created a kind of irregular meter: "from *an*guish you re*lease* me have *mer*cy and *hear* me" suggesting a mixed meter, 1-2-3-4 1-2-3 1-2-3 1-2. The brothers on the other side of the chapel picked up the next phrase: "How *long* oh *peo*ple will your *hearts* be *closed*? Will you *love* what is *fu*tile, and *seek* what is *false*?" As they chanted in unison, the brothers leaned back against the monastic benches with their eyes closed and hands either clasped at the waist or hanging easily at their sides. The chanted tones reverberated gently around the room as the brothers' voices blended into a neither unpleasant nor uniform mix of timbres and tones. As the brothers on one side came to the end of their phrase, they tapered their volume and tempo slightly. This made an opening for the brothers on the opposite side to begin the next phrase. They seemed to engage in a dialogue more than a rote exchange of verses as they maintained a steady, slow tempo.

Their simple melody followed the Gregorian tonality traditionally used for chanted psalms. The tenor and the final were a simplified version of the First Mode in which the final moves two steps down from and then returns to the tenor. However, instead of singing the final at the end of each two-line psalm verse, the brothers used it as a mediant in the middle of each verse. This means that the brothers on one side of the chapel did not end their line on a cadence, and thus with a sense of conclusion. Instead, they ended on the single tenor tone, which could then be seamlessly picked up by the brothers on the other side as they began their line.

This was important in creating the distinctive experience of antiphonal chanting, defined by the back-and-forth exchange of phrases. It is a characteristic feature of monastic prayer, and has been for centuries. It may be that this style of singing was a practical method for learning and praying the psalms in ancient and medieval communities where literacy rates were perhaps low. But really, even if literate, memorizing the entire psalter is easier if you only need to remember half of the words. Yet, this antiphonal style is a characteristic monastic practice that remains even as modern communities use psalters instead of memorizing every word of every psalm—or even half of the words.

This suggests that the practice holds a greater appeal for monastics beyond practicality. Even if it is perhaps physically easier to sing every other phrase of a psalm, this style of prayer is distinctively monastic for its capacity to foster a sense of presence to and awareness of oneself and one's brothers or sisters. If the monks simply sang every word in unison, their voices would draw them together in the act of communal singing. However, the antiphonal prayer form requires that they become aware of themselves and one another in a deeper way. As I listened from my seat in the gallery, I heard the phrases moving back and forth between the two sides of the chapel. This exchange of phrases from one side to the other created the sensation of a gentle wave that is always in motion, either moving toward or away, but never static. One is ever in the ebb and flow of this style of chanted prayer, always offering it or receiving it, never fully possessing it and never fully separated from it. Like the slight variations of rhythm that resist regular meter in the opening call to worship, this conversational style of singing creates a dialogue that requires deep listening and attention. This heightens the interpersonal unity of the experience by drawing the consciousness away from the rote repetition of memorized words to the communal performance of chanted psalms. These characteristics are at the heart of the monastic liturgical sensibility.

Brother Michael once explained to me that during the chanted psalms he sometimes stops noticing the words. He sings them, often from memory, but he does not experience them as the most important element of the prayer. Resonating with my ebb-and-flow metaphor, he said that the wonderful part of the chanted psalms for him is the experience of feeling buoyed up by his brothers. He said that there are times when he is at odds with one of his brothers; there are times when he feels angry or distressed. But after they chant the psalms together, he feels the tension melt away and he finds unity and peace with his brothers.

Voicing similar sentiments, brother John once told me that in truly communal prayer, "The separations go away and there is unity and harmony with the other." Compline is not simply a matter of gathering for prayer because monastics live according to Rules, and the Rule says to do so. It is an opportunity to end each day by intentionally fostering, through a carefully chosen series of musical practices, the personal and interpersonal experiences and ideals that are the foundation of the Benedictine life.

Yet, the pursuit of unity and harmony among twelve voices can present practical, musical challenges. When he tried to describe these challenges to me, brother John used the following image: If part of the group goes flat, then the others can either choose to go flat along with them, or they can fight them for the sake of the pitch. So, they all go flat, because the unity of voices is the most important element. In brother John's words, it is "a kind of spiritual battle within yourself that is about finding how you can be one with those who differ from you."

Similarly, brother Robert once told me that sung prayer presents a challenge to listen and remain attentive to his brothers. Chanting the psalms is not simply an act of reciting words, even though he has sung them for most of his life and admits that it is sometimes difficult to avoid falling into a sense of rote repetition and routine. He smiled as he said, "Recently, a few of the brothers said to me, very kindly of course, 'you know, you're singing too loud.'" He laughed as he went on, "And you know what? I was! I was singing too loud! And I know that because I could hear myself but I couldn't hear anyone else. I had forgotten to listen." If he stopped being attentive to the interpersonal dimensions of the experience, the prayer was less effective, not only for him but for his brothers.

Brother Mark shared a similar sentiment in the parlor one winter afternoon as we conversed before supper. He told me that the brothers used to say, "If you can't hear the brother on either side of you, you're singing too loud." He explained that this was about learning to blend as a group. They do not say this very often anymore, perhaps because the brothers have been singing together for decades, but it remains an important aspect of their sung prayer.

Brother Peter said something similar when he explained the relationship between singing and unity in prayer: "I haven't said this in a long time, but it's still a true thing. If you can hear any one of us and identify the voice, then we aren't blending. The unity of our sound comes when you can hear the brother to your right or to your left and you don't overpower their sound."

I asked him about the purpose this serves in prayer, and he explained that it is about cultivating interpersonal awareness and contributing to a communal sound: "Besides sounding nice, on a spiritual level, you are aware that you're not singing alone and that you're not trying to shine, but that you're trying to contribute what you have to a whole, which is the unified sound of all of us singing together. . . . And when you don't have this awareness, that's when you sound out of sorts, you're out of the blend."

Brother Peter explained that his experience of prayer has become deeply rooted in this unity of voices. For him, it is not just about a preferred musical style—"sounding nice"—it is also about a spiritual expression founded on the work of singing together. These musical-liturgical dimensions are not opposed, but rather exist in a rich dialectic that is brought into everyday experience in the simplicity and complexity of a psalm chanted on a single tone.

Nearly four years after he had described to me the spiritual battle of intonation, brother John returned again to the experience of sung prayer in a conversation about a draft of the present discussion of Compline. He talked about communal singing as a deep, unifying experience that is mysterious and difficult to describe: "Our music unites us in a way which is beyond our thinking. *It goes beyond our thinking, and it moves us beyond our thinking.*" He said, "You know, if we're at odds with one another, we sing terribly and it's noticeable among us. We feel that distance between us and we have to work to come back to our sense of unity."

Initially in my research, I wanted to read this emphasis on unity as a reflection of the local social structures. It clearly evoked the brothers' focus on an egalitarian model of monastic life, and it brought that into daily prayer. But brother John's comments moved me toward a more nuanced understanding of their vocal style and ideals. Their prayers were meant to foster a rich unity among the brothers, but, ideally, they would also create a shift in consciousness and sensibility. I did not yet understand the complexities of it, but Compline certainly had that effect on me. Sitting in the chapel, I was not thinking about theories of experience, the phenomenology of time, or conversations about the pursuit of interpersonal unity. Instead, my mind and body relaxed as my constant internal chatter grew quiet. I breathed deeply and slowly. Experiencing these dimensions of awareness, listening, and presence in my own way from my seat in the gallery, the brothers finished chanting the three Compline psalms. They continued to stand, leaning against the benches, as brother Placid, eyes closed and hands folded at his waist, recited a brief reading based on Jeremiah 14:9: "God, you are here among us; we bear your name as our own. May we never be far from you, God of love and compassion." Several moments of silence followed. Brother Elias then led the call-and-response of the Kyrie. He sang the opening call very slowly, with the gentle, bright clarity of his speaking voice: "Lord, have mercy." The brothers responded, also slowly and quietly: "Christ have mercy; Lord have mercy."

After several silent moments, brother Augustine leaned slightly forward. This prompted the rest of the brothers to stand and move into a semicircle around the candle to sing their closing hymn. Brother Michael and brother Augustine, who stood at the top of the circle with their guitars, looked at one another, nodded slightly, and began playing in their characteristic rolling, finger-picked style. I recognized the opening chords immediately as "Peace to You," one of several songs that the brothers used as a Compline hymn. It was a very slow, reflective song with a simple melody and lyrics in strophic form bidding peace and goodness at the end of the day: "Peace to you, and every good that life can bring."[5]

While Benedictines traditionally sing a Marian hymn—and on many evenings, the Weston monks do, too—"Peace to You" articulates foundational characteristics of the monastic life and the Benedictine motto "peace." The song became a thorough part of my own Weston way of being and, as the opening chords played that evening, I felt my tension fade as if a knot at the center of my chest was unwinding. It was an unconscious response to the ritual space and experience of Compline. I did not sing along with the psalms—visitors tend not to—but I did join in quietly on "Peace to You" along with several of the other guests in the gallery. I tried to use a gentle voice and attend to the voices of the brothers. I thought about the balance and unity they had described to me, and it seemed to deepen both the meaning of the song and the act of singing it as I felt the bidding of peace reverberate around the room.

With a repeated line, "and peace will bring the morning song," the closing hymn ended and silence filled the chapel once again as the last reverberation of the guitars faded away. The brothers stood for a moment, still and quiet. It had grown dark outside, and only the flickering white light of the candle illuminated the space. Brother Richard took a deep breath and, with closed eyes and a gentle nod of his head, offered the nighttime blessing: "May God grant us peace, and a restful night." The brothers bowed low toward the center of their semicircle. They split off into two lines and walked silently out of the chapel through the sacristy door.

I took a deep breath, feeling calm and quiet. I stood for a silent moment and watched the candle flicker in the now empty space. Quiet shuffling behind me told me that the rest of the visitors in the gallery were beginning to leave. I turned to walk out of the chapel along with the fifteen others who had attended Compline that evening. We all seemed to make an effort to maintain the quiet stillness as we gathered our things and left. A man who appeared to be in his sixties opened the heavy chapel door for me. I smiled and nodded a silent "thank you" as I passed through. Three women walked together ahead of me toward the women's guesthouse. The male guests—four, including the man who held the door—walked individually down the road toward the men's guesthouse. Each man was several feet away from the man in front of him; their flashlights made small circles of light at their feet. I looked up at the starry sky and repeated a line from "Peace to You" to myself: "Look up and see the vast and endless sky; who knows how far and wide the stars intensely shine." By participating in the nighttime ritual of Compline, I felt myself more thoroughly connected to the Weston space and the people who were sharing it with me. I also felt that I was beginning to understand the role of sung prayer in monastery life.

As I walked down the road, the gravel crunched under my feet, crickets and peepers chirped in the woods around me, and the bullfrogs that live in the Priory pond punctuated the constant chirping with an occasional deep, loud call. I attended closely to these sounds of the night as I felt myself moving ever more deeply into the contemplative sensibility of the monastic life, and the contemplative mindset necessary for my continuing research with the brothers. It had been more than a year since my night in the guesthouse basement with Lupita and the mouse, and I was aware that my struggles to position myself in the community, and my issues with my identity as a researcher, were beginning to fade. During my conversation over the dishwasher that evening, I became aware of how deeply dialogic my research was becoming. Like the conversational style of antiphonal chanted psalms, I had to hear the voices of others and bring my own into balance with theirs. By the time I finished writing my notes at the guesthouse dining table that evening, I was ready for the Grand Silence of night before returning to the dark chapel for Vigil prayer early the next morning.

We Were Simply Not in California

It was the first really nice day of the summer: seventy degrees, bright sunshine, a light breeze, and a clear blue sky without a single cloud. As it had rained hard the day before, and most of the days prior for many weeks, this was a most welcome change hinting at the season to come. The solstice was only two days away; Mother Nature seemed to be almost boasting with so many hours of perfection. I sat in the parlor with brother Michael and brother John. They each had a pile of papers in their laps—early drafts of my writing—and I had a notebook and pencil, ready for their thoughts. Not an opportunity for censorship or correction, sharing my writing was a way to continue our conversations on various topics outside of our relatively limited opportunities for personal interaction.

After chatting about the gardens for a while, we got to the topic at hand: our ongoing dialogues about music and monastic life. The brothers explained that they spent some of their June retreat days reflecting on a recent book on monasticism, Giorgio Agamben's *The Highest Poverty*. Brother John held a piece of paper with several quotes from the book. The first was Agamben's observation, "The cenobitic project is literally defined by the *koinos bios*, by the common life from which it draws its name, and without which it cannot be understood at all."[6]

I had never considered the Greek roots of the term "cenobitic." It literally means "community" (*koinos*) and "life" (*bios*). As we discussed this, our conversation came around to the topic of monastic vows. "We don't take vows," brother John said with his usual wise eyes and gentle smile, "we make a profession." He paused to emphasize the distinction and likely to leave space in the discussion to see how we would respond. I had heard the brothers speak in this way before. For them, vows can suggest a kind of superhuman perfection as well as the removal of choice: once the vows are made, one is chained, so to speak, to whatever it is one is avowed. Profession, on the other hand, can suggest choosing to pursue a way of life, or form of life. Profession suggests training, practice, dedication, commitment, and vocation.

Brother John went on to explain that when Benedictines make the final monastic profession, which occurs after a temporary novitiate period of several years, they profess three things: conversatio, obedience, and stability. Conversatio is most often translated as the conversion of life, meaning that monasticism is a lifelong process of growth and change. It is not a question of taking vows and immediately being an ideal spiritual type, nor is it a question of converting from one form of life—negatively valued, sinful—to another—properly Christian, "good," "redeemed." Brother John explained that in his experience the profession is conversatio and not simply conversion because it is not just about changing from one thing to another; it is rather about engaging in a conversation with other people about the form of life you have all entered into together. It is about the dialogue and the interpersonal process.

Brother Michael nodded his head in agreement, and I pointed out that most people assume that monks take very austere vows of silence and celibacy. The brothers laughed. Indeed, silence is very important in their lives, and they understand celibacy as part of their profession of stability to the community, but Benedictines do not take these as vows. Discussing the "Vow of Silence," brother John said, "In fact, with conversatio, our profession is to talk!" We all chuckled as he went on, "But then we have its balance in obedience. Obedience means our profession is to listen. And stability means that we will continue to do this, to live together in our chosen form of life." The monastic must at once be aware of talking and listening, but this does not mean only physical talking or physical listening. These are deeply metaphorical, even philosophical points for reflection. Conversatio and obedience are lived realities intended to support the stability of the monastery.

Returning to our topic of liturgy and music, brother Michael pointed out, "Really, it's all about the liturgy of the hours, returning each day to prayer." Brother John agreed and discussed his own experience that liturgy is really at the heart of the monastic form of life. He then connected his ideas back to conversatio: "You know, in all aspects, even in liturgy, conversatio is the most basic thing, even more basic than texts and Rules." I jotted notes in my little notebook and tried to understand all that he offered in that statement. He went on to talk about how there were many voices, even in the earliest monasteries. In their own monastery, they have many voices. Finding a common voice in the midst of such variety is a primary goal, but it is not easy. A common voice does not entail everyone agreeing all the time, or sacrificing individuality. Brother John pointed out that the Rule makes it clear that Benedict's monks did not always agree with one another, and Benedict knew that he was dealing with many personalities within a single community. As he talked about these difficulties in terms of the importance of conversatio and prayer, brother John concluded: "Singing is how the monks found their common voice."

I smiled. He had done it again. He always had a way of giving me the pieces I needed when I was ready to understand them and put them into context. With that in mind, I went back to the guesthouse and pulled out a three-ring binder that held transcriptions of all of my interviews over the course of my research thus far. I returned to a conversation brother John and I had shared early in my research when I was trying to understand how the brothers' musical and liturgical style developed. We sat in the same chairs, in the same parlor. It was an unseasonably warm day, and I was ready for a quiet conversation after spending a particularly exhausting morning with brother Daniel, a fellow female guest, and the sheep.

Dinner and None, the midday prayer, had given me a chance to refresh and refocus before my meeting with brother John. None is one of the "little hours" of the Divine Office, and it marks the transition from the morning work period and noon meal to the afternoon work or study period. I sat in the front row that afternoon, as always, with my trusty field recorder in hand. The brothers began, as always, by chanting their opening call to prayer: "Your spirit within us moves us to pray, through whom we know Christ Jesus the Lord. It is your spirit who gives grace to belief, and we all rejoice to be alive in your saving love." They leaned back on the monastic benches and sang the day's antiphon on a simple melody that used a melodic device that I heard in much of their music: each phrase stepped gently upward and then back down in a way that evoked a deep inhalation and exhalation. They sang: "Those who live by the truth are seen clearly in the light, and we know that what they do is simply done in God."

This antiphon marked the beginning of the chanted psalms. The brothers spoke often about returning to the sources, and evidence suggests that this is one of the oldest forms of Christian liturgical prayer. The Book of Psalms, sandwiched between Job and Proverbs in the Hebrew Bible, contains 150 poetic texts that encompass a wide variety of themes, sentiments, and attitudes. They are the poetry of praise, supplication, challenge, worship, and oral history. In a practice borrowed from Judaism, the psalms became what was perhaps the earliest liturgical music in the emerging Christian Church.[7]

For the first several centuries of its development, the Christian liturgy was designed, by necessity, for worshippers who were unlikely to have access to or the ability to read a psalter. With psalms as a central feature of their public prayer lives, antiphons allowed them to participate. A leader sang the antiphon, the people repeated it, and then the leader recited the psalm clearly and slowly, phrase by phrase, pausing for the people to respond with the antiphon. It was considered absolutely necessary that the psalms be declaimed clearly so that the people could understand the words and participate via the responses.[8]

Early monastics similarly developed various ways of praying the psalms together. As their communities became cohesive units—cenobitic—instead of ad hoc collections of hermits and their anchorites, prayer became a more communal and therefore increasingly ritualized activity. In some cases, a single reader recited the psalms aloud in the order in which they occur in the Bible. Perhaps spoken, perhaps chanted, this approach allowed the listeners to meditate on the words. In other cases, the whole community read the psalms together, perhaps from beginning to end, or perhaps exchanging verses between two choruses in the alternating style called antiphonal psalmody. This latter approach became the standard in Christian monasticism.[9] The terminology emerged from the practice of adding an antiphon, or repeated phrase, to the beginning and end of the recited psalm. The antiphon emphasized the meaning of the words, and thus became part of the tradition of exegesis and edification—interpreting and learning from scripture—in liturgical music.

That afternoon at Weston, when the antiphon concluded, brother Michael chanted the opening line of Psalm 119 on a simple tone that did not follow any of the Gregorian modes exactly, but with a single-pitch mediant that stepped down from and back up to the tenor: "They are happy whose life is blameless." The brothers on his side of the chapel joined him to finish the phrase with a final that stepped down two pitches on the last two syllables of the phrase: "who follow God's law." The brothers on the other side picked up the next phrase: "They are happy, those who do your will, seeking you with all their hearts." Most of the brothers looked at the small, green psalter each held in his hands, while some, even with the psalter open in front of them, closed their eyes and chanted from memory.

When they finished the last line of the psalm, all of the brothers sang the antiphon again together. Brother Elias then started Psalm 125 on the same simple tone: "Those who trust in you oh God." The brothers on his side of the chapel joined him to complete the phrase: "are like Mount Zion who cannot be shaken, that stands forever." The brothers on the opposite side picked up the next verse, and so on, until the psalm ended. They again sang the antiphon. Brother Alvaro began Psalm 126: "When you delivered your people from bondage." The brothers on his side of the chapel finished the phrase: "O God, it seemed like a dream." And again, the exchange of verses continued until the end of the psalm. They marked this as the final psalm by chanting a variation on the Gloria Patri doxology, still in the same tone, while bowing low at the waist: "To you, oh giver of all life; through your wisdom, Jesus the Christ; in your spirit dwelling in our midst; be praised forevermore." At the end, they again chanted the antiphon.

The more I experienced the Divine Office, the more I came to understand, appreciate, and anticipate these repeated elements and the sense of regulation, ritual, and relaxed order they lend to monastic liturgy: psalms, antiphons, doxologies, basic melodic movement, minimal bodily movement. Returning to these prayers, and their familiar patterns, several times each day seemed to lend a sense of calm regularity to daily life.

The midday prayer was not long—None is one of the "little" hours—but it had many of the most basic, familiar elements of monastic liturgy. When I visited Saint-Benoît, I experienced how these elements remain recognizable even in different languages and across distinct musical and liturgical styles. Popular imagination, religious tradition, and most chant scholarship would have us believe that Benedictines sing Gregorian chant. It is something of a romanticized image that casts them as a living echo of an earlier, even idealized liturgical age. Certainly, the Benedictines are known for chant, and after so many centuries of maintaining and reviving it as their own distinctive liturgical style, I understood why. But I also wondered how and why the Weston monks decided that they would use something else.

Brother John, who had been a Weston monk for more than fifty years and served as prior for much of that time, was a rich source for understanding this moment in the brothers' history. He was a close companion of Abbot Leo in the early days of the Priory and throughout his later life when the abbot retired to Weston as a brother. In 1953, while he was a diocesan priest in rural Vermont, brother John learned about the Priory when he attended an outdoor Mass in Burlington during which the diocese officially welcomed and blessed Weston Priory. He recalls being inspired by brother Leo's vision for a different kind of monastic life. He once explained to me that, at the time, he felt like he was always preaching that we are all a family, we are all one community, but then he would go home all by himself to the rectory. He felt that he was not really part of a community, and the priesthood began to feel lonely, even alienating. When he visited Saint-Benoît with his seminary friends, he was inspired by the monks there, working together on their farm, living a simple life, and praying the Divine Office each day. In moments like that, and countless others, he felt drawn to a different form of life, toward a monastic vocation.

Sitting in the parlor with him after None, I explained that I was interested in the early years at Weston and the moment when the brothers began writing their own music. He sat across from me with his usual pleasant expression and chuckled a bit as he said, "Okay, I think I can remember those days!" He folded his care-worn hands and rested his elbows on the arms of his rocking chair. "Well," he began, "brother Leo had very strong roots in the tradition at his home monastery at Gerleve, which was part of the Bavarian Beuron congregation."

He went on to explain that Beuron had a very strong German approach to Gregorian chant and the monastic liturgy. There were two principal congregations at the time in terms of liturgical styles: the French Solesmes congregation and the German Beuron congregation. The French tradition had a reputation for being much prettier and sweeter than the German tradition. Each congregation published liturgical books, psalters, hymnals, and chant manuals for their communities, and any others who wanted to use them. Meanwhile, at the Vatican, Church authorities created yet another interpretation of Gregorian chant that became the official Church-approved system.

With no fewer than three versions of Gregorian chant available to Benedictines during the first half of the twentieth century, the usual image of a singular, universal, ancient liturgical music becomes blurry to say the least. In the early years, the Weston monks were more or less perched on this shaky ground with an unsure liturgical footing. Even so, the new recruits were enthusiastic about building a Benedictine community from the ruins of an old farmhouse in the wilderness. They set to work learning the complex monastic liturgical systems, and they practiced Gregorian chant to the best of their ability.

Brother John explained that he feels as though Gregorian chant had developed into something of an art form in monasteries at the time. It is a challenging musical style, and the early brothers, while not entirely without talent, were not necessarily great musicians. Brother John smiled and laughed as he recalled that time: "Oh, you should have heard some of the sounds we made! And we had no organ, really, so someone just blew an A on a pitch pipe and away we went! Aieeeeee!" he said, as he broke into a hearty laugh, "we used to sing so high!"

We both laughed as brother John picked up the story again: "But we tried very hard. We loved the chants, and we wanted to learn to sing the monastic Office prayers." In this process, they were glad for the help of their neighbors to the north. The Saint-Benoît monks sent their own choirmaster to instruct the Weston monks. In fact, the two communities established a strong bond of mutual guidance and friendship. During this time, Father Bede took over as prior at Weston. Brother John recalls that Father Bede had a deep love for Gregorian chant, and he encouraged the brothers to continue in this practice. But he was on loan from Conception Abbey in the American-Cassinese congregation. Saint-Benoît was in the Solesmes congregation. Brother Leo hailed from the Beuron congregation. In looking back on that time, brother John smiled as he recalled that the brothers felt as though they were piecing together bits of many different liturgical systems as they tried to figure out, more or less on their own, how to sing like Benedictines.

I would reflect, long after brother John told me this story, that what he described was not all that unlike the experience of Prosper Guéranger as he looked at the liturgical systems left behind by many monastic communities in order to figure out, through a blend of careful study and everyday practice, how the Solesmes monks would sing—and live—like Benedictines. Brother John described it as a difficult but rewarding practice. He said that the brothers grew to love the prayerful aesthetic and deeply monastic character of Gregorian chant, and over the course of a decade, they became quite proficient at it.

At the time, the twentieth-century liturgical movement had gathered momentum and was pushing for change in the Catholic Church. The brothers responded to this movement by using Gothic vestments—unusual at the time—and including some communal responses in their daily Mass, which was increasingly popular among Weston locals and visitors passing through the area. As the Second Vatican Council convened in 1962, change was brewing. When the council promulgated *Sacrosanctum Concilium*—the Constitution on the Sacred Liturgy—on December 4, 1963, the Church entered what was to be an era of, among other things, more fully communal worship.[10] The constitution very specifically called for the active participation of the people, and, to foster this, opened the door for vernacular worship. The door proved to be a floodgate.

Before that moment, Latin was the language of the Church. In parishes, priests stood with their backs to the people. The people sat in pews silently praying devotional prayers from their pocket-sized Missals. They did not participate in the liturgical prayers, and, given that everything was in Latin, it is unlikely that most people understood what was being said. In any case, priests mumbled the prayers in a quiet voice through most of the Mass, indicating that the words were not for communal articulation. In this model, understanding language seems like a moot point. Vatican II suggested that it was possible, even desirable, to change that.

Monasteries and cathedrals have different liturgical practices and separate institutional structures with the Pope and Vatican hierarchy at the top of both. When Vatican II called on parishes to renew their practices, monastic communities were encouraged to do the same, but in ways that would reflect their monastic heritage. Up to that point at Weston, all of the prayers were in Latin. Brother John explained to me that a few of the brothers were ordained, and so they had a basic understanding of ecclesiastical Latin from their seminary training. However, the nonordained brothers did not. So, while hours on end of singing in Latin was effective in various respects, it did not offer the same experience that might be possible in a more familiar language. In fact, when reflecting on their developing liturgical practices, the brothers at the time noticed that daily prayer, the very thing that was supposed to bring the community together, was proving divisive because they did not share a common experience. The language of prayer, and their own varying degrees of fluency, created separations among them. "So," brother John explained, "when the Vatican Council affirmed the vernacular, we were ready for it."

They may have been ready for vernacular liturgy, but when Vatican II gave it the official thumbs-up, options for liturgical music were scarce. This resulted in a kind of "silencing" of the liturgy not unlike that described by Eamon Duffy in his study of the Reformation in England.[11] Vernacular worship and active participation required not only new hymns and songs, but entirely rewritten liturgical texts with their prayers, acclamations, antiphons, doxologies, and responses. This opened the door for musical and liturgical creativity that had been unknown in Catholicism for centuries.

Having spent a decade piecing together bits of many liturgical systems from various congregations, the Weston monks were already prepared to find their own way. Several years after brother Leo founded Weston, their founding community, Dormition Abbey in Jerusalem, became a conventual abbey, meaning it was independent of the Beuron congregation. Weston thus also became independent of founding abbeys and congregations. This meant there was no hierarchical authority to send along revised post-Vatican II liturgical books. The brothers were on their own. They embraced the moment as a new beginning. From that point on, daily prayer became a locus for ongoing creativity and innovation within the community, a place where the brothers could cultivate a liturgical style, spiritual experience, and monastic life that would reflect their collective consciousness and identity, not just as Benedictine monks, but as Weston monks.

Brother John explained that, for the community now and for those living at the Priory in 1963, the call to vernacular prayer was a deeper question than prayer in Latin or English. The question became: What does it mean to pray, to sing, indeed to live in one's own authentic voice? What does it mean for a community to pray and live with a common voice? "You know," brother John said, "if you are really using your own language, prayer becomes authentic. You are the author of it. Then it has author-ity." For him, this is the best way to think about authority, that which comes from authentic expressions offered in one's own voice. It is certainly a departure from the usual image of hierarchical, institutional Church authority. "If you use somebody else's language, no matter how versatile you become, it will always be somebody else's," brother John said. I sensed that he was speaking both literally and metaphorically.

"So for you," I began, trying to understand what he was offering, "it's the authenticity of the local that makes the language sacred, that makes it prayer?" "Exactly," he said, "you know, even in the days when we tried so hard to sing Gregorian chant, I think we were authentic in spite of ourselves! We tried really hard. We wanted to be more professional, but we were not." We both laughed as brother John explained that the brothers were who they were. They were just a group of young people trying to build their monastic life: "We had to be who we were and where we were. We simply were not in California, or anywhere else. We were here."

The brothers worked hard to figure out what their life would be, what it would look like, and what it would sound like. In deciding how to address this in their liturgies, they encountered a dilemma: they loved the prayerful aesthetic and traditional monastic style of Gregorian chant and the Latin prayers, they wanted to maintain that style in their Divine Office, but they knew that the language was a problem. Brother John explained that simply translating the chants into English seemed like the most obvious solution, but it did not produce pleasing results. Smiling, shaking his head, and laughing as he recalled this moment in their history, he said that the translated chants left a lot to be desired. The language felt awkward and the melodic movement no longer fit the accent and cadence of the words. He recalled that the brothers knew very well that the translated chants were not working, but they tried to cheer themselves up by drawing little pictures on the mimeographed sheets. In his experience, "There is a marriage between the Latin and Gregorian such that the two can never really be separated." He laughed as he said, "We learned that if you are going to sing Gregorian chant, you just better do it in Latin!"

The Weston monks had to find their own way, and they quickly learned how difficult that would be. It is an ongoing negotiation that combines two layers of performance and experience usefully illustrated in Pierre Bourdieu's suggestion of the *habitus* and his assessment of the authoritative language of liturgy. Bourdieu describes habitus as systems of dispositions generated by history, collective experience, and collective consciousness. The habitus sets up parameters for behavior: what to do or not to do, what sorts of actions are possible, which of those actions are acceptable. For Bourdieu, the habitus is unconscious, what he calls "a product of history" that "produces individual and collective practices . . . in accordance with schemes generated by history."[12]

Like brother John's discussion of authenticity and authority, habitus is particularly meaningful in ritual contexts where symbolic actions can function only when participants are conditioned to receive them. This is central to Bourdieu's theory of symbolic power and authoritative language in liturgy.[13] In liturgical contexts, the performance of authoritative language creates ritual. Bourdieu argues that words, in themselves, have no power, but rather are given power by the spokesperson, who in turn draws on delegated authority. Thus, the authoritative language of liturgy can be understood as a communal phenomenon negotiated collectively through dialogue, interaction, and shared experience. This is then manifest through the collective creation and performance of the habitus, or local way of being.

Bourdieu further observes that language in a ritual context is only effective if the gathered people determine, based on agreed-upon criteria, that it has been correct. Participants can experience various kinds of errors that render the ritual ineffective and false. Conversely, they can make choices, from the language of worship to the style of music, designed to create and maintain a ritual that is collectively experienced as effective.[14]

In brother John's description, authority and authenticity can have very basic criteria: they are the expression of the local and the personal. This does not make the issue any less complex. In brother John's experience, the challenge to sing, pray, and live in one's own distinct voice is not as easy as simply translating words into the local language. In monastic life, liturgy can thus become a kind of living nexus that is the locus for the expression, creation, and negotiation of the local way of being in all of its specificity and complexity, as it references received traditions and outside sources, and as it results from the very specific place and time of the community.

Music is at the heart of these processes. The Weston monks learned this the hard way as translated chants left them feeling as if Latin might not have been so bad after all. At the same time, a couple of the brothers who had been learning guitar played popular folk songs at evening recreation. Brother John recalled the moment when these two musical experiences came together as a brother who was a particularly gifted musician said to him: "Well, what can we do? We've got the texts, why don't we just try to write the music ourselves?" To hear brother John tell the story, it almost sounded like a last resort, but it turned out to be an exciting new beginning. It was how the brothers found their common voice.

From Gregorian to Guitars

For the Weston monks, Gregorian chant was no longer effective in the context of post-Vatican II liturgical renewal. Vernacular liturgy demanded more than translation from Latin to English. It required a shift from one style of prayer to another, from distant Latin forms to more familiar folk styles, from institutionally sanctioned musics to those that emerge from local creativity and currency.

I thought about these aspects of liturgical music as I walked from the guesthouse to the Priory on a sunny autumn afternoon. I noticed that the green leaves were tipped with red and orange. I had not noticed it the day before, when the weather was still hot and summery. A distinctively autumn-like chill was in the air, and the shift of seasons was palpable.

The rhythms of monastic life heightened my awareness of these natural cycles. In fact, they entirely shifted my consciousness and experience of time as I unchained myself from my calendars and day planners, those constant companions that render time linear as each hour, day, week, month, year marches onward into eternity. Immersed in the daily liturgy of the hours, the repeated cycles of the psalms and readings, the progression of each week toward the Sabbath, and the long-term unfolding of the seasons, I found that the monastic experience of time is far more cyclical. It is like planting a seed, waiting patiently to see what it will become, watching the resulting plant grow and thrive, and finally seeing it wither, brown, and turn back to seed so that the whole cycle can start over again.

Occasionally, the question of time came up in my conversations with the brothers. They cultivated an almost Zen-like focus on the present moment, yet they were careful to maintain an awareness of their own history, their inherited traditions, and their cultural and historical context. They looked for a balance between historical consciousness and a forward-looking, living tradition. Brother Peter once explained to me that they wanted to bring tradition into dialogue with present experiences so that their resulting form of life could remain localized, particular, and flexible even as it reflected broader practices and more ancient traditions.

I went through my usual daily rhythm that day: Morning Vigil, breakfast in the silent refectory, reading and writing in the early morning, and helping out around the monastery during the work period. Brother Daniel showed me how to switch out some of the bright, summery tablecloths and liturgical vestments for ones with more autumn-like tones. It was another indication of the changing seasons and the passing of time.

At noon, I joined the brothers and their guests for dinner, then we all cleaned the kitchen and, when the bells rang shortly after the last dish was dried and put away, we went into the chapel for None. After the chanted psalms finished and we sang a hymn based on the Beatitudes, I went to the pond to meet brother Augustine for an interview.[15] I was still working to understand not only how the brothers' music developed, but, more important, what that meant to them and how they understood it in terms of the monastic life. I sat in a plastic lawn chair under a pair of apple trees and looked out over the pond. The bullfrogs croaked every now and then, and flies danced around the surface of the water glistening in the sun. Visitors wandered the grounds or sat in chairs around the pond reading books, writing in journals, or simply looking out over the landscape.

Brother Augustine emerged from a door on the side of the monastery near the kitchen—he had just put a pan of apples into the oven to bake for that evening's supper—and he joined me by the pond. A tall man in his seventies, he sat in a plastic lawn chair with one leg crossed over the other. He was known as a multitalented monk-of-all-trades around Weston, and his well-worn work jeans attested to that. He told me that he spent the morning tending the sheep, splitting wood, and fixing a broken window. His demeanor was lighthearted and friendly; he was someone with whom I frequently conversed throughout my field research.

Brother Augustine had been a Weston monk since 1959, and he knew I was interested in his memory of the early years at the Priory. He was acutely aware of the story of Weston; his memory was sharp, his stories were engaging, and he had a knack for recalling dates and details. Like brother John, brother Augustine lived through the Gregorian chant years, the failed attempts at translation, and the period of uncertainty when the brothers tried to figure out what their post-Vatican II liturgy should be.

We talked about his background a little. He grew up in Montreal, and he said, with a broad grin, that he came to Weston on July fourth. He told me, with a laugh, "It was my own independence day!" I asked what prayer was like when he first arrived at Weston. He replied, "Oh, everything was Latin, and everything was Gregorian chant. And it was long! I mean, we would spend well over an hour at the Vigil prayer, and in those days it started at 4:00 a.m.!" We both laughed as he went on, "So we had to get up early! I mean *really* early!" I asked if he understood the Latin, and he explained that he had learned some Latin in high school, so he probably understood about half of the words. "But you know," he said, "except for brother John and Abbot Leo, I don't think many of us understood a heck of a lot more than that."

He echoed brother John's sentiments that when Vatican II gave the go-ahead for vernacular liturgies, they were more than ready for it, but they were not sure where to turn. "It was around 1964 or '65, I think, when we began to try it out. We started to translate a lot of Latin, and we tried a variety of things," he recalled, "but it was kind of poor, in a way. It just limped along and didn't have the right quality about it at all."

While all of this was happening—around 1967, as brother Augustine told the story—he decided he wanted to learn to play the guitar. Some friends had given the brothers a couple of guitars, and he loved the popular folk songs that were current at the time. With his characteristic grin and bright eyes, he sang the opening lines of "Michael Row the Boat Ashore" and "Kum Ba Yah." There were a few guests and various other visitors sitting around the pond. They heard brother Augustine singing and momentarily looked up from their books, conversations, and contemplations. Some smiled. Some looked puzzled. We both laughed. "You know," he went on, "I loved listening to singers like Peter, Paul, and Mary, and Joan Baez. Even Bob Dylan, which was, at the time, a little rebellious!" He smiled and laughed heartily, shaking his head. "It was the popular style at the time, you know, that folk style, and I would just strum away at it." He pantomimed strumming, closed his eyes, and swayed his head imitating a 1960s-era folk singer.

By this point in my research, I had gotten over any romanticized images I might have had about monks as world-renouncing, austere, holy men. I smiled, though, because I knew that a monk strumming away on a guitar and belting out some Bob Dylan would come as a surprise to many people. The popular imagination does not assume that a bunch of young Benedictines in the Vermont mountains in the 1960s would have kept up with the popular music of their time. This reminded me of brother John's observation that they were who they were, sometimes in spite of themselves. They were, and are, products of their place and time, of their musical and cultural heritage, and of the particular individuality and personality of the brothers who have called Weston home.

Brother Gregory, who was a Weston monk from the early years until the mid-1980s, learned to play guitar around the same time. The two budding musicians occasionally brought simple folk songs to the rest of the brothers in evening recreation in a kind of monastic version of a family sing-along. "So," brother Augustine began, "when we enjoyed the guitars so much, we said, well, why not try to play our guitars for prayer?" It seemed like a promising idea, and even those brothers who were skeptical of guitars in prayer agreed to try it out because nothing else seemed to be working. However, brother Augustine recalled that when the time came to play for the Divine Office prayers, he was surprised to find how nervous he was. Smiling and laughing, he said, "I was so shaky my fingers got stuck in the strings!"

There was something different, perhaps intimidating, about playing their guitars in prayer. The atmosphere was more serious and there was more at stake. There was also the added element of introducing change to the routines and traditions of their monastic life, at that time past its fifteen-year anniversary. Even if the routines were not satisfactory, monasteries thrive on the regularity of a carefully ordered life, and this makes change not only noticeable but, in some cases, unnerving or upsetting, even when the community agrees that it is best. There is always a time of transition when a newer practice replaces an older one, and the community must be patient with the process until, eventually, the new practice becomes an old, familiar one.

In spite of all of this, or perhaps because of it, the young musicians' efforts were well received. The community saw a promising potential solution to their problem of a less-than-satisfactory vernacular prayer experience. Because there was little available music, and much of what was being written at the time was intended for a parish Mass and not the monastic Divine Office, brother Gregory suggested that they try writing a few original songs. It was he who said to brother John, "Well, what can we do? We've got the texts, why don't we just try to write the music ourselves?"

Brother Augustine recalled liking the new music immediately. Brother John and brother Gregory worked especially hard to create the right kinds of songs, but all of the brothers had a voice and a role in the process. Brother Augustine said, "The songs had an organic quality to them because they expressed what we were up to, who we were, and what we ourselves were thinking and experiencing." They emerged from their lives not as Benedictines trying to sound like Benedictines should sound, but as the Weston monks singing like the Weston monks. He added, "We brothers really wanted to maintain the spirit and the quality of Gregorian chant, and yet express something that would be of our own age and our own way of life."

As he spoke, I thought about my conversation with brother John and all that he told me about how important Gregorian chant had been to the young community and their desire to maintain the spirit of the chants. The brothers quickly learned that translating the chants into English killed their spirit, which made me wonder: What is the "spirit" of the chants? After spending years researching Benedictines, and countless hours at prayer in the daily rhythm of the Divine Office, I think this spirit has more to do with the style of sung prayer than with the accuracy or authenticity of pitches, rhythms, and vocal style. These latter qualities have been the topic of much debate since the nineteenth-century revival. The Solesmes monks developed one interpretation, the Germans another, and the Vatican yet another. Solesmes and the

Vatican argued for decades over which interpretation was correct—the more florid French style or the heavier approach favored by Vatican chant scholars. Gregorian chant was understood to have come from God, in the voice of God, for worshipping the Divine, and so it was important to get it right. Musicologists and monastic scholars have long argued over who was right and who was wrong, who was more accurate, who less so. But it was all a product of its time.

These are not the aspects of chant that the brothers were interested in preserving. They were not arguing over how medieval monks did or did not sing their daily prayers, and they were not splitting hairs over neumes, meter, and the question of rhythm—does it follow the cadence of the language, or does it not? They were after something far more elusive, the quality that prompts many to experience Gregorian chant as mysterious yet beautiful. It is the ineffable quality of simple texts, chanted on simple tones, in a plain communal voice; of the chanted psalms handed back and forth phrase by phrase across a monastery chapel such that they become greater than the sum of their parts. It is the beauty and depth of the silence from which the chants emerge and to which they return when the last tone echoes into the rafters. It is the mystery of the search for the divine, the experience of standing alone before God as did the early Desert Fathers and Mothers. It is the mystery of prayer, in all its simplicity, to which the monastic returns throughout the day, every day, for the whole of life.

When the brothers talked about maintaining the spirit of Gregorian chant, these are the qualities of which they spoke. They are mysterious and ineffable, but they are the most basic elements of monastic liturgy. As brother John explained, singing in someone else's voice, however lovely, would never get them there. They had to find a truly vernacular, common voice grounded in a style of prayer they had grown to love and had come to see as their own. The new folk-inspired songs began to meet this need by resonating with their focus on present experiences balanced with awareness of tradition, history, and local context. It is this that turns their music into common prayer for a community of brothers. It is this that allows them to sing like Benedictines and sing like Weston monks.

Brother Augustine reminded me of the importance of this balance when, after nearly an hour and a half of reminiscing and remembering, he returned to the idea of a forward-looking, living tradition. He said that his favorite thing about their music is that it is always growing, always evolving. "A lot of the really early songs we just don't sing anymore," he said, "and then the songs we're creating now have an entirely new quality to them that reflects who we are. We cannot be afraid to grow and change." He explained that, in spite of a half century of life at Weston to reflect upon, he finds that it is most valuable to think in terms of the present. He said, "For myself, I try to live in the now and I don't think a lot about the past, so that every moment is in the present." This is one of the primary challenges of monastic life: to reflect the history of an inherited tradition without living in the past.

The Benedictine Monks of Weston Priory. *Front row, from left:* brother John, brother Richard, brother Peter, brother Alvaro. *Second row, from left:* brother Augustine, brother Mark, brother Columba, brother Robert. *Back row, from left:* brother Daniel, brother Michael, brother Placid, brother Elias. July 2010. Photo by Weston Priory.

Stone Chapel. October 2006. Photo by Weston Priory.

Monastery buildings. *From left:* Stone Chapel and original farmhouse, refectory and kitchen, monastic enclosure. October 2016. Photo by Weston Priory.

Original monastery farmhouse. June 2010. Photo by Weston Priory.

Inside the Stone Chapel. January 2011. Photo by the author.

Brothers and guests in the refectory. Brother Daniel sits at the desk in the corner reading aloud. December 2008. Photo by Anthony Reczek for Weston Priory.

Morning Vigil prayer. December 2008. Photo by Anthony Reczek for Weston Priory.

Evening Vespers during Advent. December 2008. Photo by Anthony Reczek for Weston Priory.

Abbaye de Saint-Benoît-du-Lac, Québec, Canada. August 2009. Photo by the author.

The organ and monastic benches in the abbey church at Saint-Benoît-du-Lac. August 2009. Photo by the author.

Brother John, dancing at the feast of Saint Benedict. July 2009. Photo by the author.

Brother Daniel preparing to put Noël the llama in his harness and leash. August 2010. Photo by the author.

The author working in the apiary. May 2010. Photo by Weston Priory.

Brother Elias, preparing supper. December 2008. Photo by Anthony Reczek for Weston Priory.

Brother Mark baking bread. May 2009. Photo by the author.

Brother Peter making pots using a coiling technique. December 2008. Photo by Anthony Reczek for Weston Priory.

Brother Augustine at the potter's wheel. June 2010. Photo by the author.

Brother Michael, brother John, and the author in the recording studio. January 2011. Photo by Weston Priory.

Chapter Four

My Novitiate

Understanding Craft

When they live by the labor of their hands, as our fathers and the apostles did, then they are really monks.

—Rule of Benedict, 48:8

If there are artisans in the monastery, they are to practice their craft with all humility, but only with the abbot's permission. If one becomes puffed up by his skillfulness in his craft, and feels that he is conferring something on the monastery, he is to be removed from practicing his craft and not allowed to resume it unless, after manifesting his humility, he is so ordered by the abbot.

—Rule of Benedict, 57:1–3

In the Kitchen with Brother Mark: The Craft of Baking

Baking bread is a practice. Inspired by brother Mark's hearty yet soft dark brown loaves dotted with raisins, and feeling confident in my baking skills, I decided to try making bread when I returned home after an early field research visit. My first loaf was a brick with a clump of raisins in the middle. "You just know when it's right," brother Mark told me. I did not know, and it was not right.

Several months after my failed attempts at bread baking, I was back at Weston. Brother John, brother Michael, and I had recently been discussing the practical work of creating new music—how they decide to write a new song, how they create the lyrics and melodies, how they introduce new music to the community—and the topic prompted a wider discussion of craft. Brother John explained that he finds it helpful to think of music as a craft in the monastery and the brothers as craftspeople, not artists. Brother Michael agreed; even though he currently does a lot of the practical work associated with creating new music, he eschews the label "composer" because it singles him out for special attention as an artist.

When the brothers said I should think about music as craft, I thought I understood what they meant. I nodded along as they spoke. But the more I considered it later back in the guesthouse living room, the more I realized how tricky the word "craft" really is. It is a multitasker in the English language, to say the least. Craft is a noun and also a verb. A person who is sly, untrustworthy, or sneaky is crafty. A craft is something made by a skilled artisan or craftsperson; but crafts also emerge from quilting bees, knitting circles, a stay-at-home mother's sewing room, and a children's art class. Attending a craft fair is not the same thing as attending an art show. Armed with bulk supplies of paper, glue, markers, and paint, I spent my college summers as an arts and crafts teacher at a local camp, "arts and crafts" here treated as a singular phenomenon. To craft is to make, most likely by hand. The concept points to creativity and creation, often emerging from a highly skilled and carefully considered activity that requires time, patience, and training. I can craft an idea, a play, an essay, or a boat. A boat is itself a craft. An airplane is a craft. Witchcraft is The Craft.[1]

I realized that treading the waters of craft, although it is such a familiar and seemingly useful term, can become a murky business. It is notoriously difficult to define. Dictionary definitions seem to agree on associating craft with the idea of skill, workmanship, and the handmade. It is the ability to do something, and to do it well, perhaps to a level that is not readily achieved and requires at least some degree of focus, practice, and planning to acquire. It results from discipline and dedication. It is intentional and directed activity that is likely, although not entirely or necessarily, physical, often manual. It is familiar, organic, and human. It is grounded in the local and ideals of tradition. It is frequently positioned as the antithesis of High Art or fine art, yet a tidy art-or-craft distinction is overly simplistic and inaccurate. Typically, craft draws the focus to process and the subject, whereas discourses of art tend to look toward product and the object. But even this becomes tricky; it is possible to focus on the object or product of craftwork, the processes of artwork.[2]

When I thought I understood, at least in part, what the brothers meant by "music as craft," I based that understanding on these assumptions about craft. As I continued to consider the idea, though, I realized that I needed to understand craft as both concept and practice from their perspective. To this end, brother John and brother Michael suggested that it might be useful for me to join some of the brothers in their craftwork. Because of my newfound interest in bread baking, I decided to make brother Mark my first stop.

As we sat in the parlor awaiting the dinner bell one afternoon a few days later, I asked brother Mark about his bread. Sitting across from me in an armchair in the corner of the room, he explained that he had suffered a stroke in the mid-1990s. He smiled and joked as he said that the community needed to find some work to occupy him since he could no longer do any of the physically demanding monastery labor. Brother Mark is known for his sense of humor and levity, and the few guests gathered with us chuckled along with the lighthearted way he told the story. "Well," he said, shrugging his shoulders and raising his eyebrows, "we had to find me *something* to do!"

Returning to a more serious tone, he said that his physical therapists suggested that baking bread would be an excellent form of therapy. The extended periods of kneading would help his body remember the rhythms of controlled movement, and the time involved in the task would foster the focused mind that monastic labor is meant to support.

"You don't learn to make bread overnight," he pointed out with a smile on his face and a tone of laughter in his voice. "There were a lot of doorstops and bricks before I got it right!" He said that it took him a long time and a lot of practice before he produced anything worth eating. After so many years, he had the whole process down to a carefully timed weekly routine. He invited me to join him the following morning so I could observe his baking process.

His timing could not have been better. I had hit something of a mental roadblock in my research. That morning at prayer, the brothers sang, "Song in Our Silence," for one of the opening psalms.[3] Based on Psalm 139, the lyrics are rich with metaphors firmly grounded in ideas and imagery familiar to Christian mysticism: "Song in our silence; light in our darkness; water of life for our thirst; you are the freshness of birth every morning; the grace that encircles our days." Brother Michael and brother Augustine picked out the chord progression in their rolling, finger-picked style, creating a steady beat and clear meter while maintaining a sense of gentle movement. Most of the visitors in the chapel sang along quietly with the simple melody, and as I listened I wondered—not for the first time—how best to describe the brothers' style and its relationship to popular American folk music of the singer-songwriter type. I thought of brother Augustine's description of his early musical influences, and I felt as though their style was more reminiscent of the light, encouraging, engaging side of James Taylor than the course timbre and gritty edge of Bob Dylan.

Later that morning, sitting at the kitchen table in the guesthouse, I tried to take some notes on the morning prayer. "Song in Our Silence" had stuck in my head for the rest of the prayer and throughout breakfast; it became a metaphor for my state of mind. I started my notes by simply remarking that the brothers had used the song that morning, and the lyrics seemed significant in terms of their spirituality and values. But that was as far as I got. I was about to continue writing the details of morning prayer, but the order of the liturgy and the number of people in the chapel did not feel like important or noteworthy details that would help me understand the monastic life around me. My mind felt blank. Not the sort of silence I was after. It was an unproductive lull in my normally chugging train of thought. "I am at a loss," I wrote, after sitting quietly and looking out the windows for a while, "for an approach to my field notes. I no longer know what to write, or how."

The next morning—with uncharacteristically blank pages staring up at me from my field journal—I went through my usual, familiar morning ritual of prayer, followed by tea, toast, and silent movement through the refectory. But after I finished eating, I did not return to my guesthouse to face my mental block. Instead, I went to the back corner of the kitchen and found brother Mark ready for our baking lesson. He had laid out his hardware the night before: large stainless-steel bowls alongside measuring cups, whisks, and spoons. He wore a red "Cota & Cota Oil" T-shirt and blue apron as he prepared the sponge by combining water, yeast, and molasses in an oversized stainless-steel bowl. The bowl reminded me of the one my grandfather used to prepare the giant Sunday dinner salad for our giant Italian-American family. Feeding big families requires oversized kitchen equipment. With twelve brothers and as many as fifteen guests, often even more depending on who is passing through, Weston is indeed a big family to feed.

Brother Mark held the bowl with his left hand and whisked slowly with the right. The whisk turned around and around the bowl, creating a gunge that resembled runny, goopy, natural peanut butter. He sprinkled flour-covered raisins over the mixture and stirred them into the brown goo. He alternated scoops of raisins with scoops of whole-wheat flour as he turned the giant whisk around the giant bowl. Eventually, the dough started to come together.

Meanwhile, guests and brothers gradually finished their breakfasts and passed through the kitchen to wash their dishes and carry on with their own morning routines. Brother Elias pulled trays of food out of the fridge for the day's meals. Brother Peter came into the kitchen to refill his coffee mug. He walked over to the large fruit bowl and picked out a grapefruit. He looked up at us, smiled, and left the kitchen.

Respecting Grand Silence, brother Mark and I spoke very little as I observed his process. When we did speak, we used a light whisper. I wondered how he knew when to stop mixing the dough. He said that, in time, you get a knack for it. One day, you just feel when it's right, whereas every day before that you could never quite tell if it was good or not.

I told him that my love of his homemade raisin bread had inspired me to learn to bake bread, but so far my skills were not great. I made many loaves, and the results varied. I explained that my recipes offered little help. They suggest how the bread should look and feel at various stages, but mostly simply imply that I will "know" when it feels right. Too spongy? Not right yet. Too springy? It was right a few minutes ago, but it's not right anymore. Too wet? Not right. Too dry? It probably won't ever be right. This is hardly a recipe; it implies a long road of trial and error, and perhaps several attempts, before a perfect, beautiful loaf emerges from my oven.

Brother Mark laughed quietly as I regaled him with my trials and tribulations. Even though the kitchen and refectory were empty, we tried to maintain our whispered conversation. But we struggled as we both found humor in the discussion, and shared humor had become an important part of my rapport with brother Mark. In light of my struggles, he pointed out that the mental and physical space of the monastery is perhaps ideal for learning to bake bread. Returning to the task each week, with fidelity and focused attention, the monastic learns to appreciate the process over the result. Learning patience, paying attention to the whims of yeast, flour, and water, coaxing goopy messes into something worth eating, the monk becomes a monk-baker with a focused appreciation for the present moment instead of an obsessive attention to goals and products. Fortunately, the results are delicious.

When the dough was "right," brother Mark set it aside to rise and told me to come back a couple of hours later. As instructed, I returned to the kitchen to find brother Mark ready to work on his bread again. Grand Silence having long since ended, we were free to converse more openly. Brother Mark was perhaps the most talkative of the brothers as far as chatting with guests is concerned. Ken and Donna, a local married couple who were friends of the community and particular friends of mine on my visits, were also in the kitchen preparing dinner for the brothers and their guests. Ken and brother Mark joked and laughed a great deal with one another. Ken stood at the stove sautéing slices of tempeh with mushrooms and zucchini in two very large cast-iron skillets. Brother Mark stood across the room and worked on his bread. Donna and I talked about my research while she washed dishes and I helped to dry and put them away. The vibrant energy of the kitchen late in the morning created a sharp contrast to the still quiet of the earlier hours.

Brother Mark stood at the counter along the sidewall of the kitchen. The sky outside was hazy and the windows were open to let the unseasonably warm, humid air waft into the kitchen. "Yeast really is amazing," he observed, when I noted how quickly the dough was rising just sitting out on the counter. "I've already kneaded it, punched it down, and really beaten it up, but there is just no stopping it!"

The spongy heap of golden brown dough bulged over the top of the bowl. Brother Mark heaved the dough out onto the counter and punched it into an oversized disc resembling a giant chocolate chip cookie. He rolled, kneaded, and punched until the disc was a log several inches thick and at least two feet long. From years of practice and experience, he knew that this log was precisely the right size to yield six three-pound loaves. He used a long knife to measure and divide the log into sections as it continued to rise visibly in the humid air.

He plopped one mound of dough onto the scale with a heavy thud. It was a bit light, but acceptably close to the three-pound mark. He grabbed a loaf pan, poured the extra oil out of the pan onto the countertop and rolled the dough ball in the oil. He shaped the ball into a loaf, lowered it into the waiting pan, and used his knuckles to squish it into the corners and flatten it out. His movements were intentional and unhurried.

After such treatment, the loaves looked a bit wrinkled on top, but brother Mark explained that his final step would be to turn them all over in their pans so that the nice flat bottom became the top and the wrinkled surface remained hidden. He took the first pan he had filled, flipped it over, and the loaf inside flopped out as a squishy blob, disinclined to maintain its rectangular shape and yet not ready to completely abandon it either. Once flipped and returned to its pan, brother Mark scored it crosswise with a knife. He repeated the process until all six loaves were flipped, scored, and ready for the oven. The monastery bells rang, indicating the end of the morning work period. We cleaned up the kitchen and waited for the clock to strike 11:55 a.m., the precise time when the bread had to go into the oven so that it would come out at the end of dinner. Throughout dinner, I could smell the bread baking. I eagerly anticipated a fresh slice at supper that evening.

After dinner, I went to the None prayer that marks the transition from the noon meal to the afternoon work or study period. The short prayer is, among other things, an opportunity to re-center and focus the mind for whatever the afternoon will bring. The brothers concluded None that day by singing their song based on the Beatitudes, and I sat in the chapel pondering the famous series of blessings from the Sermon on the Mount: Blessed are the poor, the meek, the hungry, those who mourn, the pure of heart, the peacemakers, the persecuted. I frankly felt a bit silly for worrying about my inability to produce insightful field journal entries in light of the dimensions of human experience—and problems far greater than my own—brought to light in the song. I returned to the guesthouse, determined to get over it by just writing about the details of my morning with brother Mark, whether or not it seemed insightful in the moment.

Sitting at the kitchen table with my notes in front of me, I reflected that bread baking was one of brother Mark's contributions to the community, and I could tell that he took great pride in it. Even after fifteen years of repeating the process every Wednesday, he still fretted over small details like cracks in the top of the loaves. He paid careful attention so as to time everything according to the brothers' work and prayer schedule. It was an opportunity for him to participate in a focused practice that fosters balance, physically and mentally.

I wrote down some of the things brother Mark had told me that morning about baking bread, hoping it would help in my own pursuit to get an edible loaf to emerge from my kitchen. It was then that I realized that I learned a lot from brother Mark that day not only about baking bread but also about the importance of the regular rituals of monastic life. The very notion of living according to a Rule speaks to this as the Latin for Rule, *regula*, is the root of "regular," "regulate," and a host of related words. It could become rote or even mind numbing, as had my daily return to my writing. But baking bread is about participating in the mindful repetition that is at the heart of monasticism. It is about fostering concentration and contemplation, nurturing communal relationships, and encouraging personal growth, skill, and achievement. It is about turning an everyday activity into a craft.

I began to write in my notes that this was what I needed to do. Then, I gradually realized this was what I was already doing, I just had not yet paid attention to it. The mental and physical space of the monastery was as ideal for learning to bake bread as for learning how to learn in a meaningful way. Returning to my task with fidelity and focused attention, no matter the struggles, I could, like a monastic, learn to appreciate the process over the result. I needed to stop thinking ahead to whatever product, ideas, critical theories, or sparkling revelations I would produce. I needed to live the process with a focused appreciation for the present moment instead of an obsessive attention to goals and products. I needed to start seeing my own work as a monastic craft.

Making Room for Something other than Yourself to Emerge

I continued to think through the brothers' ideals of craft when, a few weeks after my morning in the kitchen with brother Mark, brother Augustine and brother Peter invited me to join them in the pottery studio for the afternoon. It was an opportunity to see them in one of their most familiar practices. Like their music, pottery and ceramics made by the Weston monks have brought the community a great deal of outside recognition over the years and have become favorites for guests and visitors passing through the Gallery Shop.

Pottery was one of the first crafts cultivated in the young Weston community. After receiving a kiln and other supplies as gifts from generous benefactors, by 1961 the young monks were producing enough to sell a few items in their shop. In their September 1962 bulletin, they describe their approach to what they called "operations handcrafts": "In an age where factory production has satisfied the functional needs of the consumer product but for the most part has lost the beauty and humanity contained in handmade things, the individual craftsman is rising again to satisfy the need for art in useful things. Here at Weston, although we are still only in the beginning, our efforts are founded on this principle of beauty in everyday things."

This segment of their bulletin very much reflects the historical and sociocultural context of Weston Priory. The community is, in many ways, the result of antimodern, countercultural movements that emerged in Western culture in the late nineteenth and early twentieth centuries as people came face-to-face with industrialization.[4] Craft became a symbol for an imagined simpler time, a reclaiming of individuality and the human capacity for creativity in the age of machines and factories.[5] In the United States, the 1960s counterculture extended these ideals as young people resisted consumerism and manufactured goods in the midst of the postwar affluence of the 1950s. As the hippies established their alternative lifestyles and communes—and as Benedictines moved into rural monasteries—they turned toward a more rugged way of life where the handmade replaced the factory made, emphasizing skills learned in an apprentice-like process that reveres tradition and human experience.

After dinner, a short walk around the pond, and the None prayer, I was ready for my own glimpse of that process as a lived experience at Weston. I waited outside for brother Augustine, who emerged from a side door near the kitchen wearing faded jeans, old sneakers, and a blue T-shirt with a graphic showing a glass of water and the words "half full." We greeted one another and walked toward the workshop, called simply "the pottery."

The main monastery building sat at the top of Priory Hill, and a scattering of barns, workshops, and outbuildings lined the gravel road that eventually disappeared into the Green Mountain National Forest. The outbuildings were, with the exception of the barns, small, single-story, and painted dark brown. Running along the central road with ponds on either side, these simple structures were homey and rustic; they seemed to suit their natural surroundings.

On our short walk we chatted pleasantly about the summery weather. Brother Augustine opened the door to the workshops. We walked through a storage area, and then into the pottery. Brother Augustine turned on the lights, opened a sliding glass door, and showed me around the space: a large kiln sat empty in the corner, painted white on the outside, lined with tiles on the inside; there was an area for composing, mixing, testing, and applying glazes; there were shelves loaded with dripping containers of colorful liquid; there was a small counter where a box and spray gun lay idle; the near sidewall was lined with vases, bowls, teapots, cups, and shards of pottery. These shards had been used to test glaze colors in iridescent purples, glistening blues, deep reds, and emerald greens. Down the side of the room were sinks covered in the pale gray splatters and colorful glaze remnants of pottery past, washed off of hands and arms, and sent down the drain. Work aprons, tools, and supplies of all kinds, too numerous to note or recount, were neatly organized yet artistically jumbled around. A long worktable and the pottery wheels sat in the center of the room.

As brother Augustine showed me around the space, we talked about the amount of time required to make a piece of pottery on the wheel: twenty minutes of wheel time for a relatively simple piece, then days of firing, glazing, firing, and cooling. He told me about learning the craft of pottery decades ago from brother Thomas, a former member of the community. The brothers prefer working with at least one confrere, and brother Augustine was glad that brother Peter decided to take up pottery as one of his crafts several years ago. We looked at brother Peter's pots, made using a coiling technique, and we looked at some other ceramic pieces such as crosses, plaques, and hand-painted tiles.

Brother Peter arrived just as brother Augustine was beginning to roll out a slab of clay in what looked to me like a giant pasta machine. With smiles and greetings all around, brother Augustine handed me an apron and we got to work. We sat at one of the counters and stamped small, equal-armed crosses out of a slab of cold, wet clay. It reminded me of the many hours I spent each Christmas season making sugar cookies. We imprinted each cross with a design—the signature Weston downward facing dove, an inset cross, stalks of wheat, a heart, or the word "peace" in a whimsical font—and punched a hole in the top for a rawhide loop. Brother Peter paused frequently to instruct me.

We talked about the task at hand, the craft of pottery, and the monastic approach to work and community life. The conversation flowed easily with some periods of quiet; we talked freely but never in a mode of idle chatter. At one point, the conversation moved to the issue of quality control. "Good work!" brother Peter observed, as I painstakingly finished my second cross, "You pass quality control!" We laughed, and I thanked him. "Yes," brother Augustine agreed, "good quality control." He said that one of the appealing parts of pottery as a monastic craft is the experience of getting your hands in the dirt, feeling the clay, and working with something messy. At the same time, they have to keep the end product in mind. "We joke about quality control," he said, "but it's a practice we have to work at all the time." "That's right," brother Peter responded, "it's a practice of letting go, of not being possessive. But it's sometimes better not to get too philosophical about craftwork, at least not while you're doing it, because sometimes things crack and that's okay. It's part of letting go, relinquishing control. You just let it be."

Across the room, suddenly brother Augustine began to sing: "Let it be! Let it be! Let it be! Let it be! Mother Mary . . ." He trailed off as he went into the back storage room. "You know that's a song about marijuana, don't you?" brother Peter called after him. "It is not!" brother Augustine responded as he emerged with a fresh lump of clay. "Yes it is! Mother Mary is marijuana." "No! It's a spiritual song." Brother Augustine's grin and tone of voice suggested sarcasm—perhaps he agreed with brother Peter and was putting on a show of aloofness for my sake. Clearly he found humor in the conversation.

As brother Peter and brother Augustine playfully discussed hidden drug references in Beatles songs, we noticed a slight crack in one of my crosses. The brothers helped me fix it, and again we joked about quality control. This prompted brother Peter to point out, in a more serious tone, that creativity is about making room for the imperfections, making room for something other than yourself to emerge. Just like that, we flowed right back into our chat about the formative, spiritual practices of a monastic approach to craft. From deep discussion, to playful humor, to a present problem, and back again. This is the rhythm of discourse in the monastery.

Finding my place in this rhythm was a challenge. I am a talker, and, as my blended Italian-American and French-Canadian heritage nearly guarantees, I am a loud talker and active gesticulator. I am accustomed to the mode of discourse cultivated in a large family: we talk over one another constantly, and yet somehow manage to converse; we joke almost as constantly, with heavy sarcasm; and we hardly know what to do with a lull in conversation or a quiet room. The monastic mode, on the other hand, is not scattered or constant. It is not talking for the sake of talking. Rather, it grows out of a mindful focus grounded in awareness of myself, the people around me, and wider perspectives. My current needs and thoughts, the presence of others and their needs and thoughts, and questions of meaning, identity, philosophy, and the Absolute are in constant, living dialogue. Add to this a quiet posture of careful listening that avoids interruption or interjection, and the chatter familiar to the secular world fades into the distance. Like brother Peter's experience of craft, for me, this experience of conversation was one of humility and creativity, relinquishing control to see what sort of thing, outside of myself, would emerge.

We continued to chat as we sat around the high table working on the crosses. Brother Augustine joined us. I asked how often the brothers work in the pottery. Brother Augustine said he worked in the afternoons, usually three or four days a week. Brother Peter said that in the best of times he worked three afternoons a week, but lately it had been less as he had been busy with other things. "It's remarkable how many things you have going on all the time," I said. "Exactly," brother Augustine responded, "I have the sheep, too, to take care of, and then cutting wood, and other things."

Returning to the task at hand, I asked if I should start to punch holes in the tops of the crosses, indicating the growing pile now cut from the slab of clay. "Sure, sure," brother Augustine responded. "Make sure to use this end of the punch." He indicated the narrower end. "As you do, the little circles will pile up inside—see?" He demonstrated how to punch a hole in the top of the cross, and then handed me the tools. He got up to check the stock to see which styles of crosses were needed. Brother Peter and I sat quietly at the worktable. I punched holes in the top of the crosses. He scraped down the sides of fired ceramic plaques. After several minutes of silence, brother Peter said, "You know, part of the craft idea is that there is a lot of creative work that initializes the project, but then, once the creative work is initiated, there's a lot of practical skills that are needed." Brother Augustine responded from the end of the table, "Yes, there are a lot of hand skills, for example." Brother Peter then added, "The creative work is in creating the design, the concept, but then making it is very practical. Some people can be creative, but can't carry it through because there is no craft, no practical skill."

Trying to understand what he was offering, I asked, "Do you think that is part of the reason why craft is so important to you?" "Well," brother Peter began, "a big part of it is humility." He laughed as he indicated the broken shards and cracked vases around the room, evidence of projects that failed to turn out as planned. "Yes," I said, "the cracks and quality issues!" We all laughed, returning again to our conversation about quality control. It is not all dreamy imagination and creativity.

Brother Peter continued, "Learning humility, doing very practical, mundane, manual things." He paused for a moment. No one interjected or interrupted. "Also," he began again, "it is a discipline of getting things done, making your living, supporting each other. Everyone participates in that." I responded, "I also find that it seems like each brother has an individual craft, something that involves a lot of personal work but is also for the good of the community." "Mm-hmm, you're right," brother Augustine said as he stamped a design in the front of the crosses, "A lot of us have a craft in us, sort of in embryo, and it hasn't had the opportunity to come out of us, so we try to offer up the opportunity to develop a craft in that way."

I put a hole in the last of the crosses and said, "That also seems to encourage balance in your day, by having opportunities for many pursuits." Brother Augustine looked up from his work, "Right, I could be in the forest all day. It would be nice. But it isn't very balanced." After a quiet moment, brother Peter added, "And the other part too, with crafts, and making your living, and being a monk. Basically, our primary purpose in being here is to be monks, to be brothers." He paused for a moment, looked up from his work, then went on, "Some of us have varying talents and skills. No one is more important than the other, as humble as it might seem. So the major work is not to develop a particular creative gift, but to develop the human relationship of brotherhood." Brother Augustine nodded in agreement. I also nodded, feeling that the brothers were helping me to understand much more than how to make a ceramic cross.

After a few moments, brother Augustine said he should start getting his things ready to throw a pot on the wheel. He turned to me and asked, "Would you take over here?" He handed me the stamp and showed me how to press it into the center of the crosses. I carried on stamping. Brother Peter sat across from me scraping down the plaques. Brother Augustine walked to the back of the room and began slapping together a ball of clay, preparing it for the wheel.

Brother Peter then returned to his previous thoughts. He said, "You know, there can be conflict or tension if your craft isn't set in the context of brotherhood. The monastic life is our profession, and if you become an artist the question is: are you an artist-monk or a monk-artist?" He raised his eyebrows and spoke in a serious tone. "It can be very challenging because it's countercultural," he went on, "but it's that emphasis on humility, and relating as equals, and keeping your focus on the community. So the balance is in developing our persons within that context, and having a balance between creative work, personal work, community, service work, and practical work." Brother Augustine responded, agreeing with brother Peter, "On any given day, it might be more of one aspect or another, but it should become balanced."

"Okay," brother Augustine said, walking over to my workstation, "good work on the crosses, it looks like they're finished. Shall we do a demonstration on the wheel?" We went over to the electric wheel while brother Peter continued to work on plaques. The wheel itself was a flat disc with concentric gray circles moving from the center out to the edges. These remnants of past projects showed a well-loved, well-used wheel. The wall behind the wheel, the basin containing it, and the area surrounding it, for at least two feet on all sides, was nothing short of a splattered mess.

"So," brother Augustine began the instruction, "the beginning part is to center the ball of clay on the wheel, and then you wet it down." The wheel began to spin slowly, making a gentle humming sound. Brother Augustine dipped his hands into a vat of water, pulled out a sponge, and wet down the clay. He held the spinning ball in his hands, and it made sloshing noises as it took on the water and began to soften into shape.

"And then I have to squeeze the clay a little to get it going up and down, and to get it into the center." He squeezed gently, and liquid clay ran over his fingers as the ball quickly took shape. The goopy heap of clay, spinning around the center of the wheel, then became taller and narrower as he squeezed it. It reminded me of brother Mark's goopy heap of dough gradually becoming bread thanks to his patient attention. Brother Augustine periodically wet his hands as he worked, and he used the sponge to keep the clay pliable and prevent it from sticking. He spent the next few quiet moments getting the piece tall and centered.

"Okay, so now you open the clay," he said, as he used his thumbs to depress the center of the column. More water flung around the basin, and his hands were awash with the gray liquid. "I think I'll make another pitcher," he said, indicating two large ceramic pitchers nearby. He adjusted his foot on the pedal and the wheel slowed down a bit. He squeezed the opening in the top of the clay and the walls grew taller and thinner.

I watched, mesmerized by the spinning wheel and morphing clay. I noticed that brother Augustine's hands created a pattern of lines around the piece. As he squeezed, his calluses and wrinkles, the sides of his fingernails, and the angle of his knuckles made tiny impressions in the spinning clay. The developing pattern of rising concentric circles was the potter's fingerprint, a particular mark that only his hands could make. There is a certain amount of letting go involved in a monastic approach to craft, an openness to creating something that is not yourself, as brother Peter described it, and yet the resulting craft is particular to the creator and bears a distinct fingerprint, literally and figuratively.

"You have to have a sense of how thick the clay is, or you could put your finger through it," brother Augustine pointed out as he continued to shape the column of clay. "As it gets thinner, you slow it down a little bit to keep the clay from flying all over the place." He stood up, looked down into the pitcher, and continued to shape the body and narrow the slope of the top to create the mouth of the pitcher.

The rhythm of an afternoon in the pottery marched along. The wheel hummed, the water sloshed, and eventually a finished piece emerged. Brother Augustine sat in front of a pitcher that had been a lump of clay a mere fifteen minutes earlier. It was very impressive, and I asked him how long it took to learn how to do that well. He said that it took about a year, and in the interim, he sent a lot of clay flying all over the room. "It would fly over there," he said, gesturing his clay-splattered arm toward the windows, "and over there" he said as he pointed toward the wall on his left. "It would slop all over the place, and it would get all over me."

Brother Peter then began a story of brother Augustine "showing off" for some nuns from Pennsylvania several years ago. According to the story, brother Augustine failed to center the clay correctly and it went flying across the room. "I wasn't showing off! I was just trying to do it, period," brother Augustine objected, in a friendly tone. Brother Peter decided not to push the details of the story, but instead changed tactics and explained that throwing pots is much harder than it looks once you get your hands on the clay and it starts spinning. "But that's the joy of it," he said. "You have to be one with the clay. You're centering yourself as well, keeping a steady bodily feel." And just like that, we went from practical instruction, to humor, to philosophical and spiritual discussion.

This ideal of centering was exactly what I experienced in brother Augustine that day. The meditative repetition of craft becomes trancelike. The wheel spun, and brother Augustine never stopped moving as he gracefully and swiftly drew the clay up, out, and around. He never took his eyes away. He was intensely focused on the creative task in front of him. I stood mesmerized—clay, hands, water, spinning.

That night at Vespers in the outdoor Barn Chapel, a few hours after leaving the pottery, I was reminded of the focused trance of craft while watching brother Augustine's hands as he played guitar. Sitting behind him over his right shoulder, I watched his fingers from the side and observed the profile view of his hands in the repetitive motion of picking. The pinky-finger rested against the body of the guitar, grounding his right hand. The thumb picked, rocking from the lowest string, to its neighbor, and back again; it paused, and then repeated the pattern. The index and middle fingers filled in the rolling accompaniment: pluck-pluck, tap-tap, up and down over the strings. The ring finger floated up in the air; like the tail of a cat, it seemed to offer balance without getting too involved. The gentle, repetitive pattern rolled, sometimes slowing as the tempo pulled back, sometimes pushing ahead.

I thought back on an afternoon earlier in the spring when I spent the morning work period splitting enormous logs with brother Augustine and a male guest. We pulled five-foot sections of tree trunks off of a pile, stood them up under the steel plate of a huge splitter, braced ourselves as the splitter ripped the logs in half, and then slammed the pulp hook into the end of the halved logs to stand them up for another bout with the splitter. That his logger's hands were rough enough for that labor—mine were not, even in heavy work gloves—and yet agile enough for the guitar, and graceful enough for the potter's wheel, was a physical manifestation of the balanced monastic life he had spent decades cultivating.

The Ideal Balance: Understanding Craft in the Monastery

As I learned in the kitchen and pottery studio, the brothers' sensibility of craft reflects their sociocultural and historical context understood in terms of their received traditions as Benedictines. In the Rule, craft emerges as a means of fostering balance, a theme on which Benedict frequently focuses. Recognizing that spiritual, mental, and physical demands are sometimes conflicting or contrasting, he endeavors to bring them into a kind of embodied harmony in which differences become a resonant whole. For Benedict, it is only by bringing the individual self into alignment that the monastic person is able to engage fully in the community. In this way, the individual finds the points of mental, physical, and spiritual resonance that prompt the at-one-ment of a unified self within the context of a common life.

This sets up an individual-communal dialectic that is the foundational tension out of which the Benedictine form of life emerges. In our conversations, the brothers consistently highlighted the communal nature of their lives. It became something of a mantra. Whether we spoke about music, liturgy, crafts, work, cooking, cleaning, or receiving guests, everything was understood in terms of the community. However, this communal mindset was always set in terms of individuality. Each brother was his own person, not an interchangeable facsimile of an idealized monk. Monasteries may seem like a place to check your individuality at the door, pull on the habit, and align yourself with the standardized norms. In reality, though, each brother or sister takes up a unique monastic journey, set in the context of his or her own person, but also set within and animated by an intense focus on a highly unified community life. This can result in conflict, but it also offers a push-and-pull tension between selves and others that drives monastic life. It is the primordial ooze out of which everything else emerges.

This foundational tension is set within a series of contradictions and paradoxes. As I discussed with brother Michael and brother John when we talked about the monastic vows, a Benedictine professes stability, obedience, and conversatio. Stability tells Benedictines to become rooted, attaching themselves deeply and remaining steadfast. At the same time, conversatio instills a disposition of continual growth and change. Obedience tells them to listen, conversatio encourages them to talk. Never becoming static or stagnant, their lives are ever in motion; the heart, while grounded, remains open to others and to the self. Further, they must foster silence in order to nurture a contemplative and prayerful heart, yet this must not interfere with the basic necessities and ordinary problems of daily life.[6]

As brother Michael once explained to me, sometimes it is his turn to change the filters on the septic tanks. This is about as mundane and profane as it gets, and he does not need to wax philosophical about the job while he does it, nor is it useful to lament the unpleasant activity. However, in the context of his communal life grounded in a contemplative, open heart, even the most unpleasant task is a point for personal growth and active engagement with communal monastic sensibilities. Looking at this tension from another angle, a brother who is always locked away in his room, deep in meditation, contemplating the mysteries of the universe, cannot participate fully in the community life. The individual-communal becomes simply the individual as one member pulls too deeply into himself. There is a critical balance to be struck.

With these driving tensions and foundational contradictions, it is perhaps not surprising that a primary goal of the monastic life is balance. This is not simply an ascetic life of moderation, even if excess is never desirable, and it is not just the equal tempering of yin-and-yang opposites. There are times when a feast is in order. There are moments when certain tasks demand more than their equal share of time; for example, there might be only five minutes for *lectio divina*—prayerful reading—during the marathon work of haying fields or tapping maple trees. When I mentioned to brother Peter that dissertation writing had so overwhelmed my time I was not maintaining much balance, he observed that sometimes balance occurs week to week or month to month instead of through the hours of the day.

From this perspective, balance, that elusive internal oneness that resonates across the community, seems at once flexible and fragile. Anything that jeopardizes it threatens to throw individuals and the community into fragmentation, so careful negotiations of the diverse elements of the monastic life are necessary. Craft participates in this process, offering at once a point of constant challenge and contradiction—brother Peter's observations of the monk-artist/artist-monk dichotomy, brother Augustine as a monk-of-all-trades with demands on his time and person that could easily disintegrate and fragment, brother Mark's work to overcome the physical barriers and emotional defeat of a stroke—as well as a vital means of fostering self as well as self-other alignment.

The physical requirements of skilled work range from felling and milling trees to the most intricate carving in the woodshop; the repetitive, nonstop motion of the potter's wheel that demands attention and discipline, to the busy feet and hands that work in the carefully timed rhythm of backstrap weaving; the small strokes and steady hand of calligraphy, to the attentive work of beekeeping. Each of these skills requires a great deal of mental focus to learn and execute. The monastic practice seeks a high level of skill not for the acclaim or sense of achievement that results, but for the focused mind, inner joy, and experience of beauty that is fostered in the process. This is also true of the spiritual aspects of craft; it is not a matter of expecting enlightenment to come when the piece of pottery is finished, but is instead about an openness to the moments of insight and awakening that are possible throughout the process. Thus, craft becomes an ideal context for the balance of mind, body, and spirit, creating more contradictions and paradoxes of its own while providing a point for negotiating the complexities and mysteries of the contemplative religious life.

All of this is set within the communal framework of cenobitic monasticism, in which everything revolves around the life lived in common, whether the community has two members or two hundred. Benedict frames this in a variety of ways throughout the Rule, perhaps most clearly when he cautions his monks strongly against private ownership, calling it an "evil practice" that "must be uprooted from the monastery" (33:1). As far as he is concerned, unless it has been approved by the abbot, "No one may presume to give, receive, or retain anything as his own, nothing at all—not a book, writing tablet, or stylus—in short, not a single item" (33:2–3). Everything is to be held in common, and goods are to be distributed according to needs, and returned for redistribution. In this, Benedict is concerned with the spiritual development of the individual and the interpersonal relationships of the community. A monk who is free from concern over goods, possessions, and ownership is also free from the worries these can create. He has no cause to be concerned over his clothing, books, tools, food, and necessities because the community meets these needs. He has no cause for jealousy over his brothers' possessions, and has no need to fear that his brothers might covet his possessions. These barriers to brotherly relationships are avoided when all possessions are held in common.

In lived experience, this communal way of being goes well beyond the problem of possessions. An egalitarian approach to shared goods and an antimodern rejection of material wealth and consumerism is a hallmark of monasticism, and it presents particularly challenging points for the conversion from the secular to the religious life. Compared to Benedict's strict language, contemporary monasteries tend to have a more relaxed approach to the question of ownership, not seeking to accumulate possessions and individual wealth, but neither desiring to hold all things in common to the point of extremes—perhaps a brother's socks and toothbrush can be his own, even if he might be relieved of the worry associated with purchasing such items. The point here is that Benedict's concern with the communal frame of mind is understood to go beyond the mundane question of stuff, however practical; it is a basic unifying principle, and all aspects of life lived in common must be understood in this framework.

Here, a monastic perspective on craft participates in the freedom from possessions and prosperity in favor of communal sensibilities. A personal pursuit of skilled work and artistic effort must not become an individualized focus on achievement, success, or recognition. The monastic profession cannot be sacrificed in pursuit of an artistic profession. A brother cannot lose sight of the importance of the process in favor of the end result. For example, if a piece of pottery is beautiful, brother Augustine is recognized by his brothers for his fine work and he certainly has a sense of personal achievement and satisfaction in a job well done, but he does not sign his name to the piece, outsiders do not single him out among his brothers, and proceeds from the sale go into the communal funds with no consideration of whose work is the most lucrative. Brother Augustine, who is not responsible for running the Gallery Shop, has no cause for concern over the reception of his work by the visiting public and is free from worry over how he might redirect his efforts in order to achieve higher acclaim.

From this perspective, craft is not limited to skilled manual work, but rather is bound up in human relationships expressed in the collective, continued practices of tradition. Craft integrates head and hand, body and mind in the pursuit of quality, highly skilled work. Like many craftspeople, monastics often become skilled at their chosen craft, but to seek after recognition for oneself would be equal to Benedict's storing up of goods and possessions, and would jeopardize a vital foundation of communal living. A monk whose work is not set, always and already, within the framework of community runs the risk of setting himself between and against his brothers, opening up the paths of jealousy, setting the seeds of resentment, and digging trenches of separation between an individual and the group. This might seem a harsh perspective on a successful or particularly gifted member of the community, but the dangers are immediate and the threat to the community is real. The risk is so great, Benedict admonishes that an artisan who becomes "puffed up" in his craft is to be removed from it (57:1–3).

In all of these ways, a monastic ideal of craft at once participates in and brings into balance the tensions of the Benedictine form of life. Craft balances the individual and communal because it is simultaneously a dialogue with materials, skills, and knowledge, and with other persons as fellow craft workers and observers. The monastic craftsperson articulates individual presence without claiming individualized credit in the public eye, for example, in brother Augustine's fingerprint in the lines of the clay. In this way, existence becomes material and tangible, without fragmenting individuals and communities.

Craft celebrates collective wisdom, knowledge, and understanding that come together to form the concept of tradition. It requires a disciplined mind and body, and fosters concentration. There is perhaps only a thin line between concentration and contemplation, and so this supports a monastic life that resists a transcendence-based, head-in-the-clouds approach to contemplative sensibilities in favor of a focus on immanence and the everyday. Craft encourages an awareness of rhythm in the repeated practices that require disciplined commitment as well as an alertness that resists falling into stale routine. Craft is thus a dynamic process that mirrors, supports, and participates in this most basic characteristic of monasticism. Craft is a practice in letting go: mistakes happen, things break, and room must be made for something other than the self to emerge.

The Comfort of the Familiar

After the brothers and I left the pottery that afternoon, it was nearly time for Vespers. I went to the outdoor Barn Chapel for the evening prayer, then to supper afterward. After helping brother Daniel empty the dishwasher and put the dishes away, I went outside to take some notes on my day. I wrote about the details of working in the pottery. I wrote some preliminary thoughts on craft. But mostly I focused on the comfort I was beginning to experience in the predictability of life at Weston. It created a deep sense of welcome and home for me, and I wondered about how that must affect the brothers who have made this way of life their profession.

It was a relatively basic experience that got me thinking about this: I noticed that at supper I found comfort in knowing that there would be soup, crackers, cheese, bread, hummus, and salad on the table. I could anticipate the order in which they would be set out. I knew which containers, bowls, and cutting boards would be used for each food. I could anticipate the quiet movements with which I would serve myself. I imagined this kind of predictability could easily become stale or routine, as it had weeks earlier in my consistent return to my field notes. Over the course of a monastic lifetime, the experience of strict routines likely varies. But it was beginning to give me a tremendous sense of comfort. It was a far cry from the relative discombobulation of my early meals at the Priory. Knowing what to expect from day to day, hour to hour allowed me to move easily into the flow of monastic life. In this flow, I noticed things around me and engaged with people in a more focused way. This is exactly what the routines of monasticism are meant to support. I felt as if it was giving me room not only to think, but to hear my own thoughts.

As I wrote that evening, I sat by the side of the pond and looked up at Terrible Mountain defining the horizon across from me. It glowed bluish in the fading daylight. Birds, bullfrogs, and mosquitoes were the only sounds. The sky was clear and blue, streaked with impossibly faint wisps of clouds. Tiny water bugs left rippling circles on the pond such that it looked like raindrops falling on the still water. Terrible Mountain reflected in the mirrorlike surface.

As I took all of this in, two women staying in the women's guesthouse approached me, holding their cell phones up toward the sky. They asked if there was any reception anywhere. I smiled. I had not so much as thought about a cell phone, television, or Internet access in weeks. I told them that they would need to go back over the mountains and into the neighboring town. There, they might get some service. They were taken aback. They wondered how the brothers functioned without cell service. I was taken aback that they would *want* cell phone service cluttering up the internal and external quiet of the monastery. Disconnecting from the incessant connectedness of the digital age was an important part of my sense of calm, focused attention in the monastic ethos. I explained to the women that Vermont had spotty cell phone coverage because of the mountains, many of which had no towers on them because of an effort to protect the natural landscape. "That must be nice for the mountains," one of the women said briskly as she continued to pursue a cell phone signal. The other explained that they were unprepared to be without their cell phones. I knew they had traveled a long way to be at the Priory, and both had teenage children back home. I felt for them, and understood their almost frantic desperation to check in with their children. I offered to share my long distance calling card for the phone in the guesthouse if they needed to call home.

This experience of recognizing and valuing the mental and physical space that had come to define my field research and my emerging understanding of monastic life—and this reminder of the space between monastic life and the nonmonastic world—returned me to my day's pursuit to understand craft. The challenge to make space for something other than yourself to emerge seemed to require just that: space. It occurred to me that monasticism is in some ways a life dedicated to carving out, and learning to dwell within, that space. I further reflected that my work to understand the brothers was similar. I was well on my way to carving out and dwelling in my own kind of space, and this process was related to the processes of craft that the brothers described. My knowing was becoming part of my being. It was emerging gradually in my presence in and attention to the repeated practices and regular processes as well as the unexpected moments and unpredictable experiences of each day. The bells rang for Compline and I again felt the comfort of the familiar. I closed my notebook and made my way to the chapel, wondering what the rhythms of the next day would bring.

Chapter Five

Music as Craft

Creating a Tradition

> Language and silence are here engaged at the high point of their eternal dance with one another.... Uplift and transform language; use it in a different way. Create the sort of language that will always feel like it is brimming with divine silence.
> —Rabbi Arthur Green, *Radical Judaism*

"Listen": Telling the Weston Story

Several brothers, each in his own way and in different contexts, emphasized to me that their music is not composed in a vacuum, that it grows out of their experiences and reflects their lives together. To illustrate this, several of them told me the same story. On Christmas day in 1971, the Priory's founder, brother Leo, suffered a heart attack from which he recovered. Brother Leo had retired from his role as abbot of Dormition, he was living full time as a Weston monk, and he had grown very close to the still-young community. The near loss of their founder and father figure was intensely emotional for the brothers. As a reflection of this moment and as a gesture of honor for brother Leo, the brothers created the song "Listen."

I first heard "Listen" at Morning Vigil one day in the late spring. Perhaps fitting for my own participation in the Weston narratives of history, memory, and everyday life, it was the day before the burial of brother Philip's ashes. Brother Philip had passed away after living with amyotrophic lateral sclerosis (ALS). The brothers' friends and family members were beginning to gather, the guesthouses were full to capacity, and there was a more pronounced reflective atmosphere around the Priory.

I walked from the guesthouse to the chapel that morning in the bluish darkness just before dawn. I walked up Priory Hill Road from the women's guesthouse, and as I reached the top of the steep hill the chapel gradually came into view through the trees. When I entered the chapel, my eyes took a moment to adjust to the dim light within. I saw the shadowy outlines of several people scattered around. To my left, a woman sat in the back row. Her eyes were closed; her hands were folded in her lap. Brother Daniel's mother, Lupita, sat toward the front. Several of brother Mark's cousins who had arrived from New Jersey the night before sat together toward the back of the chapel. I saw a few Weston locals around the room and recognized them as regular visitors.

I sat at the end of the front row of chairs. As usual, brother Columba was already sitting on his prayer cushion with his eyes closed and a gentle grin on his face. I heard the *swish* of the chapel door and quiet footsteps as guests entered. The brothers also entered one by one from the monastery. The bells began to ring.

Brother Richard was the last to enter the chapel, indicating that the Vigil could begin. Brother Elias picked up a rain stick—around four feet tall and four inches in diameter—that had been propped against the wall next to him. Originating in Latin America, a rain stick is a hollow wooden tube that mimics the sound of falling rain. The tube is filled with thousands of tiny beads or pebbles and lined with nails or cactus needles that cause the beads to knock around as they tumble from one end to the other. Brother Elias slowly turned the stick end-over-end. The pitter-patter of tumbling beads broke the silence of night and brought the brothers and their guests from the internal quiet of meditative prayer to the collective utterance of Morning Vigil.

Brother Elias completed one very gradual turn of the rain stick. As the beads tumbled to a stop, he slowly turned the stick back over again and the pitter-patter resumed. Brother Michael held a small soprano recorder up to his mouth, poised to play. When brother Elias turned the rain stick over again and set the beads tumbling and rustling, brother Michael added a very slow, simple, rising three-note melody over the falling rain. He took a deep breath and paused for a moment, then played the three slow notes again. Taking another deep breath, he played a new phrase, which was slightly more complex, but still very slow. The open, breathy, distinctively wooden sound of the recorder seemed to gently fill the dark chapel, but its soft timbre lacked any sharpness that would cut through the stillness or echo around the room.

The rest of the brothers had large, round frame drums in their laps. Brother Augustine picked up his drum and held it about chest high. As brother Michael repeated the recorder line from the beginning, brother Augustine played a rhythmic accompaniment, a steady *dum, dum, dum-dum, dum-dum*. The rest of the brothers joined him. Using soft mallets, they struck their drums gently and repeated the pulsing rhythm over and over: *dum, dum, dum-dum, dum-dum*. Where brother Michael's melody had been played rhythmically the first time through, but without a steady beat, he now followed the meter of the drums. It evoked the rhythms of the body: exhaling breath of the recorder, beating heart of the drums.

While they played, brother Alvaro lit a tall white candle at the center of the brothers' semicircle. He then moved around the circle, lighting candles in front of several brothers. Each candle created a soft glow of light. When he returned to his seat, the brothers stopped drumming, brother Michael played a final phrase on the recorder, and brother Elias allowed the last of the beads to fall to the bottom of the rain stick. The brothers tucked their mallets into the strings across the back of their drums, set them off to the side, and returned to their previous poses.

This wordless call to prayer evoked Native American and Latin American sensibilities more than Benedictine traditions, and it could easily be seen as a problematic appropriation of a cultural Other, essentialized as spiritual and earthy. Sitting cross-legged on prayer cushions only enhanced this imagery by adding an Eastern flair to the cultural borrowing. The first time I experienced this opening to the Morning Vigil prayer, I was very surprised. It was not at all what I expected Benedictine monks to do. I very clearly recall walking into the chapel that first morning, seeing the prayer mats spread out on the floor, watching the brothers enter with their drums, and wondering what was going to happen.

When I asked some of the brothers about this call to prayer, they explained that the indigenous instruments—their term for the rain stick, recorder, and drums—remind them of their concern for issues of social justice and peace in Latin America. They have long-term, extensive connections to a community of Benedictine sisters in Mexico City who are dedicated to working with the poor throughout Latin America. In 1984 the brothers welcomed a family of Guatemalan refugees to their home, openly defying the Reagan administration as they declared their monastery a public sanctuary.[1] They visit Mexico and Latin America annually to learn about ongoing issues of peace and social justice in the region, and they purchased the rain stick, recorder, and drums on these trips.[2] This kind of work, and the liturgical practices it inspires, are what Timothy Byrnes describes as a kind of "reverse mission," where evangelization, knowledge, faith experience, and religious understanding come from Latin America to the United States.[3] In the brothers' Vigil prayer, it becomes a dialogic interweaving of musical, cultural, political, and spiritual symbols that adds layers of meaning to the Morning Vigil and narrates an important aspect of the Weston story.

Returning to a familiar Benedictine style, the Morning Vigil continued with a chanted call to prayer and two psalms—95 and 63—the first chanted antiphonally, the second set as a verse-refrain song. As I listened quietly from my seat in the gallery, I heard the music building in a gradual progression, moving from the wordless prayer, to simple chants with limited accompaniment on a single guitar, to a song with full rolling accompaniment on both guitars. I heard familiar scriptures and unfamiliar antiphons and refrains. Gradually, the sense of energy and alertness in the room increased along with the soft yellow light from the rising sun.

After the psalms, brother Daniel picked up his candle and a sheet of paper. He read a contemporary selection about the liberating power of grace and the danger of overlooking the experience of grace in the routines of the everyday. The reading talked about finding fulfillment, autonomy, and unity with God in pursuit of freedom. Listening to others and the importance of the relationship of friendship were among the primary themes. He read slowly and intentionally.

The brothers and the visitors in the gallery, who remained completely silent for the majority of the Vigil, sat and reflected on the reading for nearly a full minute. I sat in the front row and closed my eyes, meditating on the themes of listening and friendship for a few moments, but then switching gears as I started making mental notes of things I wanted to remember about the Vigil. I was particularly interested that morning in the impression that everything was perfectly timed, and yet I noticed subtle ways that the brothers seemed to be cuing one another: brother Augustine held his drum at his chest where it was clearly visible, brother Elias shook the last of the beads in the rain stick in an effort to keep the sound going while brother Michael concluded his melody, all of the drummers stopped together right when brother Alvaro returned to his seat. I could see that most of the brothers had their eyes closed, but they were clearly aware of one another.

When brother Michael sensed that the silence had lasted long enough, he leaned over slightly and picked up his guitar. Brother Augustine noticed the movement and did the same. They made very little sound, but it was enough to catch my attention. I opened my eyes. Brother Augustine gave a slight nod and the two guitarists began to play in their rolling finger-picked accompaniment, each with his own style. They played through the first chords of the song "Listen." Brother Michael, brother Augustine, and brother Elias—the schola brothers that morning—sang the opening line: "Listen, and gentle be present." The pitches of "listen" stepped down almost like a call, the response to which was "present," sung on the same two pitches at the end of the line.[4] The rest of the brothers joined in to complete the phrase: "to all you've ever close kept in your loving heart." The second half of the line had a more complex melody, making the clear, repeated melodic motion of "listen" and "present" stand out.

This was the first time I had heard the song in prayer. I recognized it from one of their albums, and I knew that it was the song that some of the brothers had mentioned to me. Several people in the chapel sang along softly. I wondered if they knew the story behind the song, or perhaps had even known brother Leo personally. I wondered if the song would, on some level, evoke brother Leo's memory for the brothers who had known him, and if perhaps this was one reason why it remained in frequent use after so many years.

The lyrics focused on the importance of listening to one another and attending to one's own inner life. They addressed a second-person-singular "you." I wondered if, when they wrote the lyrics, the brothers imagined themselves as the addressee and brother Leo as the speaker. Perhaps this was advice he had given the novice monks. The strophic form—A, A'—did not use a verse-refrain structure, and so the entire song was sung communally rather than in a style of alternating verses and refrains between the cantors and the rest of the group. This enhanced the collectivity of the experience.

During the song, some of the brothers closed their eyes, others gazed toward the middle of the circle; some sat very still, others swayed gently with the music. They sang the slow, meditative song quietly, and the timbre of their voices blended into a multidimensional unison. The visitors who were singing along seemed to be conscious of this blend; they sang very softly. The song had a slightly lower tessitura than is common in the Weston repertoire. The brothers often sang in a mid- to high-tenor range, but the lower pitches of "Listen" gave it a resonance that blended with the darkness of the Vigil and the quiet singing style to enhance the meditative affect. When the song ended, everyone in the room seemed to take a deep, quiet breath together as the notes faded away.

Brother Augustine laid his guitar on the floor next to him. Brother Elias quietly turned the page of his binder. There were several moments of silence. Brother Alvaro picked up his candle and a small book. He read a poem requesting God's mercy, help, and renewal. He blew out his candle. There was another period of silence. The energy level of the Vigil, which was never especially high, seemed to be winding down, marking "Listen" as the high point of the experience. The brothers sang a Kyrie, brother Placid read the day's Gospel, and, after a simple sung response, everyone extinguished their candles.

The brothers sat in silence for several moments. Most of them had hardly moved at all throughout the course of the Vigil. Brother Michael, still holding his guitar, strummed a slow chord. The brothers sang their closing chant in unison while brother Michael strummed down to mark the emphasized syllables.

The arc of the Morning Vigil music seemed to come full circle as the brothers gathered up their cushions, drums, and candles and left the chapel as quickly and quietly as they had entered. Brother Daniel was the last to leave, and he blew out the large center candle as he went. I sat a little while longer in the meditative atmosphere thinking about the lyrics of the song, "Listen." I wondered if the people in the chapel were familiar with the Rule of Benedict and its opening line: "Listen carefully, my son, to the master's instructions and attend to them with the ear of your heart" (Prologue:1). The song clearly resonated with the themes of listening that were part of brother Daniel's reading, and the poetic lyrics were rich with metaphors and mystical spirituality, but I wondered if other people heard the call to deep listening as a particularly Benedictine sensibility.

Hearing the song performed in the context of daily prayer, I felt that I understood its meaning more deeply than I previously had when I heard it on the brothers' album, *Listen*. As they were preparing to bury brother Philip next to brother Leo the following day, I imagined that this song was perhaps taking on new layers of meaning for the brothers and I felt myself participating in these extensions of the Weston story as I was part of that moment in their lives.

At that time, it was early in my research process and I was still struggling with my identity as guest researcher and friend. Feeling that I understood on a deep, personal level some of the multifaceted layers of meaning in the songs and prayers of that Morning Vigil was a vital step in moving beyond these struggles as I became part of the deep listening, contemplation, and conversation that shape the Benedictine way of life. I was participating in the lived realities of connecting the past to the present in the ongoing processes of creating tradition.

Much later in my research, I returned to this experience and recognized its potential to help me understand what brother John meant when he told me to think about music as a craft in the monastery. After my experiences in the kitchen and pottery studio, I had begun to understand craft as a point for connecting to the past while navigating the present. Whether called folk art, utilitarian art, or handiwork, craft focuses on process, communality, and collectivity. At the same time, craft allows people to make their traditions personal and individual. Discourses of tradition also draw attention to collectivity and communality, but it is perhaps best understood as an individual-communal dialectic through which individuals articulate their identities as distinct selves and members of a family, community, and social group. In this process, foundational texts, sources, and stories are interwoven with ethical, moral, and religious beliefs, set alongside the local oral history that incorporates important people and events of the past into present performance.[5] It becomes a liturgical utterance spoken in a common voice with the authority of the local vernacular.

"Locusts and Wild Honey": The Creativity of Tradition

A blizzard raged on a blustery winter afternoon a couple of weeks after Christmas several months after I first heard "Listen" in Morning Vigil. Brother

Placid plowed the guesthouse driveway, which was buried under a foot of new snow. I sat at the kitchen table in the guesthouse with a fresh cup of tea in front of me, having just finished shoveling the walkways outside the guesthouse door. During that winter visit, I decided to spend some time really listening to the brothers' albums to hear the development of their music. I hit "play" on my computer. The first track of the brothers' first album came through my headphones. I heard the familiar finger-picked guitars and the less familiar 1970s-era keyboard accompaniment added during the recording session. In a clear tenor voice that was more formal, full, and youthful than I had heard in the brothers' daily prayers, one brother sang: "There was a man named John the Baptist, and this is his message: Repent for the kingdom of heaven is right at hand." The melody was a bit dark, descending toward the final, foreboding line. Then a group of brothers with young, bright voices responded: "Man cannot live on bread alone, but on every word that comes from the mouth of God. For the time has come, and the kingdom of God is right at hand. Repent and believe the good news. Repent and believe the good news."[6] The melody of the response was far more uplifted, matching the brightness of the young voices and elevating the mood a little after the intense opening line. The song had an upbeat, almost peppy style and I started swaying and bouncing my head to the beat.

The song, "Locusts and Wild Honey," had fallen out of use in the brothers' daily prayers, but in 1971, when the album *Locusts and Wild Honey* was released, it would have been the first Weston song many people heard. Following Vatican II, American parishes faced the same problems monastic houses faced: a lack of vernacular liturgical music. Parishioners and musicians experimented with a wide variety of music, from Protestant hymns to secular folk songs. As has often happened throughout the course of music history, the younger generation wanted music that reflected their tastes and offered an alternative to the styles preferred by the older generation.

Troubadour-style folk singers like Joni Mitchell and groups like Peter, Paul, and Mary were popular in the late 1960s when Vatican II opened the door for musical and liturgical creativity. Teenagers and young adults were drawn to their style: the informal, anti-institutional guitar accompanying simple lyrics set to memorable melodies. It was particularly well suited to large group participation, and as Vatican II called for the active participation of the people—the renewed approach to the Catholic Mass that the vernacular was intended to support—this was an important characteristic. Singer-songwriter-type folk music began to take center stage in an emerging liturgical music movement.

As teenagers, my own parents, along with their brothers, sisters, friends, and classmates, gathered in the basement of their home parish with guitars and homemade songbooks. A young, engaging priest encouraged them as they experimented with new worship styles, and they started their own version of what came to be called the Folk Mass. They used popular songs that could be reinterpreted to suit a religious setting—Simon and Garfunkel's "Bridge Over Troubled Water" was a particular favorite, with the "bridge" interpreted as a metaphor for God or Jesus—in their search for an authentic liturgical voice of their own.

Teenagers in parish basements throughout the United States started similar groups and the populist, countercultural Folk Mass movement began to gain momentum. However, parishioners quickly realized they needed properly liturgical music if they were ever going to get out of the basements and into the church. They needed songs with expressly religious and scriptural content as well as the necessary complement of acclamations, responses, antiphons, and hymns for the Mass. "Bridge over Troubled Water" could only get them so far.

This is when the music of the Weston monks came on the liturgical scene and helped to define the changing sound of American Catholicism. It became both catalyst and mirror for the sweeping changes that followed in the wake of Vatican II. The brothers did not write their music with this in mind. It was not for the parish Mass; it was specifically for their own liturgies. But visitors loved the new music when they heard it at the brothers' weekend Eucharist services. The hybrid folk-chant style, accompanied on lute-like, finger-picked guitars was a new, exciting music based on the inherited traditions and texts of Catholicism. Friends and frequent visitors began asking for copies of the music to use in their own parishes. People passing through Weston wanted recordings so that they could take the music home with them.

Brother John and brother Augustine told me that they recall being surprised by this response. They had not anticipated that people would react so positively to their music. They found it encouraging, especially as it was still a new practice for them. They spent many hours as a community discussing what to do. They saw that everyday parishioners in local churches experienced the same excitement about and problems with vernacular liturgies that they themselves had experienced. They were familiar with groups like the Saint Louis Jesuits and singer-songwriters like John Michael Talbot who also began writing and publishing folk-style liturgical music following Vatican II. Seeing an opportunity to share some of their monastic life through their music, offer new liturgical options to those who might need them, and also establish a source of income for the community, they published their first songbook and headed to the recording studio to make an album. It was the first of many.

Weston quickly became known as the home of the famous "singing monks." New albums turned up on the Billboard Gospel charts. Visitors flocked to the Priory by the thousands. The music of Weston Priory became the soundtrack of Catholic worship for generations of parishioners who came of age in the 1970s, 1980s, and 1990s. I sang their acclamations—the Sanctus, Agnus dei, and doxology—every week in my home church. I knew every word of "Go Up to the

Mountain," "Yahweh," "Calm Is the Night," "We Thank You Father," "Spirit of God," "Something Which Is Known," and countless other songs that filled the pages of the hymnals tucked away in the back of every pew.

As I listened to "Locusts and Wild Honey" in the guesthouse that day, I tried to imagine what it would have been like to hear this as a totally new and exciting kind of liturgical music. In the 1970s, visitors came to Weston and heard something they had never heard before, a shift from what had defined their religious lives to that point. Many people were, apparently, thrilled, and they wanted to bring it home. But I wondered if they understood the rich monastic context of the songs. I wondered if they heard fifteen hundred years of Benedictine history surrounding each word, each phrase.

When I listened to "Locusts and Wild Honey" that morning, this is exactly what I heard. Benedictine-ness runs through the veins of the song. The lyrics tell the story of John the Baptist, portrayed in scripture as an unusually austere man who turned away from his everyday life to wander the wilderness, wearing a camel-hair shirt tied with a leather rope, and subsisting on locusts and wild honey. He had an urgent prophetic message: "Repent, for the kingdom of heaven is at hand."[7]

More than a simple retelling, the song interprets the story of John in terms of monastic spirituality. It was recorded in 1971, a time when the young Weston monks likely identified with the story of a man about their age who made a choice to go into the wilderness and live as simply as possible, with his mind and heart directed toward scripture and prayer. As far back as the earliest Desert Fathers and Mothers, the story of John the Baptist has long offered this kind of inspiration for the monastic life.

"Locusts and Wild Honey" uses a simple verse-refrain form and a thoroughly folk-inspired sound. The lead singer, called the cantor, acts as a troubadour who tells the story of John, while the group sings the moral of the story in the recurring refrains.[8] The lyrics create an exchange between the cantor, who relays the story of John as a distant observer, and the rest of the singers, who voice John's words as their own and reinforce the point of the story. The purpose here is not only to highlight certain aspects of the John the Baptist narrative but also to tell the participants what this story means and why it is important. It is at once storytelling and interpretation, biblical narration and exegesis.

Throughout monastic history, liturgical music has been used in this way: as instruction and interpretation, narration and exegesis. Scripture is the primary material of the Divine Office. In liturgy, musical performance interacts with text in a creative process of interpretation. It becomes a dynamic space for proclaiming and interpreting the inherited sources of Christianity and the Benedictine life. It allows monks or nuns, brothers or sisters, to articulate who they are and what they believe in a communal voice. This is particularly the case in a community where liturgical music is the result of local creativity and currency, where music allows monastics to create, embody, and perform their way of being. It becomes a sung narrative repeated daily.

The Weston monks' narration and interpretation of the story of John the Baptist is this kind of interweaving. It is an approach that is apparent in many songs in their repertoire: "Come Now My Love" is based on the Song of Songs; "Come to Me" creates a dialogue between the Gospel of Matthew and Psalm 23; "As A Deer" blends Psalm 42 and the Rule of Benedict; "Go Up to the Mountain" is based on Isaiah 38 and 40; "I Have Called You Now" draws on passages from Isaiah, Micah, Luke, and Psalm 89. Further, many songs use liturgical prayers and texts that are central to monastic worship. "Creator of All" is an interpretation of the Lord's Prayer; "Hear the Song of Your People" is a Magnificat; "Cry Out in the Stillness of Morning" is a Benedictus;[9] "Come Creator Spirit" is an interpretation of the *Veni, Creator Spiritus*, a Latin prayer and Gregorian hymn for Pentecost. As brother Gregory pointed out to brother John: They had the texts, they just needed the music.

However, narrating and interpreting foundational texts is only one dimension of their liturgical tradition. Many songs are clearly rooted in some aspect of Christian theology or monastic spirituality, but their content is original to Weston. For example, "We Thank You, Father," was written to celebrate the final profession of vows for brother Elias and brother Placid. The lyrics do not directly reference these two brothers, but rather offer a general reflection on and gratitude for community and family life. With songs of this type, the brothers draw on their life experiences and blend these with their received texts to create new liturgical material that carries deep, very specific meaning.

This is the work of creating a tradition. Creativity and tradition are often understood as opposite ideas. Dictionary definitions of "tradition" focus on knowledge or lore handed down from generation to generation. Tradition is revered and authoritative. It is the stories, customs, repeated practices, and collective knowledge that emerge from deeply interpersonal processes. Creativity as the ontological capacity to make something is often positioned as separate from or counter to tradition.[10] However, these two dimensions of human experience and everyday life are better understood as interdependent and dynamic. Tradition is an active force, not unlike Bourdieu's theory of the habitus. It is an interpersonal, collective, often unconscious creative process that allows individuals and communities, selves and others, to understand and perform their identities. Tradition is this kind of active force in the life of the Weston monks. Through musical and liturgical creativity, they take account of their past—historical consciousness and memory—in present performance. They establish, over time, a font of repeated practices, collective wisdom, and local knowledge. From deeply personal songs like "Listen," to their work in the gardens, craft studios, and sheep pens, the brothers participate in this collective process each day as they continually create and enact their form of life.

The Limitations of Language

At dinner one afternoon late the following spring, brother John passed by me in the buffet line, his plate loaded with tempeh, vegetables, bread, and rice pudding. He told me he would have some time to meet with me that day after None if I had the time. I had spent a hot and humid morning working hard with brother Daniel and a fellow guest in the gardens. I felt tired and a little gross from working in the dirt while perspiring for hours in the sun. I was not sure if I had any kind of mental focus left, but I counted on the rhythms of the monastic day—a quiet dinner and None—to reset me mentally and physically. So I agreed, hoping I seemed more energetic than I felt, and I told him that I would meet him in the parlor after prayer.

I did feel more focused by the time we sat down in a small sitting room to chat, and when I saw that brother John was carrying a pile of papers I got a burst of excitement and anticipation. At some point, after more than a year of sharing the space and conversatio of monastery life, what began as interviews—with varying degrees of confidence and success on my part—became dialogues. I could not put my finger on any precise moment of transformation, but as brother John put down the small pile of papers, I recognized that we were sharing ideas about points of mutual interest. We were both fascinated by the questions my research raised on creativity and tradition, local authenticity and historical consciousness, music and prayer.

On top of the pile was a paper I had recently presented at a conference. Because I wanted to share the products of my research with the community, I gave the brothers a copy. It was about discourses of reform in liturgical music, it touched on themes of performance and participation, and it compared the Compline prayers I had experienced at Weston and Saint-Benoît. I could see that brother John had written notes in the margins, and I was eager for his thoughts.

We talked for a while about how the brothers were inspired by the liturgical movement, and how Vatican II gave them the inspiration they needed to start working with their received liturgical traditions in a new way that reflected their experience of living as Benedictines in a particular place and time. "You know," brother John said, "language was really a big topic there, and participation. They're related, of course." He went on to point out that language can be limiting because we must deal with all of the many meanings and implications of various terms. Words carry a lot of baggage. He said, "Even that word, liturgy. I'm hesitant to even use that word anymore. It's common prayer, really."

He explained that the word "liturgy" had become so closely tied to institutional structures and ideas about ritual that its original meaning, from the Greek word for "public works," had been lost. He went on: "Benedict uses the term *opus dei*, of course, to describe the daily prayer of the monastery. The word liturgy does not appear in the Rule. He was no Greek classicist! He was closer to the peasants. The workers."

I had my notebook open in my lap, trying to attend closely to all that he said while making little notes as he spoke to remind me of follow-up ideas and questions I wanted to ask. I said, "You know, the literature on the liturgical movement and Vatican II almost universally refers to it as 'liturgical reform.' But I often hear you speak about renewal when you talk about the Council." Brother John smiled slightly. "That's right," he said, "is it renewal or reform? Pope John said that this was not just about patching up the ship. That's what reform means. To keep patching up the ship." He went on to explain how he felt the Church was entering another time of "patching up" as the Vatican was getting ready to send newly translated English versions of the Mass to American parishes. He said, "There is no doubt that the renewal of the liturgy was very imperfect, but it was an attempt." For him, it was an attempt at, among other things, reclaiming the idea and experience of common prayer.

"So terms are tricky," he said. "I see that you use the word 'performance' quite a bit. I know that this is part of the field you're talking to, but I'm not sure about that word for my experience." He looked up and hesitated for a moment, and I asked him to please go on. "For me, performance needs an audience, and common prayer does not need an audience, it needs participants." I responded by observing that participation was a major goal of Vatican II, and brother John then animatedly pointed to a section in my essay on Laurence Hemming's *Worship as a Revelation*. Hemming offers his take on the "chaos" that the liturgy has become in the wake of the liturgical movement and Vatican II. He says that rationalism is to blame for the problems with the modern liturgy. Rationalism, as he frames it, is the understanding that all things are foreseeable and controllable by humans. According to rationalism, liturgy can be made to suit human needs, can be crafted into a "feel good" kind of experience that makes worshippers feel communal, participatory, and happy, but does not maintain the appropriate focus on worshiping God. He argues that the liturgy is not the work of the people, but the work of God, and so the modern focus on human work is misguided because it wholly misunderstands the meaning of liturgy. He suggests that singing is a form of social relation that makes present the assembly's common being in God, and so the choice of music ought to reflect the nature of singing up toward God in union with the choirs of angels.[11] He forwards Gregorian chant as the only music proven to accomplish this.

To say that Hemming has the music, practices, and perspectives of the Weston monks—among others—in his crosshairs is an understatement, but his view of the changes that followed Vatican II is not uncommon among liturgists, philosophers, scholars, musicians, clergy, and lay Catholics. Brother John reacted strongly to this perspective—he was not defensive, and never mentioned feeling personally attacked, but he certainly disagreed.

However, this is not to say that brother John was completely at odds with Hemming's ideas. Hemming talks about singing as social relation aimed toward common being. He discusses music as a reflection of that being, directed toward God. This is exactly what the brothers and I had been discussing. But it is clear that, on balance, Hemming and brother John would disagree on the interpretation and application of these ideas, as well as on the relationship between liturgy and participating people. It was this that brother John focused on in our conversation.

"You know," he said, flipping through the pages, "what Hemming says—about liturgy not being the work of the people—it's very disagreeable to me!" He laughed lightly and smiled as he said it. He then talked about how important it is for him to think about prayer as being the work of participants, the common work of gathered people. I considered that each had a very different perspective, but they were both looking toward similar issues of understanding what liturgy is and how it is meant to function.

"His words did strike me," brother John said. "Common prayer deals with authority, and that's what he's talking about. But what is authority? Authority over, or authority that comes from within?" I recalled our earlier conversation when he said that he prefers to think of authority as coming from within, having the author-ity of a truly vernacular voice and experience. He then said, "I think we can allow people to define and use certain words in ways they want to, and we can use other words. If Benedict didn't need it, we don't need it!" he said, referring to the arguments over interpretations of, and use of the term, liturgy. He then said, "To get back to some of what we said earlier: reform, renewal, revival, restoration. Each has its own flavor. Each one thinks it is doing something the others aren't!" I smiled, agreeing that words are tricky. He went on to point out that you can get yourself into a mess if you start thinking too hard about the problems of language. No matter what word you choose, it assigns a certain "flavor" to the discussion, excluding nuances particular to the others while bringing other nuances that might be inappropriate or unhelpful but are unavoidable. For example, he explained that brother Leo wanted a renewal of monastic life, not a revival, while some might have called it a reform and others before him saw themselves as working toward restoration. He then laughed a bit as he noted how you can really talk yourself around in circles.

It was the laugh that got us onto the topic that would conclude our discussion that day while opening up new directions for our ongoing pursuit to understand the role of music in communal prayer. He said, "You see, we always have to keep a sense of humor, a perspective of joy and play. We can't take ourselves too seriously!" This prompted him to tell me that the brothers had lately been talking a lot about the idea of play in their conversations about their music and the opus dei of the daily Divine Office. He said that he thought it was a useful way of thinking about all of the terminology and ideas we had just discussed. "We tried to think of opus from a musical point of view, that opus can be playful work, and we're having great fun with it! It's creativity, playfulness, chaos, and it's all wonderful!" He explained that they had been working on some new music, and really trying to work the idea of play into the experience. He suggested that I talk with brother Michael a bit about those ideas since he was lately doing a lot of the practical work with the music.

Brother John then wrapped up our conversation by returning to some of the ideas with which we began. He told me that he had lately been using a reading at morning prayer. It was a selection from Rabbi Arthur Green on silence and speaking. I thought it was significant that, after spending so much time talking about the problems of language, he brought our discussion back to a monastic perspective by emphasizing silence. He then said, "It's all about the conversation, really." And I knew that, for him, a balance of speaking, silence, and listening went into any experience of conversation. "The conversation is critically important. Even though sometimes it brings us to crisis!" He pointed to my essay, referencing our earlier discussion of Hemming and the post-Vatican II liturgical changes, which have prompted so much discussion—and argument—and caused many to experience this moment in Church history as a "crisis" of the liturgy. He said, "For us, music takes us beyond conversation. It moves into *conversatio*. It engages something beyond the words." Apologizing for overloading me with ideas—and smiling as I emphatically told him never, ever to apologize for that—he stood up and we both continued with our afternoon.

Playful Serenity

After dinner that day, brother Michael motioned for me to come over to his seat at the reader's desk after everyone had eaten. He was the reader for the week—slowly working his way through a massive book on the history of Christianity—and so he was still at the desk eating his dinner when everyone else started cleaning up. He said that he heard I had chatted with brother John earlier that day, and he had something for me. He handed me a CD with the title *Playful Serenity* handwritten in marker on the front. He explained that it was a work-in-progress that would give me an idea of the direction in which they were working for their newest album. He emphasized that it was just an in-progress version of where they were at the time, and he was interested in my reflections.

Because the brothers treat music as a craft—and had lately been thinking about it even more intentionally as play—it became a constant, ongoing locus for navigating the dynamic spaces between creativity and tradition, individuality and collectivity, self and other, and, in the case of monastic life and liturgical practice, self and God. In recording their new album, the brothers opened up an avenue for me to participate in this process and learn how it worked in the everyday, lived reality of the Benedictines who called Weston home.[12]

I knew that the brothers had turned the music room in one of their workshops into an at-home recording studio and were working on the new album, which would eventually be titled, *Wisdom at Play*. When we talked about the album later, brother Michael explained that the brothers were trying a new recording process: a few brothers—called the "schola brothers" following the Gregorian chant tradition of naming the choir after the medieval music schools—went to the studio once or twice a week to record vocal tracks. On other days, brother Michael acted as both producer and accompanist as he recorded guitar tracks and set to work mixing tracks. In the past, a friend of the community, who was a record producer and engineer, had helped them with their albums. When they had twelve new songs, they set up equipment in the Stone Chapel and did marathon-like recording sessions for a few days. "We just hammered through, *boom, boom, boom, boom, boom*," brother Michael said, as he described their former process.

When it was time to start work on *Wisdom at Play*, their friend had retired and was no longer able to help. The brothers had also aged. Long days in the recording studio proved a challenge for many of them, not to mention the difficulty of getting all twelve monks into the studio—the firewood does not chop itself, the roads do not plow themselves, and, as I learned countless times, the sheep do not scoop their own messes. Brother Michael explained that they wanted to try a new process, something that felt more playful. They wanted something that was work but less like exhausting labor and more like the creative process of craft.

The morning after brother Michael gave me the CD, I was in the guesthouse anxious to hear the new music. I poured myself a cup of tea, sat on the living room couch, fired up my computer, loaded the disc, and hit "play." As soon as I heard it, I knew it was something different for the Weston monks, not just in the recording process, but in the style. There were just three songs on the album, but each one had multiple parts. There were preludes, postludes, and interludes. Rather than marching through twelve songs one after another—"boom, boom, boom, boom, boom"—these songs became like suites with several movements allowing the material to unfold. The terms "prelude," "postlude," and "interlude" suggested that the brothers were not just playing with the recording process, but playing with time, extending the moments before, after, and between the songs. The "-ludes" were all instrumental, played on the guitar. They picked up on the melodic and rhythmic themes of the songs and created a series of variations and improvisations on the themes. To me, they sounded like extended instrumental meditations. I could hear the inspiration for the title, *Playful Serenity*. These were not the folk songs of *Locusts and Wild Honey*, and the troubadour-plus-chorus approach seemed long gone. Yet it was familiar to the brothers' liturgical style. It still sounded like them. I heard the distinct chant-like quality and simple, memorable tunes and lyrics. The guitar had a distinctively classical sound, often trading the rolling finger-picked accompaniment—which itself had grown more ornate over the years—for more open, melodic, occasionally complex improvisations that reflected brother Michael's approach to the instrument.

In an interview early in my research, brother Michael talked to me about his early years at Weston and what prompted him to become a monk. He explained that in the early 1980s, after graduating from college and teaching English in Pakistan, he experienced what he calls a series of intuitions that led him to monasticism. The desire to make a statement of peace and social justice with his life was chief among these, but music also played a role. By the time he came to Weston, the brothers had been recording their music for ten years and were at the peak of their popularity. Like most people who heard of the Weston monks after the mid-1970s, brother Michael encountered the brothers through their music. He was already a skilled guitarist when he arrived. He explained that when he was growing up in Canada in the 1970s, the instrument held a Fleetwood Mac, rock-and-roll appeal. In fact, one of the ways he learned to finger pick was by copying Lindsey Buckingham's signature style. He also took formal lessons from a young age, eventually learning to play in a Western classical style, finger-picking on a wide-necked nylon-stringed instrument. In talking to him, I knew that his approach to the guitar was something other than the folk guitar of the sixties that so inspired his brother monks.

I listened to the CD over and over that day. I took notes in an effort to keep track of my reflections, but I was unsure what to make of it all. I thought about it over the course of the next few days until I met with brother Michael in the music room, which had been transformed into a recording studio. We sat in the small room with windows overlooking the pond and gardens in front of the Priory, and we talked about a wide variety of topics relative to the brothers' music.

"I was very interested in some of the things you were saying about the connections between our music and Saint-Benoît," he said as we sat down, referring to the essay I had recently discussed with brother John. "I never really knew about the connections between the early community and Saint-Benoît. And it's quite interesting to think about that whole sense of tradition, and thinking about how Saint-Benoît-du-Lac's tradition is as authentic as our own."

He explained that he really had been working at thinking through that idea, and said that he appreciated how I was pushing him to open up questions he would not have otherwise thought about. It was a thought-provoking moment for me as I came face-to-face with my own shadows in the field—to borrow the title of Gregory Barz and Timothy Cooley's volume on field research in ethnomusicology.[13] There was no question: I was not capturing objective facts. Certainly, I was working hard to understand music and monastery life from the brothers' perspectives, but my presence at Weston, and myself as a thinking, participating, conversing, questioning observer, were shaping the very practices and ideas I was there to understand.

Our conversation took off from there. I told him that was exactly what I was interested in: the complexities of tradition and what creativity has to do with it. Brother Michael pointed out that, because of the kinds of questions I was asking, he had lately been thinking a lot about how he relates the Weston tradition to other traditions. He explained that he saw their practices as one kind of expression of a tradition, but then suggested that maybe "story" would be a better word than tradition. It resonated with how I had been thinking of the brothers' music as a way of not just narrating their story but bringing their story into dialogue with received texts and traditions, and then living that dialogue in their daily prayers. It also reminded me of my recent conversation with brother John about the problems of terminology. "Tradition" carried baggage and nuance that brother Michael was finding unhelpful for what he wanted to express.

This train of thought got us into the problems of language and, like brother John, brother Michael pointed out that he noticed I used "perform" and "performance" a lot in the essay I had given them. He was struggling with the word, but in different ways than had brother John. Brother Michael is the leading cantor for the community. In the brothers' daily prayers, he sings both with the schola brothers and as a solo leading voice. He said that he tries to think of music as a craft, and for him that is distinct from thinking of being a performer or performing. Then he said, "But there's no doubt about it, to a certain extent it's performance." He explained that recording the new album had meant working on voice and diction with a friend of the community and brother John. Their friend, a liturgist and musician, had worked with the brothers for years as a kind of conversant and consultant on their music. She had lately been helping brother Michael to form words differently so that his lyrics would be clear on the recordings. He said, "If it's not performance, then why correct my vowels? Why worry about where I'm placing my consonants?" In short, he described being aware of the listener, and so, like brother John, he thought of performance as having an audience.

He said that sometimes visitors complimented him on his voice, and he was uncomfortable with that kind of attention. He said brother John gave him great advice for a reply: "Tell them it's the only voice you have!" And that was really the summary point for brother Michael: "The call to monastic life is just as mysterious to me as that I can sing. I'm here. I enjoy singing. So I'm making something from it." He emphasized "making" in a gesture toward our discussions of the creative work of craft. With this, we moved into a discussion of his work to create and record new music.

Brother Michael laughed a bit when I asked about his process for writing a new song, using the song "Wisdom at Play" as an example. Even though he had emphasized to me on more than one occasion the collective nature of their process, he had also recognized that, at the moment, he did a lot of the practical work to write new music. "Well," he began, "first there's just the inspiration. Wisdom at play. That's provocative. It's inspiring. It gets you going." He described looking for scripture references relative to the idea of wisdom at play, then writing things down as they inspired him. Then he said he would get some lyrics down and show them to brother John. He said, "I'm trying to learn from brother John how to make things more poetic. I'm very didactic. Solid language. Brother John is very much more poetic. He hears the music in things and I don't always." He said that they would go through several revisions, with other brothers looking at their developing ideas. He said it really ended up being very collective, which was good because there is also what he called a "pragmatic reality" involved: he had to pay attention to how much time he gave to writing and recording music. This was an important part of maintaining his processes as a craft. He said, "This morning, for instance, I was in the garden, I went out to the woodshop, and now we're here. There has to be a balance to it." He felt that this balance was vital for maintaining his inspiration and energy for the project, but it also reminded me of all that I had learned about craft in the kitchen and pottery studio. Craft also meant maintaining balance so as not to be absorbed in one pursuit for the attention, renown, or sense of accomplishment that results. And it required a balance between individuality and collectivity.

Brother Michael then returned to the idea of play. He said that recently brother John had asked him, "What's at the center of your being?" And brother Michael had responded, "It's grace. Because we're all rooted in God and God's free gift of love. So it's grace." But brother John challenged him by saying, "That's just a fancy word for play." "It struck me afterward," brother Michael explained, "that that's a real challenge for myself. Do I dare call the center of my being play?" He went on to talk about how play has always been part of the community; they try to include some kind of recreation in each day to provide balance and joy in the monastic life. But in the context of thinking about music and craft, as well as the creativity of work and play, this way of looking at play as the very center of his being was opening up new ways of engaging with the recording process. He said, "We first started recording in October, and those recordings—I have them here somewhere—they're terrible! Really horrid! We sound like metronomes!" We both laughed as he said the brothers decided they needed to step back and rethink what they were doing, because clearly they were not having fun with the process. This was when they decided to slow down—not to do twelve songs "boom, boom, boom"—but to take their time with a few in the fall, a few in the spring, and then see where they were. He said that was also when he started sharing his ideas for the preludes, interludes, and postludes. The brothers responded well, to both the idea of slowing down their process and playing with the time before and between songs on the album.

The entire conversation was eye-opening for me in terms of my emerging understanding of music and craft, the relationship between creativity and tradition, and all that these ideas implied about musical, spiritual, and monastic processes. When we finished talking, we both moved on with our day, but brother Michael had opened up new ways of thinking through the ideas brother John had prompted just days before.

Thanksgiving

Because of the way my research unfolded gradually, it was several months before we returned to these topics or the work of recording the new album. In the meantime, summer turned to autumn and Thanksgiving arrived, marking the transition to winter. A monastery may sound like an unpleasantly austere destination for a holiday dedicated to feasting, but Thanksgiving was tailor-made for the Benedictines. For fifteen centuries, they have perfected the art of hospitality and they know how to celebrate a feast, liturgical or not. A day devoted to gratitude, home cooking, family, and celebration is as thoroughly Benedictine as chanted psalms and hooded black scapulars.

I woke up early Thanksgiving Day and went through my usual morning routine. I was already in the chapel when the bells tolled for Morning Prayer. Most days began with Morning Vigil at 5:00 a.m., but Tuesdays and Thursdays started an hour later to give the brothers a little variety and a more relaxed morning schedule. The later hour—on monastery time, 6:00 a.m. *is* a later hour—and the Thanksgiving holiday meant that the Morning Prayer was unusually well attended that day.

When I arrived, nearly twenty guests and visitors already filled the chapel. I sat in my usual seat in the front row, but I felt a little off of my routine with so many people in the seats around me. My mornings typically featured a healthy dose of personal space for a quiet, meditative start to my day. I not only enjoyed this, I had come to depend on it as a vital part of my own monastic rhythm. Already Thanksgiving felt like anything other than business as usual around the monastery.

We were nearing the shortest days of the year, but as I looked out the chapel windows I saw that the bluish predawn light had turned Terrible Mountain to the east into a dark shadow against an inky sky. Frost shimmered on the grass and what remained of the autumn-flowering plants. Dim overhead lights illumined the chapel. The shuffling of feet and *swish* of the heavy door were the only sounds. I sat and waited, feet flat on the floor, eyes forward, recorder in my left hand. I looked up and saw brother John enter the chapel carrying a book for the morning's contemporary reading. Seeing him with his nonscripture book, wearing something other than a typical Benedictine habit, preparing to sit not on the monastic benches but on a round prayer cushion on the floor, I was reminded of all that we had discussed about the relationship between historical consciousness and local authenticity.

I had lately been thinking about those ideas in terms of the relationship between creativity and tradition. As part of that dialogue, brother John talked to me about their Morning Prayer. It is a combination of the morning prayers of the full Divine Office: Vigil, Matins, and Lauds. Doing a slightly different prayer twice weekly added variety to the daily liturgies. Such variety seemed to counteract the potential for the highly regularized monastic rituals to become stale routine.

The prayer began with brother Richard striking a prayer bowl and letting the sound reverberate around the room. The brothers bowed toward the center of their semicircle. With the silence of night thus broken, brother Michael and brother Augustine played their guitars as the brothers sang one of their own songs about how life is a journey that we travel together, our different lives coming together like a woven cloth. They followed this with "Wisdom at Play," the song brother Michael and I had talked about.[14] The lyrics sing of the playfulness of God's wisdom evident in the created world. It reminded me of the themes of the Morning Vigil early in my research when I was inspired to start paying attention to the world around me and the small moments of each day. Brother John then read the selection by Rabbi Arthur Green that he had mentioned months earlier: "Language and silence are engaged at the high point of their eternal dance with one another."[15] He pronounced the words slowly, intentionally, as if reciting poetry. They became a meditation. Brother Augustine picked out a quiet series of notes on his guitar, adding a subtle musical quality to the reading and emphasizing the meditative experience of the words. Language and silence, words and music, contemplation and conversation, playfulness and wisdom, self and other in an eternal dance.

Toward the end of the hour-long prayer, the Thanksgiving theme began to take shape. The brothers sang a song inspired by Catherine of Sienna as the gathered people, monks and visitors alike, walked up to a central table: "You are the bread, and you the table, the love who serves at our feast; You are the leaven of promise among us, the life in every seed."[16] Each person pulled a section of bread from a communal loaf and handed the loaf to the next person, making eye contact and smiling. On Thanksgiving morning, the song offered a reminder of the monastic perspective on feasting as an opportunity for love and service.

A few hours later, the bells rang for the special Thanksgiving Eucharist service. Guests and visitors filled the chapel again, this time beyond capacity. Fresh fruits, vegetables, stalks of wheat, grasses, and flowers filled a cornucopia in the center of the room. In their call to prayer, the brothers sang: "There is a way of truth and life, of hope and strength. Gather all people of every land, a harvest of compassion is at hand."[17] The song had an upbeat tempo, but the melody emphasized some of the more dissonant minor intervals in the major-key song, giving an air of seriousness. Hardly a rote repetition of the daily Mass, this Eucharist service took full advantage of the holiday, making it a liturgical event.

After Eucharist, the gathered people headed out to their own Thanksgiving festivities. I left the chapel and followed the brothers, their guests, and a group of invited friends to the living room of the original monastery farmhouse. The room was warm and inviting. A table covered with a green tablecloth held an array of wines and ciders, striped red-and-orange candles, and flowers. Brother Augustine, still in his plain muslin cowl, made a fire in the woodstove: "I'm just making some ambiance," he said with a smile. I walked in with Sister Mary, a fellow guest and nun from New Jersey. As the brothers and their friends gathered, the din in the room grew to a roar of happy voices and friendly conversation. The brothers made a point to greet every person, welcoming them and wishing them a happy Thanksgiving.

I chatted with the brothers and caught up with friends who lived in the Weston area. Brother Michael poured wine and cider into little plastic cups. Brother Mark made sure everyone had something to drink. Brother Columba and brother Alvaro handed out beverages as people milled about the room. Brother Peter joked that maybe I should not mention the wine cellar in my book. He said, with his characteristic sense of humor, "We are austere monks, after all. No indulgence!" "I won't tell if you won't," responded brother Augustine, with a grin. Brother Mark chimed in, "Who are you kidding? No indulgence? I'm having at least two pieces of pie! That is, if brother Peter doesn't beat me to them." Brother Placid smiled and laughed, "I don't know if we'll have enough pie for the both of them!" The fire crackled in the living room of the cozy farmhouse as the brothers laughed and joked with one another. Brother Augustine was right. It was the perfect ambience for a Thanksgiving afternoon.

When the meal was ready, brother Elias called us to the refectory where we all gathered around in a circle. The buffet table was set with a feast in a homey mish-mash of the brothers' nicest serving ware. Brother Richard tinkered with the food as we made our way in, making sure everything had plenty of serving spoons. The tables, normally in a U-shape, were spread around the room. Each had a yellow tablecloth, festive napkins, flowers, and candles. The familiar buffet table was dressed for the occasion with a colorful tablecloth and flowers. At the back of the room, a long table held wine, cider, and many, many pies. The whole atmosphere was festive, exciting, and abundant in a way that most people would not readily associate with monastery life. The refectory was transformed into a banquet hall.

Brother Richard welcomed everyone and expressed the brothers' gratitude that we could all be there together. He explained the contents of the buffet table, going through each dish and telling us what was in it: local, fresh, Vermont turkey; vegetarian stuffing made with mushrooms; traditional stuffing cooked in the bird; gravy; squash from their garden made with herbs, also from their garden; broccoli with garlic, capers, and lemon; homemade cranberry sauce; a tray of olives and artichokes; rolls made by a neighbor; pies brought by friends. The brothers had spent the whole morning cooking so that each could contribute something of himself to the communal table. The aspects of their shared life and hard work—garden vegetables, their own herbs, favorite Priory recipes—were part of their individual expressions—vegetarian stuffing, an Italian antipasto tray—and the necessary Thanksgiving fare—a perfectly roasted turkey, gravy, potatoes, pies. I thought about how this was an example of the very ideas of creativity and tradition that I was trying to understand.

We all loaded our plates and sat around the room. Brothers mingled with guests and friends. A local friend and I sat across from brother Robert and brother John. We chatted about a variety of things. It was the first time I talked during a meal in the refectory. The reader's desk in the corner sat empty. The room came alive with the vibrant energy of love, gratitude, and family. It was an aspect of monastery life I had neither envisioned nor anticipated.

Eventually, the feast began to wind down. Brothers and guests cleared their plates to the kitchen, abuzz with people cleaning up and continuing to converse. Finally, when the dishes were done, the kitchen put to rest, and the guests gone home, I walked back to the guesthouse for the traditional Thanksgiving nap. As I walked, I recalled my sense earlier in the day that this would be a holiday unlike any other I had ever experienced. Even in the midst of a Thanksgiving feast, questions of historical consciousness, the authenticity of the local, the balance between individuality and collectivity, and the relationship between creativity and tradition continued to emerge as consistent, important, puzzling themes that had become the constant accompaniment of my work to understand the Weston monastic life and the role of music therein. I felt that I was finally beginning to put the pieces together. By the time the brothers were again in the chapel chanting the evening psalms at Vespers, the crowds were gone and the rhythm of monastery life resumed. As I sang along with the Magnificat, I felt myself joining in with the collective Weston voice and beginning to understand what that meant.

The O Antiphons

I sat toward the front of a moderately crowded chapel on Sunday evening just three days after the Thanksgiving feast. Brother Michael and brother Augustine began finger-picking their guitars, and the brothers sang their call to prayer: "We are grateful for the stillness of this day, a time in which creation finds rest in God. Holy, holy is this day. We are saddened to see Sabbath's end."[18] The melody evoked the simplicity and repetition of chanted psalms but with slightly more motion and a subtly minor tonality. The schola brothers sang the verses, then the brothers responded with the second refrain: "The stillness of your Sabbath is healing for our souls, a time in which the eternal touches our heart. Holy, holy is this day, we are saddened to see Sabbath's end." The schola brothers sang the second verse, and we all responded with the first refrain to finish the call to prayer.

There was a time when the order of the Office prayers was thoroughly confusing to me. I could not make sense of the string of psalms, songs, canticles, and readings in each prayer hour, nor could I establish a strong sense of continuity between or among the prayers, aside from their sharing a similar style. Gradually, though, I came to know the order for each prayer so well, I found myself settling into the familiar comfort of the Divine Office. I closed my eyes that evening and listened to brother Mark read from a text on the light of the Sabbath. I breathed deeply and listened as the brothers chanted the evening psalms. Eyes still closed, I listened to the back-and-forth flow. My breathing slowed as I unconsciously aligned myself with the rhythm of the chants. I found a sense of calm in the simple, unadorned, familiar music.

I opened my eyes when the final antiphon ended the chanted psalms. Brother Richard picked up the lectionary and read the day's scripture, from the Letter to the Romans. It was a message about preparing for salvation. "The night is far gone," brother Richard read, "the day is near." The brothers sang a hymn and we all stood for the closing Magnificat.

I stood in my place in the chapel, ready for the antiphon. But when brother Augustine and brother Michael began to play their guitars, I snapped out of the contemplative rhythm of a familiar Vespers. Synapses fired in my brain. They were playing something I had never heard before. In unison, the brothers sang: "O Wisdom, flowing from the mouth of the most high."[19] The melody was slightly melismatic with an upward sweep on "wisdom" followed by a gentle downward motion through the rest of the line. The short antiphon continued, calling on wisdom to teach the way of truth. Each line had the same gentle melismatic motion giving brightness and energy in the upward sweep and answering downward movement.

I realized I had just heard my first *O Antiphon*, but in true Weston fashion this was no Latin *O Sapientia* like those I had seen in books on Gregorian chant. I knew that Sunday was the beginning of Advent, so I was surprised to realize that, being so immersed in the Benedictine life, I had not anticipated the O Antiphons. They are special refrains traditionally sung with the Magnificat at Vespers during the week leading up to Christmas. There are seven, each taking its lyrics from the titles of the Messiah: O Wisdom, O Adonai (O Lord), O Root of Jesse, O Key of David, O Rising Sun, O King of the Nations, O Emmanuel. Each antiphon refers to the prophecy of the Messiah in the Book of Isaiah, one of the central scriptures of the Advent season. They are among the most familiar, well-loved aspects of Gregorian chant and Divine Office liturgies. They have been for centuries. They are not something that most people, even devout Catholics, have heard of these days, but for chant scholars and enthusiasts, medievalists, musicologists, and monastics, they represent the best and finest of the liturgical year, musically speaking.

I hardly paid attention to the Magnificat that followed. Hearing an O Antiphon was a thrill that perhaps only a student of liturgical music would experience, but in that moment I felt surrounded by the dynamic interplay between the ancient sources of monastic life, the inherited traditions repeated for centuries by countless Benedictines, and the particular voice of the Weston monks. When the brothers repeated the antiphon at the end of the Magnificat, I attended fiercely to every word, every note, in an effort to take it all in even though I knew very well that my recorder was dutifully working and I would hear the antiphons again and again throughout Advent. I needed to memorize the excitement and visceral awareness of that moment when conversations, discussions, and explanations turned into knowledge in the reality of lived experience and musical performance.

"I just *love* this season," brother Elias said the following afternoon as we put away the baking dishes and serving platters that brother Placid had washed in the sink. "The O Antiphons are so beautiful." He added, "most places sing them just during the week of Christmas, but we sing them all throughout the season of Advent. They're too lovely not to!" The weather was beginning to turn from fall to winter, the days were growing shorter, the forest was cold and gray, but the new liturgical season was bringing brightness and excitement.

Collective Composition

A few days later, I sat down with brother Michael and brother John to return to our conversations about their new music. We met in the Franklin Room of the original monastery farmhouse in the early afternoon. It was the same welcoming room where we had spent such a lovely Thanksgiving, the room that was once the primary living space for the early community. It felt larger and more open without the Thanksgiving crowd, and I could better appreciate the warmth of its farmhouse character.

I sat in a green upholstered armchair next to a large window looking out over the snowy gardens, ponds, and mountains beyond. Brother Michael sat across from me in an equally cozy armchair. He wore jeans and a wool sweater in muted dark colors. Brother John sat to my right in a wooden rocking chair, completing our friendly trio. He wore faded jeans and a denim work shirt. He got up to stoke the fire as we were all getting settled. I wondered how many times he must have stoked that fire in the more than fifty years since he first moved into that little farmhouse. He pulled a log off of the stack, opened the door of the black woodstove, and tossed in the log. "There," he said with a broad smile as he closed the woodstove door with a heavy metallic *clang*, "that will keep us toasty warm in here. It's cold out there today!" The fire crackled and I looked out the window to see the light dusting of snow flying around in the blustery wind.

Brother Michael had given me a more recent copy of their work-in-progress album, and I had listened to it repeatedly in the guesthouse. "Well, I'm eager to hear your reflections on the disc," brother Michael began, a little hesitantly. Usually, I was the one asking questions, the one asking for thoughts and reflections. Being on the receiving end of inquiry was new territory, and, having learned from my time in monastery life, I tried to participate in the process instead of obsessively analyzing it and wondering what it all meant for my work.

I told the brothers that to me the album felt as though it had a lot of space for each song to take shape, and something about that was appealing to me. I noted that the lyrics were poetic and filled with rich metaphors, as usual, but they seemed to have a more deeply contemplative, mystical character. I said, "I don't know what it is, exactly, but something about the rhythms and melodies seems to give each word more space." "Well," brother Michael responded, "I appreciate your reflections, because really that is the goal, we want to create space for people to really *hear* the words and experience the music as prayer. We want room for each song to breathe. We want to offer some of our own experience of prayer." Brother John nodded encouragingly, saying, simply, "Yes."

The brothers were trying to use this new album to convey something of the monastic sensibility and spirituality of listening. Rather than a practical means of giving people access to their music outside of the Priory setting, this album would ideally allow them to share some aspect of their way of life and their style of prayer. Brother John's simple "yes" highlighted that. When space is given for experiences of conversatio and, its counterbalance, listening to unfold, each word, each sound, each silent gesture is rich with meaning. It opens up and welcomes in so that the singers and listeners participate in creating and experiencing that meaning.

As the conversation went on, brother John explained that they were trying to focus on really enjoying the recording process and being playful with the material. Because they recorded a little bit at a time, one track at a time, this opened up an opportunity for me to join in. The brothers often included instrumental accompaniment on their albums. In the past, they had used keyboard, bass, sometimes a violin or two, usually one or two wind instruments such as flute or oboe, and occasionally a trumpet. These instruments added some extra depth to the texture of their recorded albums. Typically, musician friends of the community played these parts. Knowing I am a flutist, brother Michael and brother John asked if I would try writing and recording some flute parts while I was visiting.

I eagerly accepted the offer. Not only was this kind of participation exactly what ethnomusicologists seek out—the founders of the field long ago understood the importance of being a part of the musical life about which we want to learn—it was an opportunity for me to join in the playful, craft-based, gradual process of creating the new music. I said, "Yes," and that was it. The brothers gave me copies of the sheet music to go along with the CD, and they handed me some manuscript paper. They did not give me instructions. They offered no ideas. They just handed me the music and away I went.

After Vigil and breakfast the next morning, I again sat on the couch in the guesthouse living room with the CD playing on my computer. I looked out the picture window at the rolling mountains, bare of leaves and dusted lightly with snow. The brothers and I decided that we would record accompaniment parts for "We Desire You" first, so I listened again to the recording. Brother Michael's clear tenor voice sang through my headphones: "God our God, we long for you, for life, for bread, and for truth."[20]

The tempo was incredibly slow, and each word unfolded gradually. The melody was simple and chant-like, with little motion. The guitar picked a rolling, arpeggiated accompaniment in the background. The schola brothers singing on the album joined in on the refrain: "We desire you, oh you who desire us. Come with the gift of your love."

The refrain had a bit more movement and lightness than the opening lines, but still the slow tempo allowed the words to unfold gradually. During our conversation in the Franklin Room, brother Michael told me that "We Desire You" was the last song that brother Philip wrote before he died. He expressed awe that while his brother was dying from ALS, completely unable to move or speak, he was filled with such remarkably peaceful thoughts. Brother Michael called this "grace," and I could tell by the impassioned way he spoke that the lyrics held intense meaning for him. As I listened to the song, I could not help but think of brother Philip and wonder at his wisdom and grace as he faced a painful, incurable illness. His heart seemed to be filled with the joy and optimism that were always part of his personality. Instead of being angry with God, he expressed the longing for God that is so familiar in Christian mystical writings like those of Teresa of Avila, John of the Cross, Hildegard of Bingen, and modern monastics like Thomas Merton.

As I stood in the guesthouse in front of my music stand, manuscript paper on the table beside me, flute in hand, pencil behind my ear, I considered what kind of accompanying part to write. My intention was to work out a countermelody, something complementary that would add interest and highlight melodic and harmonic movement. But as I stood there staring at the blank staves, I struggled to figure out how to counter the simple, open, slow tones of the song. I began by jotting down a series of arpeggiated chords based on the accompaniment. It seemed like a promising start. I hit "play" on the recording and added my part on top of the brothers' voices and guitars. Immediately I knew I had created a mess of notes and rhythms. I recoiled with disappointment at the resulting sonic mud. The intensity of the lyrics drowned in the sludge.

I was unsure what to do. My music theory training had taught me that the notes I wrote should have worked. I dutifully played along with the chord changes. I took account of the melody. I worked with the existing rhythm and meter. But it was all wrong. I needed to take a different approach. I decided not to write a countermelody, but to counter my own inclination to create a melody for my flute on top of what was already present. Living as I was in the Benedictine ethos, independent and flashy did not seem suitable, but quiet and open did.

I got rid of the quick notes and arpeggiated chords and instead wrote out a series of long, low tones: not quite an ostinato, but the same idea of reinforcing and grounding harmonic motion. When I hit "play" again and added these low tones underneath the brothers' voices and guitar, I suddenly felt myself resonating with them, literally and figuratively. Low tones created a new timbre, a rich under-layer that drew the ear more deeply into the words. I wrote down my accompaniment. It was my series of notes and rests, arranged in my own manuscript handwriting on lines and spaces, yet I felt the communal act of its creation. Would I have written this line at home? I am inclined to think not. At home, I would likely have made something for me, beautiful and showy, not open and contemplative. In that moment, I began to understand how the individual-communal dialectic works in musical performance and composition.

Two days later, I was in the workshop-turned-studio. I stood in front of a black music stand. A large gray microphone hung overhead. Wires ran across the floor linking microphones and headphones to the recording equipment. Windows on the back wall of the small room looked out over the pond. An old wool rug covered the concrete floor. Two bookcases filled with various music books—guitar methods, folk song collections, Gregorian chant books, the Weston psalter—stood against the wall opposite the windows. The white walls were simply decorated with a framed photograph and a colorful painting. A grand piano against the back wall left just enough space in the middle of the room for three music stands, the microphones, and a few people. Brother Michael sat in the corner of the room managing the recording equipment. Brother John sat in an armchair next to the grand piano in the back corner. I stood in the middle, flute in hand. We all wore headphones.

It had taken some trial and error, but I felt confident in my accompaniment parts. I had the sheet music for "We Desire You" in front of me with my parts written out on manuscript paper set off to the side. When everyone was settled, brother Michael hit "play" and the tracks for "We Desire You" came through the headphones. I played along, adding the low accompaniment phrases I had written. There were a few places where my pitches clashed unpleasantly with the guitar, and there were moments when the flute part seemed to fall flat. I made mental notes to fix those spots, but overall I thought it sounded pretty good. It complemented the melody. It blended nicely with the guitar chords. It added another layer to the texture. It was everything I thought it should be. Even so, I sensed that something was not quite right. Where the flute part had seemed to work perfectly when I played it in the guesthouse, it now felt like something was missing.

When the song ended, everyone was quiet. I looked up. Brother John looked at me, then at brother Michael, then back at me. I looked back and forth between brother Michael and brother John. Brother Michael looked at me, then at brother John, then back at his music stand. No one spoke. I raised my eyebrows and gave a little shrug, saying, "Thoughts?" Brother John spoke first: "Well, it offers a nice harmony line, but the question is: where do we bring it in and where do we leave it out? It's too much throughout the whole thing."

After a few moments, brother Michael spoke up. He began on a positive note. "Well," he said, slowly, "I really like what you've got there—it's got some really nice moments." However, he agreed with brother John's assessment: it was too much throughout the whole thing and seemed to weigh down the words. He wanted to make sure the accompaniment complemented the lyrics without distracting from them, so we reconsidered what to do with the flute part. We discussed where and how to bring it in, where to leave it out. We considered whether or not certain places worked the way I had written them. Some sections had too much motion and became distracting, so we scaled them back. Some of the more complex parts were stripped down to their bare bones. Some of the simpler parts were made more complex.

I played the parts over and over. Each time we made little adjustments here and there. I stood in front of the music stand, pencil in hand, scribbling, erasing, crossing out, and otherwise amending what I had originally written on my manuscript paper. Finally, brother Michael hit "record" and we laid down the flute track. It required several takes. During the first one, we realized my snow boots were squeaking every time I moved. I took them off and we tried again. During the second one, some of the parts did not work, so we adjusted them and tried again. After nearly an hour and a half, and countless iterations of flute accompaniment, we had a final recording.

When brother Michael played the finished recording, I looked back at the original parts I wrote in the guesthouse living room—what I could still see of them, anyway—and I could hear my original ideas and intuitions in the final version. The flute playing was still my own distinctive sound and style. Like my voice, I could recognize it as me and not someone else. It reflected my sensibilities as a flutist, but it was no longer only about me. The parts I wrote on my own were fine flute parts, but they were not yet Weston music. They lacked a necessary monastic affect that could only emerge in the musical and interpersonal dialogues of creativity and craft. Musical performance at Weston is not a platform for showing off one's skills. It is about communal prayer. I could not create this on my own. It is collective, and yet a reflection of the individuals present in the moment of its composition. At the same time, it is rich with the long line of people who have created the Weston tradition and have contributed to the story that it tells. It resonates with centuries of monasticism while evoking a very specific place and time, among a particular group of people.

I sensed this throughout my research. The brothers had told me as much many, many times in countless conversations around the kitchen, in the parlor, in the pastures, in the pottery, in the garden, and at the apiary. They communicated it several times a day every day, each time the bells rang and we again gathered in the chapel for the Divine Office prayers. They showed me time and again that this was their reality. I tried repeatedly to puzzle it out in my field notes. I read books on tradition, craft, folklore, liturgical music, and ethnography. But all of this could only get me so far in the process of understanding the unfamiliar, in the dialogues of learning and creating knowledge. Until that morning in the recording studio, I was missing a critical piece: experience. It was only through experience that I really learned what music means as a collective, interpersonal, prayerful process. It was only by becoming a part of it that I came to understand it.

Brother Michael, brother John, the schola brothers, and I repeated the recording process periodically throughout the winter until all of the songs on the album had flute accompaniment. I always worked out my ideas in the guesthouse first. I wrote down various possible harmony parts after learning in the first session that I would likely need alternative plans in case the first ideas did not work in the communal space of performance. I knew things would likely change, but in order to contribute my voice to the dialogue I had to work through some ideas first. Each time I played a new iteration of a phrase or section, we discussed it, I made changes that I thought reflected the discussion, and then we played it through again. We all paused and waited to see who would speak first. There was no jump to fill in the silence, and I had to actively remind myself not to speak just because no one else was talking. Brother Michael and I looked a lot to brother John for his reactions, but he was sparing with his words. Sometimes a simple nod was enough. Brother Michael was more likely to talk through his thought process. Brother John helped him work through his ideas. "You seem to be thinking more about something," brother John would say, picking up on brother Michael's affect. "Well, I'm just reflecting," brother Michael would begin, before unfolding his train of thought. Brother John would nod along and occasionally ask brief questions, encouraging brother Michael. I would suggest some changes that reflected his ideas, and then we would play through the whole thing again.

This became our usual way of working together in the studio. Occasionally other brothers would drop by to hear our progress, and they became part of the dialogue, too. They mostly just offered words of encouragement and told us they liked what we were doing—too many opinions or suggestions might have created a too-many-cooks-in-the-kitchen situation, but their positive reactions helped us to feel as if we were on the right track. By the end of these sessions, my manuscript paper was always filled with notes, corrections, changes, and what I called my "road map," a series of lines, arrows, and symbols telling me what to play and when to play it. The parts usually ended up being very different than anything I wrote in the guesthouse. I felt that I finally understood the brothers' refusal to assign a single composer to their songs. Claiming the individualized credit of "composer" of the flute parts was not an accurate reflection of the communal process that went into their creation. In fact, looking back at my sheets of manuscript paper, I cannot decipher them. I understood what they signified in the collective moment of composition well enough to play and record them, but they seem to have lost that meaning now.

When I picked up my flute in the Weston context, it was not my own skill as a musician that mattered but my ability to understand the brothers, who had become my musical community when I was included in their process. The microphones in the studio were pointed at me, and it was very individual in that way. And clearly I needed a flutist's skills and training. However, in the end, it was about my ability to listen, silencing my individualized self so that the communal voice could emerge. It was about my ability to access, participate in, and create the Weston tradition. By opening myself up to what the brothers had told me about the communal nature of their music, I could recognize and move beyond my expectations of the creative process, participating fully in the music-as-craft ethos and its contemplative awareness of interpersonal spaces and social relationships.

At Weston, music is craft. It is a process of creating and performing tradition, the collective wisdom and systems of knowledge that tell the local story. It allows the brothers to connect to their past while situating themselves in their present. It participates in the dynamic individual-communal paradox that animates monasticism. One cannot navigate these processes independent of the collective context. My flute parts—and myself as flutist—became part of the vibrant whole of Weston Priory, performed in song.

Chapter Six

Monastic Spirituality

Learning to Listen with the Ear of the Heart

> The unknown, the mystery, shows itself and withdraws in words and in music and in friendship, or put the other way around, our loving and our knowing ebbs and flows.
>
> —John Dunne, *Music of Time*

> We live a reflective life in the hope that our words come from a deeper silence.
>
> —Brother Philip

The Glamorous Job:
The Mystical Spirituality of Monastery Labor

It was mid-January. I dressed accordingly and stepped out of the guesthouse door for Morning Vigil into a mixed precipitation of freezing rain and snow. With the strong winter wind, I felt as if I were being pelted in the face with frozen slush. I could see only as far ahead as my headlight shined. Driving to Vigil was an option in less-than-appealing weather, but my car was encased in thick ice. I wrapped my face as tightly as possible in my scarf, leaving only my eyes exposed. I put my head down against the driving slush, and I got on with my walk. In an effort to think about something other than my discomfort, I tried to shift my attention to the world around me. I noticed the quiet stillness of the forest in winter: no little critters scurrying around, no birds singing, no crickets or peepers filling the air with their distinctive, not-unpleasant din. There were also no bugs. I tried to appreciate that as I winced against the pelting ice. I also tried to notice, if not appreciate, the distinctive chill of the wind and crunch of my feet on the frozen ground. Step, step. Crunch, crunch. Eventually the monastery came into view and the warm chapel welcomed me inside.

Back in the guesthouse after breakfast, the icy precipitation had turned to a heavy snowfall. I sat on the couch facing a large picture window looking out over snow-covered mountains. The world was steeped in the deep silence of a snowy winter's day. From this comfort, with my field journal open in front of me, I spent some time reflecting on my morning. I wondered about my relatively unpleasant walk, and the challenges it posed for appreciating the world around me, my presence in it, my movement through it, and what I might be learning from it. I wrote: "How to live fully each moment, even in the discomfort?" It was the start of a wider train of thought on monastic spirituality, and the challenges it posed.

I put down my notes and picked up the book I had been reading that week: Esther DeWaal's *Seeking God: The Way of St. Benedict*. DeWaal is a Benedictine oblate who has written extensively on the Benedictine form of life and how she connects it to her own as a nonmonastic woman. I certainly related to her pursuits. That morning, I read part of her section on work and balance. I had lately been struggling with feeling as though the marathon work of researching and writing a dissertation was overwhelming all of my time and mental focus. It felt at odds with the Benedictine life I was trying to experience and understand.

As I read, I underlined DeWaal's observation that, in Benedictine life, "there is contentment with the familiar, the ordinary, the monotonous."[1] I wrote in the margin: "but how not to become stale routine?" I thought back to my conversations with brother Elias and brother Augustine about how each of them came to monastic life as an alternative to what they experienced as the rote repetitiveness of daily life. I considered that, phrased differently, the rituals and rhythms of monasticism could simply be called repetitive routines. I had seen how the Weston monks tried to resist this by aiming for variety in their daily tasks and including recreation and craft. They talked about it as the pursuit of balance, and DeWaal makes similar observations. She points to the importance of turning the many parts of life into a "harmonious whole" rooted in the ideal of balance: "The monk moves between praying and studying and working with his hands, going in turn from chapel to library to kitchen to farm."[2] This resonated strongly not only with my experience of monastic life, but with my developing understanding of the Benedictine ways of being and knowing and musicking.

DeWaal goes on, though, to direct this ideal of balance toward a monastic spirituality that is distinctly mystical: "The ideal of Benedictine equilibrium is not an end in itself. It is a means for total integration, the transforming of the whole man or woman so that a more complete experience of God becomes possible."³ There it was. The phrase I had danced around, and more or less avoided, in my research and writing so far: experience of God.

Perhaps I had thus far avoided the topic of monastic spirituality because I was not yet in a position to understand it in a meaningful way. But I also avoided it because it can be tricky territory. Talking about music in religious life, while not without problems and struggles, is one thing. Getting into the discourses and experiences of spirituality and divinity is quite another. Religion suggests doctrine and ritual as well as discourses of tradition, authority, and belief. But dealing with less observable phenomena—like the nature and experience of God—is less straightforward, especially in an anthropological context. I had seen that discussions of mysticism or spirituality can tend toward psychologizing or can provide scholars with an opportunity to interpret what is *really* happening—socially, politically, physically, mentally, emotionally—when people *say* they encounter the divine. Fanella Cannell makes this point strongly and directly when she observes: "Religious phenomena in anthropology may be described in detail, but must be explained on the basis that they have no foundation in reality, but are epiphenomena of 'real' underlying sociological, political, economic, or other material causes."⁴

I wanted to understand the Benedictine ways of being and knowing from the brothers' perspective without dismissing, judging, or explaining away what was less concrete, observable, or easy to understand. I recalled my very early difficulties as I sought to understand the unfamiliar. But this seemed to go beyond the unfamiliar into a far murkier territory: the Absolute, the depths of mystery and reality, the outermost limits of being and knowing. Whatever the difficulties, I knew it was time to think—and write—about Benedictine spirituality as I was encountering it at Weston, and to try to understand what music had to do with it. It was time to go back through my experiences, interviews, notes, recordings, and conversations in an effort to know what I sensed the brothers had likely been telling me all along. It turned out to be a line of inquiry that would tie together and bring into focus everything I had been working to understand about monasticism, music, and ethnographic research.

In the pursuit of balance, I put down my reading and picked up the skeins of wool I planned to knit into a hat. The soft, slightly scratchy balls of cream-colored yarn had been spun from the coats of the brothers' sheep. I gazed out at the snowy landscape and entered the meditative repetition of knitting. The soft click of bamboo needles. The gentle tug of the yarn around my fingers. Loop upon loop, stitch upon stitch, the yarn began to take shape. It was the perfect metaphor for the way I would stitch together bits and pieces of my experiences to build a wider sense of understanding and more complete picture of the way of life I had entered into when I knocked on the monastery door.

Considering the sheep who gave their coats for the wool, I thought back to a particularly memorable work period one late spring morning several months prior. When I sat in the parlor waiting for brother Daniel that day, I knew what to expect. Mucking out sheep stalls became something of a weekday tradition for us as we did what he called "the glamorous job" with pitchforks and muck boots. A fellow female guest joined us that day. She and I sat in the parlor chatting about the Priory. I was well into my research, and by that point I had become something of a human guidebook for guests who wanted to know more about life at Weston. It was her first visit to the Priory, and she had yet to figure out the bells. I was in the midst of explaining when and why they ring as brother Daniel entered the parlor.

I wore old jeans, a T-shirt, old shoes, and a wide-brimmed hat. Brother Daniel looked at me, then looked at my fellow guest for a few awkward moments. I remembered those awkward moments from my first visit. In his deep voice and thick accent he said, "Well, you are wearing long sleeves which will be good, but I don't think you'll want to wear those sandals with the sheep." She looked puzzled and stared at her turquoise-blue flip-flops. She responded, in a thick southern drawl, that she thought they would be okay. Even though she had never heard the term "mucking," she did not recoil at the thought of getting dirty.

Brother Daniel smiled slightly and searched for the right words to explain that the sheep were, in his words, "not good housekeepers." He said that we would find that they were quite messy, and her shoes might not offer much protection from their "mess." I sensed that he was looking for a polite way to say "poop." My fellow guest looked confused. She expected that working with the monks would involve some kind of crafting or cooking. She had not yet realized what she volunteered for. Brother Daniel asked for her shoe size and went to fetch her the smallest pair of men's muck boots he could find.

My fellow worker and I walked outside, through the courtyard, and past the Gallery Shop. I lifted the gate of the split-rail fence and we entered the pasture. It was a warm, sunny day and the sheep bleated as we approached. Noël, the resident llama, looked at us, seeming skeptical. When brother Daniel emerged from the back door of the monastery, he took long strides toward us across the pasture. The sheep began to bleat louder and louder. They ran toward the gate where they knew he would enter their pen. He called out to them in Spanish, "Buenos dias! Buenos dias!" He entered their pen and they crowded around him with excitement. A flock with one ram and at least eleven ewes and lambs bumped into each other as they jostled for a space near brother Daniel. They rammed up against his legs and pushed each other around as he patted their heads and greeted them in a flurry of Spanish. Noël, on the other hand, headed immediately for the far side of his pasture. He did not yet know that his morning would feature a manicure and vaccinations, but he did not plan to stick around to find out. The whole scene was simultaneously chaotic and utterly endearing.

Brother Daniel handed us gloves and pitchforks. He looked to the sheep, to the llama, then to the pastures, apparently trying to develop a plan. Brother Augustine had already set out the water in the new pasture, and brother Daniel needed to bring the sheep around the back of the workshop to the new pasture as quickly as possible so that Noël would not escape. He opened a gate, instructed me to close it quickly behind him, and asked my fellow guest to be sure Noël stayed put. Having had experience with Noël, I was not sure how brother Daniel expected her to do that, but I put on my most encouraging smile and braced myself as the sheep banged around in their pursuit to pass through the gate all together. The entire herd followed brother Daniel, except for one lamb, whom he picked up and carried upside down, holding her legs and hugging her close to his chest while she bleated loudly and wiggled. I closed and latched the gate. Noël stood in the farthest corner of the pasture, apparently having no intention to follow either the sheep or brother Daniel.

Brother Daniel returned to the now-empty pen and gave us our instructions. He would work on getting the new pasture ready for the sheep while we scooped the "messes" from the now empty pens into a wheelbarrow. We were then to empty the wheelbarrow into a holding pen. We set to work. I was grateful for a companion who was not at all averse to scooping poop. She certainly seemed to appreciate brother Daniel's foresight in providing her with boots, and I appreciated having her there to help. The pen was beyond messy and we were in this thing together.

My companion chatted happily as we worked, discussing the poop and making observations about the size of the piles she scooped. Monastic silence seemed not to be part of her retreat experience. "Can you come scrape me off—this one's *real* sticky!" She called from the wheelbarrow, hanging on to the word "real" with her thick southern accent. A dark greenish clump was stuck to her pitchfork. The sheep had recently been moved from the barn to the pasture, switching their diet from hay to green grass. This turned their normally pellet-like piles into green, gooey mounds as their digestive systems adjusted to the change. More than unglamorous, this was downright nasty. In my everyday life, I was not really one for scooping "messes," but in my Weston life, pitchfork in hand, I hunted and scooped like a farm girl. Even the smell stopped getting to me after a while, which simply meant that I myself smelled like manure and so could no longer distinguish it in my surroundings.

We worked quickly to clean out the pen and lay down fresh bedding. It was not a task to meander over. Our efficiency left us with enough time to visit the apiary—a far more appealing chore. Brother Daniel brought us up to the large barn at the back of the Priory grounds where the beehives sat at the edge of the woods. He handed me a beekeeping suit. We had done this work before, and I was accustomed to wearing the heavy, white canvas suit made for a six-foot-tall man. I put the suit on in the barn and emerged looking something like a clown. I pulled the long, heavy gloves over my sleeves and put on the hat and veil. My companion was already wearing a white long-sleeved shirt and long pants, and she was not afraid of being stung through her clothing. I marveled at her bravery. She put the long gloves over her sleeves and donned the hat and veil. Brother Daniel, the bravest of all of us, wore the hat and veil but no gloves.

By the time we got to the apiary, the sun was shining brightly and it was unseasonably warm. Brother Daniel filled the smoker with pine needles and lit them, pumping the bellows until a heavy, cool smoke poured out of the spout. For the rest of the morning—nearly an hour and a half—I worked the bellows on the smoker while the others checked on the bees. They lifted the covers of the hives, pulled out the frames, and checked on the health of each queen. By the time the bell rang for the end of the work period, we had only enough time to quickly change our clothes before the dinner bell called us to the refectory. We were hot, tired, hungry, and surely a little smelly. When we sat in the parlor with our fellow guests and they asked how we had spent our morning, I was unsure if they were just making pleasant conversation, or if they were reacting to our appearance and our smell.

During a similar morning a couple of months later, I hauled beekeeping equipment up a small mountain for an injured brother Daniel. I wore the canvas beekeeping suit and suffered in the heat of a bright summer day as I lugged a fully loaded hay cart up the steady incline. When we finally descended the mountain—a task as difficult as the uphill climb as I fought gravity to keep control of the cart—I went immediately to the kitchen. It was a few minutes before dinner, and I was exhausted, overheated, and relatively certain that my legs were turning to jelly. I grabbed a glass from the shelf, desperate for a drink of water. Brother Michael came in and laughed when he saw me standing at the sink, red-faced, drinking glass after glass of cold water.

"What has brother Daniel had you doing this time?" he asked, with a knowing smile. I told him about the hay cart loaded with equipment, and his eyebrows went up when I explained where I had hauled it. "To the upper meadow?" he exclaimed, laughing. "You know, you can tell brother Daniel 'no,'" he said, still smiling. I told him it was fine, I did not mind, and I would probably recover eventually. I said, "I always feel more like I belong here when I come to dinner sweaty and starving." Brother Michael laughed heartily and observed that it was a very accurate assessment of monastic life. It is not all meditation and contemplation.

Indeed, it was not, but as I learned over the course of many work periods, meals, and prayers, the contemplative and the spiritual emerge within the nitty-gritty, often very dirty, aspects of the everyday. To say that sheep manure offers a contemplative monk an experience of God seems to be a bit much. However, it is in this deep, thorough participation in the rhythms of the natural world that the contemplative finds knowledge of the divine. During my time at Weston, I cleaned the sheep stalls and hauled hay bales for fresh bedding. The manure I scooped fertilized the garden, fueling the bountiful harvest on the dinner table. One evening, there were new potatoes on the buffet and brother Michael scooped them, leaned in closely to look at them, and said, "I recognize you!" He marveled at his own participation in the cycles of life and rhythms of nature that brought the potatoes to the table.

When I knitted my hat from the sheep's wool, I thought about how their coats, so filled with muck, straw, and a distinctive *eau-de-*barn aroma during the summer, were spun into soft white yarn that would protect me from the January blizzards. As I worked the yarn in the guesthouse living room, I felt deeply connected to the earth, the sheep, and the world around me. I was grateful to the sheep for the gift of their wool. Maintaining a clean home for them did not seem so unglamorous after all.

Sitting on the couch, yarn in hand, snow blowing outside, I recognized that this was a mystical experience. It reflected the distinctive epistemology and ontology, or way of knowing and being, that emerges in the monastic form of life. When the brothers explained to me that their music emerges from the community, they were telling me about language, narrative, collective composition, tradition, creativity, and local authenticity, but they were also telling me about this way of knowing. They were saying that the sheep are in the music. The gardens, the bees, the forest, the workshops, the solar panels, and the pigpens are in the music. The lyrics may not literally sing about the circle of life, from mucking pens, to knitting wool, to eating potatoes, but everything and everyone participates in the cycle. Everything becomes part of the unity of selves, others, and all of creation. It is a mystical epistemology and ontology.

Grounding Spirituality in Everyday Experience

The sermon, called a homily in Catholicism, is a familiar element of Christian worship. It is an opportunity for presiding clergy to instruct, and perhaps inspire, the faithful. In monasticism, often the superior in the community, whether an abbot or prior, abbess or prioress, gives a homily after the Gospel reading during the Sunday Eucharist. It is an opportunity to teach the monks or nuns about their monastic lives, interpret scripture for them, or explain doctrine to them. It is typically intended to be instructive and enriching, but a homily is not traditionally a dialogue or conversation.

That the Weston monks have rethought the traditional homily in their liturgical practices is not surprising. While the experience doubtless varies from one monastery to the next, the genre can be counter to their egalitarian ideals. They prefer a format more like a conversation or Quaker Meeting.

During their evening Vespers and weekend Eucharist services, the time after the Gospel is set aside either for silent reflection or an open discussion. Any brother who feels inspired to speak can take the microphone and offer his reflections on the day's scripture readings. Sometimes no one speaks, sometimes only one or two brothers offer their thoughts, and sometimes it becomes an animated exchange of ideas as the microphone is passed around.

During a Wednesday evening Vespers in the middle of winter late in my field research, while I was in the midst of thinking through the brothers' spirituality, brother John offered a humorous reflection on an article he had recently read. There were only around twenty guests and visitors gathered in the chapel; a blizzard made the roads around Weston treacherous, so the crowd was smaller than usual. Brother John engaged not just the brothers, but the group in the gallery as well. He looked around, smiled, and spoke in an animated tone of voice. Everyone listened intently, and many of us laughed along with him as he spoke in his usual manner blending a light-hearted tone with deep reflection:

> I don't know how many have seen it lately, but there was an article saying that the Church is going to start training more exorcists because there's too many demons around right now. (*He chuckles, the crowd in the visitors' gallery laughs*)
>
> The article is kind of interesting in a way. It seems that the exorcists are going to be *really* trained. Up until now, we've all been exorcized if we've been baptized because there's a little exorcism ceremony there. The poor little child gets the demons drawn out of him! (*laughter*)
>
> And I don't know about others, but for my own experience, it makes room for seven more demons to enter in! (*laughter*)
>
> (*In a more serious tone*) I think that to over-spiritualize at the present moment may be missing an opportunity for a reality check. I don't know about everybody else, but I experience my demons. Every once in a while I am just not myself. Somebody else is taking over my body. (*Brother John chuckles*)
>
> I'm not sure what kind of exorcism I need, but I suspect it requires a lot of help from others. My brothers can help me to practice certain disciplines of our monastic life more seriously instead of needing one of us ordained to be our exorcist. They can encourage me to more discipline, to really practice—perhaps a little more seriously—prayer, kindness, forgiveness, and all of those other wonderful practices that Jesus lived out in his life and that we follow in our monastic life. I think somehow this does help to make us free to be who we want to be instead of who we sometimes just feel driven to be.

Brother John's thoughts reminded me of some reflections that brother Placid had shared a week earlier during the Wednesday evening Vespers Eucharist. He talked about his reactions to that day's readings: the first letter of John, as well as the Gospel of Mark with the well-known story of Jesus walking on water. I sensed something of a theme running through the brothers' remarks, and when I returned to my guesthouse after Compline that night I turned on my computer and pulled up the recording. Brother Placid was the third brother to speak that evening in a lively exchange that considered the nature of perfect love:

> Reflecting on the readings we've had this evening, I was very struck, as others were saying, in the first letter of John: perfect love casts out fear. I think the perfect love that John talks about is love that is practiced, love that is attempted and tried, love that is put in a place where there is no love.
>
> In the Gospel, I also think Mark is perhaps critiquing the apostles. He compares the apostles who have hardened hearts with nature. Nature is all around them and seems to be accepting Jesus. It's not that Jesus suddenly had miraculous buoyancy or something, and he floats on water that way, so much as the water refuses to let him go down. The wind stops when he gets in the boat. Again, it's Mark's play on how the disciples had to struggle with faith while all those around them—the foreigners and nature in this story—were accepting this man Jesus of Nazareth. I think it becomes a real challenge for us to open our hearts more and more, not to let them be hardened. Not to let them be fixed in whom we love. Rather, always to be open and reaching out to our neighbor and the stranger in our midst. In practicing hospitality. In the welcome and the care that we offer.

This resonated with brother John's caution against over-spiritualizing, and as I listened back to brother Placid's thoughts it reminded me of something brother Michael had said in his reflections during a Eucharist service a few months prior. His words were memorable enough to stick with me, but it took a lot of hunting through recordings before I found the right one. As I searched, I felt as if I were following breadcrumbs that the brothers had left for me along the way, piecing together the bits and pieces as I tried to make sense of their spirituality.

I found the recording in question. It was another Wednesday evening Vespers Eucharist. I looked back at my field notes and recalled that it was the week before Labor Day and the Priory was especially crowded with visitors passing through at the end of the busy summer season. The Barn Chapel, which can hold a few hundred people, felt very full as the eighty or so people who came for the evening Eucharist spread out around the space. After the readings, brother Michael offered his reflections on the miracle stories in the Gospel and that day's reading from Paul's letter to the Corinthians:

> These were extremely engaging readings. What I heard Paul saying, basically, was that although he has preached, there was something more for the Corinthians than simply listening to preaching. It was their actual experience of believing. And I think Paul was trying to ask them really the question: what do you believe?

I think that's such an open question for ourselves right now, when there's a lot of information, a lot of preaching, a lot of answers given to us. But the same basic question remains: what is our experience of our beliefs?

For myself that was the real window into the Gospel today that talks about the miracle stories of Jesus. These stories are not about the suspension of natural laws. The Gospel writers are trying to tell us that something new was happening. I think that Jesus was somehow able to wake people up, to cure them and heal them of their dis-ease. I think that there was something in his message: the reign of God is close at hand. What does that mean? What does that experience signify for us? I think it brings it right into our own time, into our life together. Trying to move into our experience of believing, of living, of loving, and finding within it, within the many challenges, that that's where our hearts are fully engaged.

It may seem radical for a man in a Christian vocation to call the literal truth of the miracle stories into question, but this is exactly the kind of grounding that brother John and brother Placid spoke to in their own reflections. Just as brother Leo admonished his monks to take the Rule of Benedict very seriously but not to take it literally, so the brothers took matters of spirituality, scripture, and faith very seriously but with an open-mindedness grounded in the immediate reality of experience. For them, over-spiritualizing could miss a present, tangible point. However, a focus on immediate experience need not dismantle spirituality by over-rationalizing or over-intellectualizing. As in all aspects of the Benedictine life, there is a balance to be struck. During my time with them, I noticed that the brothers were open to mystery and the ineffable, but that the mysterious did not require suspension of the rational or the intellectual. For them, the rational mind and the spiritual heart coexist. Head and heart, rational and spiritual, need not stifle or silence one another. Both are necessary as the brothers position themselves toward an experience of God that is immediate yet distant, familiar yet ineffable, immanent yet transcendent, and as rational as it is unknowable. This spirituality is decidedly monastic, marked by a mystical way of knowing that is open to and firmly grounded in the limits, the possibilities, and the paradoxes of the everyday.

Stanislaus, Stanislaus, or Stanislaus

I asked brother John during an interview early on in my field research, "Do you think it is accurate to call your spirituality mystical?" He responded, with his characteristic grin and raise of the eyebrows, "Only if you do it with a smile on your face." Mysticism has a long and varied history in Christianity, and it has an abundance of spiritual, religious, psychological, and cultural associations. In other words, it comes with a lot of baggage.

The Benedictine monastic sensibility supports a subdued spirituality directed toward the loving desire for God and the pursuit of God's presence through contemplative remove from the world. In the Rule, Saint Benedict focuses on the internalized presence of God in the midst of the worshiping community.[5] This contemplative orientation is focused not on union with God, but more generally on an experience of the divine presence. It is an experience of vision through knowledge, wisdom, and perception rather than union. The focus is on love and unity as the driving power of this experience.[6] The monastic turns inward in a spirit of listening, outward in a spirit of wonder and awe, and toward the community in an effort to find unity with others.

The turn toward the community is primary as the contemplative, cenobitic monastic life becomes a family life supported by loving commitment and the bonds of brotherhood or sisterhood. Commitment is entirely voluntary, but it is taken very seriously. The experience of making a profession—"taking vows"—is primary, but the tradition of taking a new name is also significant. Most of the Weston brothers changed their names to something from scripture or early Christian history on the occasion of their monastic profession.

I shared a humorous conversation about the importance of names with some of the brothers and a few guests one afternoon. We had just finished cleaning up the kitchen after a festive Sunday dinner, and brother Richard, brother Elias, brother Daniel, two male guests, a female guest, and I stood in a corner of the kitchen chatting. Brother Richard had recently discovered my grandfather's business card in a drawer of his desk, and he pulled the card out of his pocket to show me. My grandfather, who was an attorney, had done some legal work for the brothers in the 1970s. As brother Richard handed me the old business card, he asked if I planned to keep my name when I got married the following summer. He had a very slight, rather sly grin as he asked the question. I told him I did not plan to change my name. He smiled broadly and said, "Oh good! Maria Guarino is a nice Italian name. You must keep it."

He pronounced my name with an Italian accent. Like me, he was raised in an Italian-American family. He understood my desire to hold on to my heritage, but he also understood that it is not an easy choice to make. Brother Daniel chimed in, "But, Maria Zimmerman would make a nice German name." He pronounced it with a heavy German accent. "But she isn't German! She's Italian!" Brother Richard objected, with a smile. "Her husband can be the German, she can be the Italian." From across the room, brother Mark, also Italian-American, added his voice to the discussion: "Well, our resident scholar is certainly a liberated woman. No husband is going to tell her who to be. She should keep her name. Changing it seems so old-fashioned."

In the refectory that week, we had been listening to a book on John Muir, the nineteenth-century naturalist. That afternoon, we heard a rather vivid section of the opening chapter describing Muir's overbearing father, Daniel, as an extremely strict Scottish man who exerted careful control over his wife and children. Our discussion of my name brought us to a discussion of the book. Brother Augustine finished packing the last of the leftovers into the walk-in refrigerator and he joked that my fiancé must have some Scottish in him, so I should plan on being a very carefully controlled wife. We all laughed as I sarcastically commented, "Sure, I'll be really well controlled, starting with refusing to change my name!" The female guest standing next to me, a woman who appeared to be in her sixties, nodded her head and patted my arm in a show of female solidarity. "You keep your name," she said quietly, "I did, and that was at a time when it was considered a very strange thing to do!"

With the discussion of my name causing quite a stir, and uncovering some of the markedly liberal, feminist political orientations of the Weston monks and their guests, brother Elias chimed in. He said he was with me on the name change question. He observed that, socially and politically, women perhaps should not change their names anymore because the practice is caught up in an outdated model of submissive wives and domineering husbands. However, he said that his own monastic experience had taught him that changing one's name is also about marking a commitment to a new way of life and a new family. He said that when it was time for him to become a novice, brother Leo asked what name he wanted to take. He replied: "I'll give you three options: Stanislaus, Stanislaus, or Stanislaus." Brother Elias, who is of Polish descent, wanted to be named for the eleventh-century Polish bishop and martyr. Brother Leo, who was still Abbot Leo at the time, was not happy with that choice. He told the young novice monks that he really preferred brothers take a name from the Gospels or the Hebrew scriptures. They could choose something from early Christianity or early monasticism if they wanted to, as brother Augustine and brother Placid did, but he really preferred that they go no later than that. He asked brother Elias to think about it some more.

Later, brother Leo asked him again, and he again replied: "Stanislaus, Stanislaus, or Stanislaus." Brother Elias explained that he was too stubborn to consider the purpose of the name change at that time in his life. He recognized later that it was about making a commitment to the community and putting himself fully into that commitment. It was about becoming the person he would be in his family of brothers. But at the time, brother Elias saw it instead as a problem of obedience to authority. In refusing to choose a name from an accepted source or time period, he pushed back against authority and rejected the challenge of obedience.

During the Sunday Eucharist at which a young brother Elias made his vows, brother Leo leaned over to him and whispered: "I'm sorry, I'm going to have to disappoint you." Brother Leo sat in a chair that was set up in front of the Eucharist table and gave a homily in which he talked extensively about Elijah, whose name was translated into Latin as Elias. "Oh no you don't!" brother Elias recalled thinking as he knelt in front of brother Leo, preparing to make his final profession. Lo and behold, brother Elias received his name. "But you see," he said, "brother Leo knew better than I did, and he chose well for me. It's amazing how the name suits me."

He went on to talk about the person he was then and the little ways in which he would resist authority. "It's just evidence of where I was in my life and on my journey back then," he said. He offered another example. His cousin, who was also in a religious vocation, visited him once when he was still a young monk. "At the time," he said, "the Franklin room was the kitchen, the dish pantry, the refectory, the library, and the laundry." One day, the doorbell rang, and when he answered it he was surprised to see his cousin on the other side. She stayed for a short visit and as she was preparing to leave she turned to brother Elias and said, "I'm telling them I don't like it." He asked what she meant, fearing she would give a negative report on the monastery to their family back home. "Your beard!" she replied as she turned and went away.

We all laughed at the story. Brother Elias explained that, in those days, the brothers all decided that they wanted to grow beards. Brother Leo hated the idea. As the story goes, brother Leo's primary objection was that one of the brothers at Dormition had such a long beard, it was always in the soup. But because brother Leo was still abbot of Dormition and had to split his time between Jerusalem and Vermont, he was not always at Weston to monitor the presence or absence of beards. Brother Elias said that for them at the time, not shaving for three days was enough to say they were growing beards. So they all decided they wanted to do it, and by the time they told brother Leo they were already three days into their facial hair rebellion. Brother Elias explained that they were not really asking permission: "If he said yes, well, it was already happening, and if he said no, well, we would just continue to forget to shave!"

We all laughed. Brother Augustine chimed in: "Oh, yes," he said, "I had a beard! And long hair! It was a thing we all did when we were young. We thought we were pretty hip at the time." Brother Elias responded, "What was nice, was that we all did it together. It ended up being a wonderful bonding experience." One of the male guests said that the cover of one of his old Weston records had a photo of the whole community in full beards. Brother Augustine made an exaggerated expression of embarrassment and said, "Yes, I think it was on one of the album covers, maybe *Wherever You Go*. We're all there in our beards. We're quite a sight!" We all laughed and continued to talk about their rebellious days when they found communal unity in resisting authority and bonding over beards and long hair.

The conversation reminded me of brother Daniel's reflection during the Saturday Eucharist the day before. He spoke about competition. He said that when he first came to the community, the brothers played volleyball for recreation. Brother Daniel explained that, in order to make a competitive sport fit into the monastic way of life, they removed all competitiveness: "You got three chances to serve, everyone had to hit the ball before it could go back over the net, the ball could bounce off the ground, we rotated around both sides so there were no teams, and no one kept score!" The crowd of people in the Barn Chapel laughed. The brothers smiled. Even in competitive sports, their focus was always on fostering a strong brotherhood.

Turning Outward and Turning Inward

Brother Daniel called me over to the windows in the kitchen as the last of the dishes were being put away one Saturday evening. The cloudy sky outside was a dramatic shade of inky indigo blue, but Terrible Mountain, the small peak that defines the horizon to the east of the Priory, was glowing bright green as though a giant spotlight shone on it. The whole brilliant scene reflected in the mirrorlike pond. "Isn't it amazing?" brother Daniel remarked.

I went outside to try to capture the dramatic landscape on camera. Brother Elias and brother Augustine were nearby fixing a window that had been blown out by strong winds the night before. It started to rain lightly, and I heard brother Elias say, "Look! A rainbow!" A rainbow arched above our heads high in the sky against the backdrop of blue clouds. The sun was so low and it cast the rainbow so high, it was nearly a circle of colored light around the mountains. Brother Peter came outside to take in the scene. Brother Daniel appeared beside us. The five of us stood there in the driveway, looking up, marveling, and silently taking it all in. "I *love* living here!" Brother Daniel exclaimed, "In all seasons, it is beautiful." The rainbow faded and we went in different directions, returning to our tasks before Compline.

This disposition of looking around, taking it all in, and being left breathless was fundamental to my experience of life at Weston. Nothing was too small for notice. Brother Peter, whose crafts included photography, had recently taken to photographing bees, bugs, and flowers. Even cracks in the pavement were artistically rendered through his camera's lens. Likewise, no large-scale phenomenon was too broad to appreciate: the relentless march of the changing seasons, the increasingly visible effects of climate change, the immediate importance of conservation.

In the fall/winter 2011 bulletin, the brothers state, "In our monastic life the promise of stability clearly roots us in the soil of this earth in a particular place and with each other in a way that brings us into relationship as brothers to all persons and to all of creation." This deep connection to and rootedness in the earth is a familiar trope throughout the history of Christian mysticism. For the mystic, nature, also called creation, is evidence of the hand of the Creator. In this orientation toward the natural world, God becomes accessible and visible.

The Absolute becomes tangible. In the same bulletin, the brothers state, "Jesus invites us to discover the mystery of God's Incarnation that has been unfolding from the beginning, when the Creator Spirit brooded over the emptiness and breathed life into the universe."

This is an earthy, pastoral mysticism, which can sound a bit idyllic. But it is not always so. I spent a lot of time at Weston listening to birds chirp, watching sunrises and sunsets, weeding the garden in perfect weather, and walking through the quiet woods. However, I also encountered more than one bear; I got close enough to a baby moose to wonder where mommy and daddy moose were lurking and consider whether or not I could outrun them; I walked back and forth from my guesthouse to the Priory in a blizzard so severe my eyelashes turned to ice crystals; and I battled seemingly endless swarms of black flies. While these experiences—along with my participation in the daily labor of the monastery—are part of the wonder-and-awe trope of amazement in the presence of the natural world, they are also thoroughly grounded in the reality of the everyday. They cured me of any romanticized notions I might have had about life and spirituality at Weston. At the same time, it was only through them that I really came to understand what it means to ground spirituality in the tangible and present, to look for the Absolute in the quotidian, and to allow the rational and reasonable to uncover the mystical. This outward-turning spirituality of wonder and awe is counterbalanced by an inward-turning spirituality of listening and silence. Silence allows the monastic person to make room, to open up the self to the possibilities of experience. This fosters an orientation toward the presence of God as the mystic becomes attuned to the divine in the world.

Kathleen Norris remarks on the importance of ceremony in the monastery, as in the practice of eating in silence while someone reads aloud. In her experience, the ceremony of monastic life forces the monastery guest to slow down, but this is not always easy. It can feel like slamming on the brakes and, in her words, "skidding to a halt."[7] Perhaps it is this sense of "skidding" that causes some guests to find the silence of monastic life a difficult adjustment, particularly at meals. For several days, I sat next to a female guest who told me that she found it rather difficult to be read to during meals. This surprised me, as I had come to enjoy the monastic mealtime *lectio*. To me, it was a quiet, focused way to eat in the company of others. I asked her why she found it difficult, and she said she was bothered because she could not focus enough on the reader. Maintaining silence during meals caused her mind to wander as she got absorbed in other thoughts. Then, when her attention was recalled to the reader, she realized she had lost several sentences of the book and could no longer follow what the author was saying.

I recognized immediately that I did exactly the same thing. As much as I had come to enjoy the quiet, reflective atmosphere of the refectory, I was not entirely attentive to the reader. I paid attention enough to keep up with the material, but my mind wandered. This was also true when someone read aloud at prayer. My mind often wandered during the daily scriptures, the psalms, the Gospels, the prose, and the poetry. My conversation with my fellow guest caused me to realize that I was really a rather poor listener in terms of a contemplative monastic ethos. Recognizing this helped me to understand that reading aloud is not only about entertainment or edification. Hearing a book read aloud is certainly informative, fun, and interesting. I learn something, I engage with the community on an intellectual level, and I have something to discuss with my neighbor at the dinner table when the meal is over. We are all better for it. But this Benedictine tradition also participates in the overarching monastic sensibility that cultivates a spirit of listening in all aspects of everyday life. Listening is a practice. It is a deep and complex monastic virtue. This is not as simple as it might sound. If I cannot listen to someone reading to me, how can I really hear that person in the other aspects of life? How can I be part of a community?

Benedict recognized the importance of this kind of listening. The first words of his rule—listen with the ear of the heart—point toward a general spirit of quiet reflection and attentiveness to the other people in the monastery. But the call to listen with the ear of the heart becomes distinctly mystical for Benedictines. This kind of listening suggests, among other things, seeking the presence of God within, or at the heart of, each person. In liturgy and in everyday life, monastics strive to achieve Saint Benedict's spiritual listening by cultivating an attentiveness that looks for the presence of God within oneself and among the members of the community.

This is not unlike the *imago dei* in Christian theology, according to which humanity is created in the image of the divine, and so the center of the human being is the image of God. Therefore, movement toward God is paradoxically movement toward self, or a participation in the deepest reaches of the soul. It requires an inward turn as the transcendent is discovered to be immanent. This also applies to other people: the imago dei is also their center, and so movement toward God requires movement toward others.

This language of turning resonates with Jean-Yves Lacoste's "coaffection," a term he offers for understanding the nature of the presence of God and the interpersonal, communal turning toward God that is the focus of the liturgical ritual.[8] It is a positioning of the internal self toward the Absolute. In monasticism, this constitutes a turning toward oneself and one's brothers or sisters. It is as individual as it is interpersonal, and thus picks up on the together-alone tension of monasticism and allows monastics to negotiate the individual-communal dialectic while also complicating the paradox of that dialectic and rendering it distinctly mystical.

Whenever I arrived at Weston for a visit there was a period of transition from the outside world to my monastic self as I worked to quiet my mind and open up my contemplative awareness to turn, so to speak, toward myself and the people around me. I went through what I often called a "de-tox" as I left behind the mental clutter created by the demands of everyday life and constant access to technology and media. I had no cell phone service, no Internet connection, and no television. While this remove from the noise of life created a quiet mental and physical space, it also set a stark, immediate, even startling contrast to my usual way of being in the world. Silence, initially, can seem deafening.

As I have explored throughout the preceding chapters, it took time for me to adjust to the monastic mode of conversation. In the pottery with brother Peter and brother Augustine, I learned to leave room for others to finish their thoughts. In the recording studio, I learned about a collective consciousness. I learned not to fill the silence with constant chatter. In the kitchen, conversations that were not about the work at hand had to flow with it. In the silence of the refectory, I learned to eat quietly. At prayer, I learned to dwell in the stillness of the monastic liturgical affect. Moving through the schedule of the days, weeks, and seasons, I learned to be patient and let the passing of time unfold without compulsively planning each moment or attempting to control the future. I learned the openness of the monastic ethos that creates space for the possibilities of experience. I learned to live fully each moment.

Brother Michael and the Musical *Metanoia*

Brother Michael, brother John, and I spent more than an hour one winter afternoon working, reworking, and finally recording flute accompaniments for one of the songs on the brothers' new album. Brother Michael deemed the days' work finished and we started to pack up our respective equipment. Brother John put on his jacket and left to attend to his other tasks; brother Michael and I cleaned up the equipment and chatted about the recording. It snowed hard and fast outside the little studio. A strong, steady wind blew. We wondered whether or not the microphones had picked up the wind, and brother Michael said he was not going to worry about it. "Some people might think, 'Oh, this is noise on the recording, we can't have that!' But for me, I think, this is real, this is life, and this is where we were when this song was recorded. It was windy. The wind is part of the life of that song now."

That certainly seemed to be an optimistic approach to something that might bother other recording engineers. After all, since their longtime friend and record producer retired, this is what brother Michael had become for his community: a recording engineer. It is not something he ever thought he might become, and it is certainly not a job that most people associate with the monastic profession. Sitting next to a sound board filled with knobs and lights, cords winding around and feeding into digital recorders and hard drives, he hardly struck a traditional image of a Benedictine at work at his craft. With his guitar set behind him, and his own music stand next to his chair, he wound cords and shut down electronics until everything was ready to be put away for the day. On the other side of the room, I cleaned my flute and packed it away in its case, returned my manuscript paper to my bag, and began lacing up my snow boots to make the blustery trek back to the guesthouse.

Normally, we did not hang around after a session; having spent enough time on one task, the brothers were eager to move on to whatever else required their attention, but that afternoon brother Michael asked if I would stay for a few minutes so that he could ask me some musical questions. Earlier in the week, I gave him a copy of some of my working notes for a postlude we were planning to record. I had taken a copy of "Wisdom at Play," applied a basic Roman numeral chord progression analysis, transferred that to a blank piece of manuscript paper, and jotted down ideas for melodic lines and harmony parts for the song. Brother Michael said that when he looked at the manuscript and all of my harmonic analysis with neat little Roman numerals lined up in rows under his chords, he thought it looked like he was a little harmonically scattered. Not wanting my need for controlled visual representations of chords and harmonies to influence his composition process or make him feel that he was doing it wrong because he did not think in these terms, I told him that after so many years of training in a Western music theory model, I had come to think about music this way.

Brother Michael then told me that he feared getting wrapped up in that sense of rules and prescriptive devices if he got too interested in music theory. He felt that his intuitions tended to serve him well, and he did not want to start questioning that because of some rule he read in a book. After talking a little bit about how I wrote the flute parts—I looked at the guitar chords, figured out which chord tones were already present in the melody, picked a different chord tone, and then used nonharmonic neighbor and passing tones to make it interesting—I explained that this method often failed me once I was in the recording studio with the brothers and heard the clashes that my flute parts created against the rolling guitar accompaniment. Even in applying every rule I could pull out of my internal music theory reserves, I was unable to control the collective composition process. Things that looked on paper as if they should work often sounded unappealing in the moment of performance.

As brother Michael and I continued our discussion about rules and techniques, I asked him about his guitar technique. I had started to learn the instrument in an effort to better understand the brothers' style, and I was hoping for a little guidance. I was interested in finding the right way to hold a classical guitar because I had yet to find a comfortable way to play. Brother Michael grabbed one of the Yamaha nylon-string guitars propped up against the wall, and, sitting in his chair, demonstrated the body position that is taught in most classical guitar method books. He pulled out a foot stool, propped his left foot on it, placed the music stand a little left of the center of his body, sat straight up on the edge of his seat, and positioned the guitar on his leg so that the neck extended up toward his shoulder.

He explained that this position is advocated by most people. He hated it. He found it uncomfortable, and I must say that it did seem a bit awkward: the small guitar extended up across his body and his long arms and legs were positioned at odd angles. He said that if he is not sitting comfortably, then he is not going to want to play. It becomes a struggle for mind and body. He removed the footstool, setting his feet square on the floor; he sat back a little in his chair, relaxing his posture; he moved the stand directly in front of him, squaring his shoulders; and he held the guitar across his lap, resting the body on his right knee and holding the neck parallel to the floor. In this position, he looked natural and relaxed, and his body was at ease.

We decided that I should try it. I sat down, held the guitar, and we immediately saw that I could not use brother Michael's preferred method. I am at least a foot shorter than he is, and the guitar became ungainly across my lap. My hands are small and could not maneuver from that angle. Whereas he could wrap his long fingers around the neck with room to spare, mine struggled to reach the farthest strings and my thumb did not provide a stable support. For me, the footstool was necessary to make up for my small stature, and the upward extended neck that seemed so awkward on brother Michael brought the instrument into a comfortable range for playing.

"You see," he said, "you need to find what works for you and go from there. If you are comfortable, you will want to play, but no method book can predict what will work best for you. And the most important thing is: don't be afraid to move." The accepted wisdom and "rules" of guitar playing did not always suit his way of life, failing to serve some of the fundamental needs of the monastic musician. Brother Michael did not reform himself to fit the rules, curbing his need for a comfortable physical center; rather, he rethought the rules, recognizing the terms in which they developed and the times at which they are useful, but accepting that his lived experience might not always fit within those limits.

Next, I asked brother Michael to talk about his finger-picking technique. He said that he had been playing for so long, it came naturally and he did not feel that he had a particular technique. He described some of the many standard methods and showed me the books he used when he was first learning. I told him that I felt as though I were still stumbling around the strings, trying to pluck out patterns but only ever going extremely slowly. I had not yet achieved the meditative rolling fingers that he and brother Augustine had mastered. My guitar playing hardly felt like prayer. He said that it would come with practice;

eventually, I would get to a point where I would not think about what my hand was doing. He remembered very clearly the first time he felt his hand functioning separately from his conscious mind. As an enthusiastic young guitarist, he had worked hard on "Second Hand News," a song from the Fleetwood Mac album *Rumors*, and finally, after countless hours, he was able to play it. Suddenly, his hand seemed to be separate from his brain. It did exactly what he wanted it to do, but without his thinking through every motion.

This conversation brought me to a new level of understanding and a perspective on monastic musicianship that I had not considered before. The monastic approach opens up musical practices to a full immersion in the internal, mental, emotional, and spiritual aspects of musicking, whether it is Fleetwood Mac, original hymns, or chanted psalms. I think of this as a musical *metanoia*, a transformation of the mind that moves beyond current thought patterns and limitations to a new plane of awareness. This opening up through mindful practice and careful attention allows music to become prayer as it releases the monastic musician from the confines that restrict the experience, whether physical impediments or stifling rules. When brother Michael plays the guitar, it is transcendent, a mystical expression founded on a contemplative approach to his instrument.

I returned to Weston Priory for a brief visit several months after concluding my field research. I was working on the present chapter at the time. The brothers sang a new song during Morning Vigil on the third day of my visit. It was similar in style to the music on the new album: a lot of open space; quiet, meditative affect; simple, deeply spiritual lyrics. Brother Michael used the same classical guitar techniques that he had used on the album. The song had an openness that resisted a standard musical form. It was like a verse-refrain form, but brother Michael extended the space in between the single-line verses and the refrains by playing solo variations on the melody. The refrain was very brief and meditative. Instead of calling it a refrain, brother Michael described it to me as a mantra.

Brother Michael played the mantra melody on guitar as an introduction, then the brothers joined in to sing the refrain, very slowly with little melodic movement: "Gather; gather in wonder and trust." After the mantra, brother Michael strummed a chord and then picked out a few notes one at a time. He let the notes ring and added a little vibrato to the sound. The brothers then sang the first verse, also slow and chant-like: "In simple, ordinary ways, the presence of God is revealed." Brother Michael played another solo guitar section followed by the return of the mantra. This back-and-forth style continued through a second single-line verse—"Listen and be attentive, with the ear of the heart"—and a third verse—"Together we journey in faith, into an open future." It was as if the piece—which was like a meditation on a theme or a poetic word painting—unfolded gradually in the silence and contemplation of the Vigil prayer. Each word was articulated slowly, and the solo guitar interludes created space for the words to reverberate in the consciousness of each person in the chapel.

I made note of the song that day because it struck me as a condensed version of the brothers' approach to their new album, with its preludes, interludes, and postludes surrounding each song in improvisations and meditations. To me, it sounded improvisatory in a way that echoed the resistance to strict meter in the Compline call to prayer, for example. In describing it for my field notes, the form of the song became clear—refrains and verses alternating with solo interludes—but in performance, this sense of structure was subdued as the guitar solos extended the time between phrases, and the single-line lyrics never seemed to assemble into substantial verses. When the predictability of common song forms was removed, and the notion of a refrain was substituted by the idea of a mantra, the experience became a deeper act of listening and attending to the music. It allowed us all to join in the metanoia.

Brother Michael and I discussed this new music as we washed the dinner dishes later that same day. I explained to him that I heard the song as a condensed version of the new style he had been using for the album, and I told him that it struck me as improvisatory. This is not to say that it sounded as though it were created on the spot in the Vigil. I could see that he was reading from a piece of manuscript paper and it sounded thoughtfully prepared. Rather, it had the feeling of an improvisation or meditation on a theme. He said that another friend had made a similar observation, and he had been thinking about the notion of improvisation. He said that his process lately had been to just sit down with his guitar and see what emerged. He would write down the things that he liked so he could recall them and play them again later, but in the moment of creation it was very much an improvisation on a general idea or guiding sense of what a song could be. We discussed how different terms could be substituted for improvisation to reflect the spirituality of the experience: revelation, epiphany, or even inspiration. The lyrics came to him in much the same way, the result of meditation and prayerful reading, what Benedictines call *lectio divina*. In performance, the lyrics maintained the sense of *lectio*.

Brother Michael observed that this is very much grounded in the mentality of music as craft. His approach to composition will necessarily grow, change, and evolve over time, otherwise it might become static and a critical sense of inspiration could be lost. Music-as-craft fuels an ever-expanding tradition. It also further illustrates and extends the idea of musical metanoia by offering inspiration and improvisation—and the parallel spiritual notions of revelation or epiphany—as experiences of transcending, via musical performance, current ways of being and ways of knowing to reach a new kind of awareness or a new layer of understanding expressed in the creative moment of composition and performance. The new Vigil song, called "We Gather," created a meditative atmosphere in communal prayer that offered the brothers and their guests an experience of metanoia fostered in the space of contemplative listening.

I watched brother Augustine's hands that evening during Vespers as he picked out the rolling accompaniment to a song. As I tried to make sense of the repeated patterns of fingers on strings, an out-of-place note sounded from someone's guitar. Brother Augustine's downbeat did not line up with brother Michael's downbeat, and for several beats thereafter their normally complementary finger-picking styles became a clash of slightly out-of-sync notes.

Pulling his consciousness from the trance of guitar and voice, but never stopping the motion of his hands, brother Augustine glanced quickly at brother Michael, who had also very subtly turned to meet his gaze, and they reestablished synchronicity. The guitar accompaniment was a joint craft, created at once by two people with unique fingerprints and styles. Both had to be grounded in the same downbeat, whatever the rolling fingers did in between. Likewise, communal prayer is a collective craft. All of the brothers were unique individuals who contributed their own sound to the Weston voice, but they had to align themselves not only musically but also spiritually. In this unity, they could allow music to become prayer as it transcended the confines that limit the experience.

It was in the space of a contemplative ethnographic disposition that I reached this layer of understanding about the relationship between music, monastic life, and mystical spirituality. I participated in the dialogues prompted by conversations with the brothers. I expanded these dialogues through experience in the kitchen, pastures, parlor, guesthouses, forests, and craft studios. I pondered the developing ideas in daily prayer. I applied them to my own participation in the brothers' music. I continually returned to my dialogues with the brothers. Finally, near the end of my research process, in a conversation with brother Michael over guitars and manuscript paper, my research had fully shifted from an individualized pursuit to a collective inquiry into the role of music in monastic life. I was not interviewing brother Michael, and I was no longer sure who was asking the questions and who was providing the answers. My work had become a true dialogue, an experience of the Benedictine profession: conversatio, obedience, and stability. Or: talking, listening, and fidelity to the process.

Over the course of my work with the Weston monks, I gradually gained a new perspective on myself, the world around me, and my work as an ethnomusicologist. The Benedictine epistemology and ontology became intertwined with my own, and I came to recognize that the pursuit of learning, creating knowledge, and gaining understanding that is at the heart of humanities scholarship is itself a kind of metanoia. It requires moving past current thought patterns to a new level of awareness and a new layer of understanding. It calls for a contemplative focus on experience, intersubjectivity, and the individual-communal processes of being and knowing. It is steeped in the ideals and challenges of craft. It is marked by gradual shifts of consciousness, knowing, and being. It demands the mystical turns: outward in a spirit of wonder and awe at the everyday lives around us; inward in a spirit of deep listening and conversatio; and toward others in ongoing dialogues and shared inquiries. So turned, the scholar stands amazed at what she sees.

Notes

Preface

1. Following the Weston monks' own usage, brother is written with a lowercase "b." The monks do this because they prefer to think of "brother" as a reminder of fraternal relationships rather than a title or distinction.
2. For examples of scholars celebrating the reforms, and the resulting musical creativity, see: Collins, *Contemplative Participation*; Harmon, *Mystery We Celebrate*; Kubicki, *Liturgical Music* and *Presence of Christ*; and McGann, *Exploring Music*. For examples of scholars decrying the reforms as a "crisis" of the liturgy, see: Crouan, *Liturgy Betrayed* and *History and Future*; Day, *Why Catholics Can't Sing*; and Hemming, *Worship as a Revelation*.
3. Some scholars, including musicologists, liturgists, philosophers, and Vatican authorities, argue that Gregorian chant is the most effective and authentic liturgical music. See: Bourdieu, *Language as Symbolic Power*; Crouan, *Liturgy Betrayed* and *History and Future*; Day, *Why Catholics Can't Sing*; Hemming, *Worship as a Revelation*; Kroecker, *Music in Christian Worship*; Mahrt, "Toward a Revision of Music"; Meeks, *Landscape of Praise*; Ratzinger, *Spirit of the Liturgy*. Others, including ethnomusicologists, liturgists, and American Church authorities have applied a broader definition of liturgical music, admitting many styles and drawing the focus to the communal act of worship. See Deiss, *Visions of Liturgy and Music*; DjeDje, "Change and Differentiation"; Dufner, *Sing a New Church*; Foley and McGann, *Music and the Eucharistic Prayer*; Harmon, *Mystery We Celebrate*; Joncas, *From Sacred Song to Ritual Music*; Kubicki *Liturgical Music*; McGann, *Exploring Music*; Walser, "Polka Mass"; and Bishops' Committee, *Sing to the Lord*.
4. Cannell, *Anthropology of Christianity*.

Introduction

1. Weston Priory Bulletin, 1961.
2. Following terminology current among people in monastic vocations, I use the term "monastics" instead of "monks and nuns." This term includes monks as well as cloistered nuns and noncloistered sisters without the need to distinguish between male and female monastics.

3. See McGinn, *Growth of Mysticism*, on monastic history and Saint Benedict's cenobitic turn, especially as it relates to mysticism.
4. All quotes from the Rule of Benedict come from Fry, *RB 1980*. They are cited by chapter and verse.
5. Casey, *An Unexciting Life*.
6. See Wathen's *Silence* for a thorough discussion of silence in the Rule of Saint Benedict.
7. Bergeron, *Decadent Enchantments*.
8. Geertz, *Interpretation of Cultures*, 6–7.
9. Watson, "Introduction," 3–4.
10. On the reflexive turn and the "crisis of representation" in anthropology and ethnomusicology see, respectively, Clifford and Marcus, *Writing Culture*, and Barz and Cooley, *Shadows in the Field*. See also scholars who have addressed reflexivity following the "crisis," and negotiated their relationship to a movement that remains controversial. Some have drawn on terms such as dialogic, for example, Clifford, "Introduction"; Tedlock, "Analogical Tradition," and "Questions Concerning Dialogical Anthropology"; and Sawin, *Listening for a Life*. Jackson, *Paths Toward a Clearing*, and Comaroff and Comaroff, *Ethnography* deal with historical consciousness. Kisliuk, *Seize the Dance!* and Westbrook, *Navigators of the Contemporary*, discuss conversations and the performance perspective. Davies, *Reflexive Ethnography*, discusses a realist ontology. Denzin, *Performance Ethnography*, engages performative autoethnography. Drewal, *Yoruba Ritual*, focuses on intentionality.
11. Watson, "Introduction," 5.
12. This approach to field research resonates both with an extended engagement in a single long-term field research project, as in my own work, and with multitemporal field research of the type described by Howell and Talle in *Returns to the Field*, where researchers return to their field sites after the initial research period, sometimes repeatedly. Expanding the temporal boundaries of "the field" not only allows for critical engagement with themes of continuity and change but also allows for a wider perspective and greater cumulative knowledge from shared experiences.
13. The full opening phrase is: "Listen, my son, to the master's instructions, and attend to them with the ear of your heart."
14. Gupta and Ferguson point to the importance of listening, noting that one thing that has traditionally distinguished anthropology as a discipline is a favored research method—fieldwork—that, among other things, is grounded in listening to, and taking seriously, those we study. "Discipline and Practice," 36.
15. See Halstead, Hirsch, and Okely, *Knowing How to Know*, for a discussion of the processes of creating knowledge in ethnographic contexts.
16. Kohák, *Idea and Experience*, 3.
17. Ibid., 4–5.
18. On the intersubjective perspectives of dialogical anthropology, see Jackson's discussion of "radical empiricism" in *Paths toward a Clearing*.

19. See the writings of Thomas Merton, for example, *New Seeds of Contemplation*. See also Butler's *Western Mysticism* and McGinn's *Foundations of Mysticism*. On the history of contemplatio in mysticism, theology, and philosophy, see Hart, "Contemplation."
20. Hart, "Contemplation." McGinn, *Foundations of Mysticism*.
21. Actuality and possibility in the history of contemplatio is discussed especially by Hart, "Contemplation."
22. See Becker, *Deep Listeners*, and Oliveros, *Deep Listening*.
23. Dwyer, "On the Dialogic of Fieldwork"; "The Dialogic of Ethnography," and *Moroccan Dialogues*.
24. Dwyer, "On the Dialogic of Fieldwork," 147.
25. Dwyer, *Moroccan Dialogues*.
26. Ulin, "Critical Anthropology," 63.
27. On these issues in philosophy, see Morris, "In Defense of Realism," 319, 324–25.
28. Ibid., 325.
29. Geertz, *Works and Lives*, 98.
30. Husserl, *Crisis of European Sciences*.
31. Merton, *New Seeds of Contemplation*, xiii.
32. On the value of "being there" as a methodological foundation in anthropology, see Gupta and Ferguson, "Discipline and Practice," and Watson, "Introduction."
33. Coleman and Collins, "Being . . . Where?" 9.
34. On "deep hanging out," see Geertz, *Available Light*.
35. Coleman and Collins, "Being . . . Where?" 12.
36. See Lewin, "Writing Lesbian Ethnography," in particular her argument that there are many "selves" in field research, and these selves are always in flux.
37. This speaks to recent work on the critical and comparative dimensions of field research. For example, in multisite research, see: Hannerz, "Being There"; Hillhouse, "Reaching Out"; Marcus, "Ethnography." On multitemporal research, see Howell and Talle, *Returns to the Field*. On nonspatial research sites, such as those of digital ethnography, see Underberg and Zorn, *Digital Ethnography*.

Chapter One

Epigraph. "Prophet" is sometimes translated as "psalmist."
1. Except for the music of the Saint-Benoît monks discussed in chapter 2, lyrics quoted throughout this book are the Weston monks' own original lyrics and are reproduced here with permission. If a song has been recorded or published, that information has been included in the relevant notes. For a complete list of the Weston monks' recordings and songbooks, visit their website, www.westonpriory.org.

2. Throughout this book, quotations from chanted psalms are taken from the Weston monks' own translation and chant settings. They are reproduced here with permission. If a psalm has been recorded or published, that information has been included in the relevant notes.
3. For a selection of the stories of the Desert Fathers, see Ward, *Desert Fathers*.
4. My knowledge of the Weston founding narrative comes from my discussions with the brothers and brother John's biography of brother Leo: Hammond, *A Benedictine Legacy of Peace*.
5. Monasteries are typically part of hierarchical congregations with an abbey—or archabbey, if the congregation has many abbeys—at the top. An abbot is in charge not only of the abbey but of all the monasteries and priories beneath it in the congregation. Priories are typically small communities that are dependent on and offer support to their founding monastery or abbey. Monasteries found dependent priories in order to have a source of financial support and personnel in an area outside of the main monastery.
6. On the nineteenth-century monastic revival, see Bergeron, *Decadent Enchantments*, and Combe, *Restoration of Gregorian Chant*.
7. On the history of American Benedictine monasticism, see Rippinger, *Benedictine Order*.
8. On the social shifts that marked the transition into the 1960s, see Gitlin, *The Sixties*.

Chapter Two

1. Translation: God, come to my aid! Lord, to our help.
2. This is the French translation of the *Gloria Patri* doxology.
3. The Examination of Conscience is a prayer of confession of one's sins and faults, to God and to the community. The Latin text: *Confiteor Deo omnipotenti quia peccavi nimis cogitatione, verbo, opere et omissione: mea culpa, mea culpa, mea maxima culpa. Ideo precor beatam Mariam semper Virginem, omnes Angelos et Sanctos, et beatum Patrem nostrum Benedictum, orare pro me ad Dominum Deum nostrum.* While not a literal translation, the standard English version is: I confess to almighty God, and to you my brothers and sisters, that I have sinned through my own fault, in my thoughts and in my words, in what I have done and in what I have failed to do. And I ask Blessed Mary, ever virgin, all the angels and saints, and you, my brothers and sisters, to pray for me to the Lord our God.
4. Translation: I confess to God the almighty, I recognize before my brothers, that I have sinned in thought, in word, by action and by omission; yes, I have truly sinned. It is why I beg the Virgin Mary, the angels and all the saints, and you also, my brothers, to pray for me to the Lord our God.
5. On Gregorian tonality, see, for example, Suñol's *Textbook of Gregorian Chant according to the Solesmes Method*, especially chapter 2 on the singing of the psalms.

6. The *Kyrie Eleison* is one of the few remaining Greek elements of the Latin Rite. In Greek, the words are: *Kyrie Eleison, Christe Eleison, Kyrie Eleison*. Translated to English: Lord have mercy, Christ have mercy, Lord have mercy.
7. The monks sang the hymn as printed in the *Liber Antiphonarius pro Diurnis Horis II, Psalterium* published by the Abbaye Saint-Pierre-de-Solesmes (2006). For reference, see the *Ave, Regina* simplex (*A Feria II Hebdomdae I per Annum Usque ad Feriam IV Hebdomadae Sanctae,* day two, week one during the year through day four, Holy Week).
8. For a thorough discussion of Mariology, see Warner, *Alone of All Her Sex*. See also Mooney, "Voice, Gender," on the hagiography of women saints. For an intensive ethnomusicological study of these issues relative to Marian devotion and musical performance, see Sklar, *Dancing with the Virgin*.
9. Crocker, *Introduction to Gregorian Chant*, 1.
10. Bergeron, *Decadent Enchantments* and "Virtual Sacred."
11. Bergeron discusses this at length in "Virtual Sacred," in which she compares the performance style of the *Chant* album to that of early music ensembles, such as Ensemble Organum, that aim for the most authentic practices.
12. Bergeron, *Decadent Enchantments*, 8–9.
13. Ibid., 19.

Chapter Three

1. See, for example, Morrow, *Names of Things*.
2. For more on the kitchen as a space for performing family and social identity, see Sklar's discussion of kitchen choreography in *Dancing with the Virgin*, 77–93.
3. Trinitarian prayers reference the Holy Trinity of the Christian cosmology: God the father, Jesus the son, and the Holy Spirit. A doxology is a song or hymn of praise in Christian worship. It is usually very short and is often added to the end of chanted psalms and canticles in monastic liturgies. The Latin text of the Gloria Patri is: *Gloria Patri, et Filio, et Spiritui Sancto. Sicut erat in principio, et nunc, et semper, et in sæcula sæculorum.* While not a literal translation, a common English version is: Glory be to the father, and to the son, and to the Holy Spirit; as it was in the beginning, is now, and ever shall be.
4. See Britto, "Gender of God," on debates over the gender of God in Judaism and Christianity.
5. "Peace to You" is recorded on the album and published in the songbook, *Calm Is the Night*. Copyright © Weston Priory, Gregory Norbet, O.S.B., 1974.
6. Agamben, *Highest Poverty*, 11.
7. For a thorough study of the psalms in Christian and Jewish liturgical traditions, see Attridge and Fassler, *Psalms in Community*.
8. See Taft, *Liturgy of the Hours*.
9. Taft argues that the conventional use of the term "antiphonal psalmody" to denote the alternating two-chorus arrangement is in fact inaccurate. He

suggests the term "alternating psalmody" be used instead, but as antiphonal psalmody is an accepted term among monastics, I continue to use it here. *Liturgy of the Hours*, 19.
10. See Abbott, *Documents of Vatican II*.
11. Duffy, *Stripping of the Altars*.
12. Bourdieu, *Logic of Practice*, 54.
13. Bourdieu, *Language as Symbolic Power*.
14. Boynton addresses a similar issue in a discussion of liturgy as the primary public performance of authoritative language in monastic life. She suggests that "to understand liturgy not just as a product, but as practice and performance is to apprehend its full range of functions: praise, prayer, teaching, exegesis, expression of spiritual self-identification and affiliation, and much more besides." *Shaping a Monastic Identity*, 3.
15. "Beatitudes" is recorded on the album and published in the songbook, *Locusts and Wild Honey*. Copyright © Weston Priory, Gregory Norbet O.S.B., 1971.

Chapter Four

1. On the language of craft and workmanship, see Betjemann, *Talking Shop*, and Sennett, *Craftsman*. On the nature and value of handwork, see Crawford, *Shop Class*.
2. On utilitarian art, see Jones, *Exploring Folk Art*. On the "strained" relationship between fine art and craft see, Risatti, *Theory of Craft*. On the nature of craft as processes carried out in specific materials or media, see Adamson, *Thinking through Craft*.
3. "Song in Our Silence" is recorded on the album and published in the songbook, *Song in Our Silence*. Copyright © Weston Priory, 1990.
4. On the history of craft in Western culture, see Bronner, *Creativity and Tradition*.
5. On the emergence of craft in the face of industrialization, see Crawford, "Ideas and Objects."
6. DeWaal similarly emphasizes the tensions and paradoxes of the monastic profession in *Living with Contradiction*.

Chapter Five

1. The brothers' declaration of sanctuary is available on their website, http://www.westonpriory.org/sanctuary/declaration.html (accessed January 29, 2017).
2. Their association with Latin America is explored in depth on their website, http://www.westonpriory.org/bulletins/ss2000a.html (accessed January 29, 2017).
3. Byrnes, *Reverse Mission*.

4. "Listen" is recorded on the album and published in the songbook, *Listen*. Copyright © Weston Priory, Gregory Norbet, O.S.B., 1973.
5. This way of thinking about craft and tradition is especially evident in Cashman, Mould, and Shukla, *Individual and Tradition*.
6. Lyrics to the song "Locusts and Wild Honey," recorded on the album and published in the songbook, *Locusts and Wild Honey*. Copyright © Weston Priory, Gregory Norbet, O.S.B., 1971.
7. Scripture references: Matthew 3:1–4, 4:4; Mark 1:15.
8. It is interesting to note that the musical *Godspell* (1971) and rock opera *Jesus Christ Superstar* (1973), which were released around the time of *Locusts and Wild Honey*, use similar soloist/ensemble methods to narrate scripture and offer interpretation.
9. The Magnificat and Benedictus are also known as the Canticle of Mary and the Canticle of Zechariah, respectively.
10. Hart uses the phrase "ontological capacity" in his discussion of contemplation and phenomenology to describe the ability to create, "Contemplation," 457.
11. Hemming, *Worship as a Revelation*, 39–40.
12. "Musicking" is a term suggested by Christopher Small, *Musicking*. It highlights that music is a process and not an object. It takes into account all phenomena and activities that happen in, around, before, after, and during the sounds we hear and name "music."
13. Barz and Cooley, *Shadows in the Field*.
14. "Wisdom at Play" is recorded on the album, *Wisdom at Play*. Copyright © Weston Priory, 2011. The music is also published in files downloadable from the Weston Priory website: http://www.westonpriory.org/esales/wisdom_toc.html.
15. Green, *Radical Judaism*, 91.
16. "You Are the Bread" is recorded on the album and published in the songbook, *Parting the Waters*. Copyright © Weston Priory, 1991.
17. "There Is a Way" is recorded on the album and published in the songbook, *Pilgrimage of the Heart*. Copyright © Weston Priory, 2007.
18. "Sabbath's End" is recorded on the album and published in the songbook, *With an Everlasting Love*. Copyright © Weston Priory, 2003.
19. "O Wisdom" is published in the songbook for the album, *Go Up to the Mountain*. Copyright © Weston Priory, Gregory Norbet, O.S.B., 1978.
20. "We Desire You" is recorded on the album, *Wisdom at Play*. Copyright © Weston Priory, 2011. The music is also published in files downloadable from the Weston Priory website: http://www.westonpriory.org/esales/wisdom_toc.html.

Chapter Six

1. DeWaal, *Seeking God*, 92.
2. Ibid., 91.
3. Ibid., 94.

4. Cannell, *Anthropology of Christianity*, 3.
5. On the development of monasticism and its relationship to mysticism, see McGinn, *Foundations of Mysticism*.
6. The twelfth-century monk and founder of the Cistercian Order, Bernard of Clairvaux, picks up on this thread in his sermon *On the Song of Songs*. The fourth-century bishop Saint Gregory of Nyssa provides the foundation for such exegesis and much monastic and mystical spirituality in Gregory of Nyssa, *Commentary on the Song of Songs*.
7. Norris, *Cloister Walk*, 99.
8. Lacoste, *Experience and the Absolute*.

Bibliography

Abbaye Saint-Pierre-de-Solesmes. *Liber Antiphonarius pro Diurnis Horis II, Psalterium.* Solesmes, 2006.
Abbott, Walter M., S.J., ed. *The Documents of Vatican II.* New York: Herder and Herder, 1966.
Adamson, Glenn. *Thinking through Craft.* London: Berg, 2007.
Agamben, Giorgio. *The Highest Poverty: Monastic Rules and Form-of-Life.* Translated by Adam Kotsko. Stanford, CA: Stanford University Press, 2013.
Attridge, Harold W., and Margot Fassler, eds. *Psalms in Community: Jewish and Christian Textual, Liturgical, and Artistic Traditions.* Atlanta: Society of Biblical Literature, 2003.
Barz, Gregory F., and Timothy J. Cooley, eds. *Shadows in the Field: New Perspectives for Fieldwork in Ethnomusicology.* New York: Oxford University Press, 1997.
Becker, Judith. *Deep Listeners: Music, Emotion, and Trancing.* Bloomington: Indiana University Press, 2004.
Bergeron, Katherine. *Decedent Enchantments: The Revival of Gregorian Chant at Solesmes.* Berkeley: University of California Press, 1998.
———. "The Virtual Sacred: Finding God at Tower Records." *New Republic* 212, no. 9 (1995): 29–34.
Bernard of Clairvaux. *On the Song of Songs*, 1–4. Kalamazoo, MI: Cistercian Publications, 1971.
Betjemann, Peter. *Talking Shop: The Language of Craft in an Age of Consumption.* Charlottesville: University of Virginia Press, 2011.
Bishops' Committee on Divine Worship. *Sing to the Lord: Music in Divine Worship.* Washington, DC: United States Council of Catholic Bishops, 2007.
Bohlman, Philip V. et al., eds. *Music in American Religious Experience.* New York: Oxford University Press, 2006.
Bourdieu, Pierre. *The Logic of Practice.* Translated by Richard Nice. Cambridge: Polity Press, 1990.
———. *Language as Symbolic Power.* Cambridge, MA: Harvard University Press, 1991.
Boynton, Susan. *Shaping a Monastic Identity: Liturgy and History at the Imperial Abbey of Farfa, 1000–125.* Ithaca, NY: Cornell University Press, 2006.
Britto, Francis. "The Gender of God: Judeo-Christian Feminist Debates." In *Gender and the Language of Religion*, edited by Allyson Jule, 25–40. New York: Palgrave Macmillan, 2005.
Bronner, Simon J., ed. *Creativity and Tradition in Folklore: New Directions.* Logan: Utah State University Press, 1992.

Butler, Dom Cuthbert, O. S. B. *Western Mysticism: The Teaching of Augustine, Gregory, and Bernard on Contemplation and the Contemplative Life.* 2nd ed. (reprint of the 1922 edition). New York: Harper Torchbooks, 1966.

Butler, Melvin L. "Dancing around Dancehall: Pentecostalism, Popular Culture, and Musical Practice in Transnational Jamaica and Haiti." In *Constructing Vernacular Culture in the Trans-Caribbean*, edited by Holger Henke, Karl-Heinz Magister, and Alissa Trotz, 63–99. Lanham, MD: Lexington Books, 2008.

———. "'Nou Kwe nan Sentespri' (We Believe in the Holy Spirit): Music, Ecstasy, and Identity in Haitian Pentecostal Worship." *Black Music Research Journal* 22, no. 1 (2002): 85–125.

Byrnes, Timothy. *Reverse Mission: Transnational Religious Communities and the Making of U.S. Foreign Policy.* Washington, DC: Georgetown University Press, 2011.

Cannell, Fenella, ed. *The Anthropology of Christianity.* Durham, NC: Duke University Press, 2006.

Casey, Michael. *An Unexciting Life: Reflections on Benedictine Spirituality.* Petersham, MA: St. Bede's Press, 2005.

Cashman, Ray, Tom Mould, and Pravina Shukla, eds. *The Individual and Tradition: Folklorist Perspectives.* Bloomington: Indiana University Press, 2011.

Clifford, James. "Introduction: Partial Truths." In Clifford and Marcus, *Writing Culture*, 1–26.

Clifford, James, and George Marcus, eds. *Writing Culture: The Poetics and Politics of Ethnography.* Berkeley: University of California Press, 1986.

Coleman, Simon, and Peter Collins. "'Being . . . Where?' Performing Fields on Shifting Grounds." In *Locating the Field: Space, Place and Context in Anthropology*, edited by Simon Coleman and Peter Collins, 1–22. Oxford: Berg, 2006.

Collins, Mary, O. S. B. *Contemplative Participation: Sacrosantum Concillium Twenty-Five Years Later.* Collegeville, MN: Liturgical Press, 1990.

Comaroff, John L., and Jean Comaroff. *Ethnography and the Historical Imagination.* Boulder: Westview Press, 1992.

Combe, Dom Pierre, O. S. B. *The Restoration of Gregorian Chant: Solesmes and the Vatican Edition.* Washington, DC: Catholic University of American Press, 1969.

Crawford, Alan. "Ideas and Objects: The Arts and Crafts Movement in Britain." *Design Ideas* 13, no. 1 (1997): 15–26.

Crawford, Matthew. *Shop Class as Soul Craft: An Inquiry into the Value of Work.* New York: Penguin Press, 2009.

Crocker, Richard L. *An Introduction to Gregorian Chant.* New Haven, CT: Yale University Press, 2000.

Crouan, Denis. *The History and Future of the Roman Liturgy.* Translated by Michael Miller. San Francisco: Ignatius Press, 2005.

———. *The Liturgy Betrayed.* Translated by Marc Sebanc. San Francisco: Ignatius Press, 2000.

Davies, Charlotte Aull. *Reflexive Ethnography: A Guide to Researching Selves and Others.* 2nd ed. New York: Routledge, 2008.

Day, Thomas. *Why Catholics Can't Sing: The Culture of Catholicism and the Triumph of Bad Taste.* New York: Crossroad, 1991.

Deiss, Lucien. *Visions of Liturgy and Music for a New Century.* Collegeville, MN: Liturgical Press, 1996.
Denzin, Norman. *Performance Ethnography: Critical Pedagogy and the Politics of Culture.* London: Sage, 2003.
DeWaal, Esther. *Living with Contradiction: An Introduction to Benedictine Spirituality.* New York: Morehouse, 1989.
———. *Seeking God: The Way of St. Benedict.* Collegeville, MN: Liturgical Press, 1984.
DjeDje, Jacqueline Codgell. "Change and Differentiation: The Adoption of Black American Gospel Music in the Catholic Church." *Ethnomusicology* 30, no. 2 (1986): 223–52.
Drewal, Margaret Thompson. *Yoruba Ritual: Performers, Play, Agency.* Bloomington: Indiana University Press, 1992.
Duffy, Eamon. *The Stripping of the Altars: Traditional Religion in England 1400–580.* New Haven, CT: Yale University Press, 1992.
Dufner, Delores, O. S. B. *Sing a New Church.* Portland, OR: OCP Publications, 1994.
Dunne, John S. *The Music of Time: Words and Music and Spiritual Friendship.* Notre Dame: University of Notre Dame Press, 1996.
Dwyer, Kevin. "The Dialogic of Ethnography." *Dialectical Anthropology* 3, no. 1 (1979): 205–24.
———. "On the Dialogic of Fieldwork." *Dialectical Anthropology* 2, no. 1 (1977): 143–51.
———. *Moroccan Dialogues: Anthropology in Question.* Baltimore: Johns Hopkins University Press, 1982.
Foley, Edward, and Mary McGann. *Music and the Eucharistic Prayer.* Collegeville, MN: Liturgical Press, 1988.
Fry, Timothy, ed. *RB 1980: The Rule of St. Benedict in Latin and English with Notes.* Collegeville, MN: Liturgical Press, 1981.
Geertz, Clifford. *Available Light: Anthropological Reflections on Philosophical Topics.* Princeton, NJ: Princeton University Press, 2001.
———. *The Interpretation of Cultures.* New York: Basic Books, 1973.
———. *Works and Lives: The Anthropologist as Author.* Stanford, CA: Stanford University Press, 1988.
Gitlin, Todd. *The Sixties: Years of Hope, Days of Rage.* 2nd ed. New York: Bantam Books, 1993.
Green, Rabbi Arthur. *Radical Judaism: Rethinking God and Tradition.* New Haven, CT: Yale University Press, 2010.
Gregory of Nyssa. *Commentary on the Song of Songs.* Boston: Hellenic Press, 1987.
Gupta, Akhil, and James Ferguson. "Discipline and Practice: 'The Field' as Site, Method, and Location in Anthropology." In *Anthropological Locations: Boundaries and Grounds of a Field Science,* edited by Akhil Gupta and James Ferguson, 1–46. Berkeley: University of California Press, 1997.
Halstead, Narmala, Eric Hirsch, and Judith Okely, eds. *Knowing How to Know: Fieldwork and the Ethnographic Present.* New York: Berghahn Books, 2008.
Hammond, Brother John, O. S. B. *A Benedictine Legacy of Peace: The Life of Leo A. Rudloff.* Weston, VT: Weston Priory, 2005.

Hannerz, Ulf. "Being There . . . and There . . . and There! Reflections on Multi-site Ethnography." *Ethnography* 4, no. 2 (2003): 201–16.
Harmon, Kathleen. *The Mystery We Celebrate, the Song We Sing: A Theology of Liturgical Music.* Collegeville, MN: Liturgical Press, 2008.
Hart, Kevin. "Contemplation: Beyond and Behind." *Sophia* 48, no. 4 (2009): 435–59.
Hemming, Laurence Paul. *Worship as a Revelation: The Past, Present, and Future of Catholic Liturgy.* London: Burns and Oates, 2008.
Hillhouse, Andy. "Reaching Out, Turning Home: The Musical Projects of Fillipo Gambetta, Genoan Organetto Player." *MUSICultures* 40, no. 1 (2013): 100–20.
Hinson, Glenn. *Fire in My Bones: Transcendence and the Holy Spirit in African American Gospel.* Philadelphia: University of Pennsylvania Press, 2000.
Howell, Signe, and Aud Talle. *Returns to the Field: Multitemporal Research and Contemporary Anthropology.* Bloomington: Indiana University Press, 2012.
Husserl, Edmund. *The Crisis of European Sciences and Transcendental Phenomenology.* Evanston, IL: Northwestern University Press, 1970.
———. *Phenomenology of Internal Time Consciousness.* Bloomington: University of Indiana Press, 1964.
Ingalls, Monique, Carolyn Landau, and Tom Wagner, eds. *Christian Congregational Music: Performance, Identity, and Experience.* Burlington, VT: Ashgate, 2013.
Jackson, Michael. *Paths toward a Clearing: Radical Empiricism and Ethnographic Enquiry.* Bloomington: Indiana University Press, 1989.
Joncas, Jan Michael. *From Sacred Song to Ritual Music: Twentieth-Century Understandings of Roman Catholic Worship Music.* Collegeville, MN: Liturgical Press, 1997.
Jones, Michael Owen. *Exploring Folk Art: Twenty Years of Thought on Craft, Work, and Aesthetics.* Ann Arbor, MI: UMI Research Press, 1987.
Kisliuk, Michelle. *Seize the Dance! BaAka Musical Life and the Ethnography of Performance.* New York: Oxford University Press, 1998.
Kohák, Erazim. *Idea and Experience: Edmund Husserl's Project of Phenomenology in Ideas I.* Chicago: University of Chicago Press, 1978.
Kroecker, Charlotte, ed. *Music in Christian Worship: At the Service of the Liturgy.* Collegeville, MN: Liturgical Press, 2005.
Kubicki, Judith Marie. *Liturgical Music as Ritual Symbol: A Case Study of Jacques Berthier's Taizé Music.* Leuven: Peeters, 1999.
———. *The Presence of Christ in the Gathered Assembly.* New York: Continuum, 2006.
Lacoste, Jean-Yves. *Experience and the Absolute: Disputed Questions on the Humanity of Man*, translated by Mark Raftery-Skeban. New York: Fordham University Press, 2004.
Lewin, Ellen. "Writing Lesbian Ethnography." In *Women Writing Culture*, edited by Ruth Behar and Deborah Gordon, 322–35. Berkeley: University of California Press, 1995.
Mahrt, William. "Toward a Revision of Music in Catholic Worship." *Sacred Music* 134, no. 1 (2007): 54–60.
Marcus, George E. "Ethnography in/of the World System: The Emergence of Multi-sited Ethnography." *Annual Review of Anthropology* 24 (1995): 95–117.

McGann, Mary E. *Exploring Music as Worship and Theology: Research in Liturgical Practice.* Collegeville, MN: Liturgical Press, 2002.

McGinn, Bernard. *The Foundations of Mysticism: Origins to the Fifth Century.* New York: Crossroad, 1991.

———. *The Growth of Mysticism: Gregory the Great through the Twelfth Century.* New York: Crossroad, 1994.

Meeks, Blair Gilmer, ed. *The Landscape of Praise: Readings in Liturgical Renewal.* Valley Forge, PA: Trinity Press International, 1996.

Merton, Thomas. *New Seeds of Contemplation.* New York: New Directions, 1961.

———. *The Seven Storey Mountain.* New York: Harcourt, Brace, 1948.

Mooney, Catherine M. "Voice, Gender, and the Portrayal of Sanctity." In *Gendered Voices: Medieval Saints and Their Interpreters*, edited by Catherine Mooney, 1–15. Philadelphia: University of Pennsylvania Press, 1999.

Morris, Brian. "In Defense of Realism and Truth: Critical Reflections on the Anthropological Followers of Heidegger." *Critique of Anthropology* 17, no. 3 (1997): 313–40.

Morrow, Susan Brind. *The Names of Things: A Passage in the Egyptian Desert.* New York: Riverhead Books, 1997.

Norris, Kathleen. *The Cloister Walk.* New York: Riverhead Books, 1996.

Okely, Judith. "Knowing without Notes." In Halstead, Hirsch, and Okley, *Knowing How to Know*, 55–74.

Oliveros, Pauline. *Deep Listening: A Composer's Sound Practice.* Lincoln, NE: iUniverse, 2005.

Ratzinger, Joseph Cardinal (Pope Benedict XVI). *The Spirit of the Liturgy.* San Francisco: Ignatius Press, 2000.

Rippinger, Joel, O. S. B. *The Benedictine Order in the United States: An Interpretive History.* Collegeville, MN: Liturgical Press, 1990.

Risatti, Howard. *A Theory of Craft: Function and Aesthetic Expression.* Chapel Hill: University of North Carolina Press, 2007.

Rommen, Timothy. *"Mek Some Noise": Gospel Music and the Ethics of Style in Trinidad.* Berkeley: University of California Press, 2007.

Sawin, Patricia. *Listening for a Life: A Dialogic Ethnography of Bessie Eldreth through Her Songs and Stories.* Logan: Utah State University Press, 2004.

Sennett, Richard. *The Craftsman.* New Haven, CT: Yale University Press, 2009.

Sklar, Deidre. *Dancing with the Virgin: Body and Faith in the Fiesta of Tortugas, New Mexico.* Berkeley: University of California Press, 2001.

Small, Christopher. *Musicking: The Meaning of Performing and Listening.* Middletown, CT: Wesleyan University Press, 1998.

Suñol, Dom Gregory, O. S. B. *Textbook of Gregorian Chant according to the Solesmes Method.* Translated from the sixth French edition with an introduction by G. M. Durnford, O. S. B. O. Tournai, Belgium: Society of St. John Evangelist Desclée & Co, Printers to the Holy See, 1930.

Taft, Robert. *The Liturgy of the Hours in East and West: The Origins of the Divine Office and Its Meaning for Today.* Collegeville. MN: Liturgical Press, 1996.

Tedlock, Dennis. "The Analogical Tradition and the Emergence of a Dialogical Anthropology." *Journal of Anthropological Research* 34, no. 4 (1979): 387–400.

———. "Questions Concerning Dialogical Anthropology." *Journal of Anthropological Research* 43, no. 4 (1987): 325–37.

Titon, Jeff Todd. *Powerhouse for God: Speech, Chant, and Song in an Appalachian Baptist Church.* Austin: University of Texas Press, 1988.

Ulin, Robert. "Critical Anthropology Twenty Years Later." *Critique of Anthropology* 11, no. 1 (1991): 63–89.

Underberg, Natalie, and Elayne Zorn. *Digital Ethnography: Anthropology, Narrative, and New Media.* Austin: University of Texas Press, 2013.

Walser, Robert. "The Polka Mass: Music of Postmodern Ethnicity." *American Music* 10, no. 2 (1992): 183–202.

Ward, Benedicta, ed. and trans. *The Desert Fathers: Sayings of the Early Christian Monks.* New York: Penguin Books, 2003.

Warner, Marina. *Alone of All Her Sex: The Myth and Cult of the Virgin Mary.* New York: Knopf, 1976.

Watson, C. W., ed. "Introduction: The Quality of Being There." In *Being There: Fieldwork in Anthropology*, edited by C. W. Watson, 1–24. London: Pluto Press, 1999.

Wathen, Ambrose C., O. S. B. *Silence: The Meaning of Silence in the Rule of St. Benedict.* Washington, DC: Cistercian Publications Consortium Press, 1973.

Westbrook, David A. *Navigators of the Contemporary: Why Ethnography Matters.* Chicago: University of Chicago Press, 2008.

Index

Abba Poeman, 26
Agamben, Giorgio, 76
Augustine, brother: on craft, 99–104; on monastic vocation, 41; on Weston music, 86
authenticity, 121, 130, 132, 148, 165n3; in Gregorian chant, 58–59, 88; music and, 83–85, 118; tradition and, 65, 126–27; vernacular and, 20, 83–84
authority, 116, 123, 144, 153–54; tradition as, 120; music and, 83–85

balance, 29, 60, 66–67, 74, 89, 96, 101–2, 104–10, 128, 143–45, 151; *conversatio* and, 12, 77, 124
Benedict, Saint, 2, 40, 47, 62, 63, 77, 122, 152, 157; on balance, 104; on craft, 91, 107; on listening, 14; on order of liturgy, 53; on ownership, 106–7; on Psalmody, 53, 65–66; on silence, 2; on singing, 53. *See also* Rule of Benedict
Benedictines, American, 40–41; American-Cassinese congregation, 41, 81; Swiss-American congregation, 41
Benedictines, history of, 40–41, 58–60, 119; nineteenth-century revival, 40–41, 58–60
Bergeron, Katherine, 6, 57–59
Beuron Congregation, 80–82
Bourdieu, Pierre, 84, 120, 165n3
Byrnes, Timothy, 113

Cannell, Fanella, 144

Casey, Michael, 3
Catholicism, 5, 20, 36, 82; American, 20, 41, 117–21
chant, 21–22, 43–46, 57–60, 65–67, 79, 126, 136; antiphonal, 71–75, 78–81, 113–14, 169n9 (chap. 3); chanted psalms, 70–74, 89, 133, 161, 169n3, 169n9 (chap. 3); Compline, 54–57, 69–74; language and, 52, 83–85; Morning Vigil, 2, 21–23, 27–28, 115; *None*, 86; spirit of, 88–89; spirituality and, 88–89; Vespers, 51–52, 133–34. *See also* chant, Gregorian; psalmody
chant, Gregorian, 4, 20, 38, 43–46, 48, 51–52, 54–60, 65–67, 79, 80, 86–89, 122, 125, 134, 165n3; nineteenth-century restoration, 57–60, 83–85
coaffection, 157
Coleman, Simon, 17–18
collectivity: collective consciousness, 3, 20, 83, 107, 158; in ethnography, 14, 18, 163; individuality and, 128, 132; in liturgical music, 71–74, 120–21; in monastic life, 2, 108, 133, 139; in prayer (liturgy), 23, 27, 28, 57, 71–74, 83–84, 112, 115, 120–21, 163; tradition and, 107–8, 116, 120–21, 125. *See also* composition, collective; unity
Collins, Peter, 17–18
community life, 13, 64–65, 99, 104–8
Compline, 4, 21, 28, 52–57, 67–75, 110, 121, 150, 155, 162
composition, 128–29, 159–64; collective, 134–41, 148

contemplation, contemplative, 1, 13–16, 16–17, 29, 41, 60, 75, 97, 105–6, 108, 116, 130, 133, 135, 137, 140, 147–48; in anthropology, 15–16; criticisms of, 15–16; definition of, 15; monastic spirituality and, 152, 157–58, 161–64. *See also* contemplative ethnography; sensibility, contemplative
contemplative ethnography, 3–4, 13–16, 18–19, 157–64
conversatio, 10–15, 19, 76–77, 105, 121, 124, 135, 163–64
craft, 91–110, 125, 128, 139–40, 143: as counterculture, 98; as distinct from art, 91–92; as monastic sensibility, 104–10; baking, 91–97; definition of, 92; ethnography as, 13, 163–64; music as, 20, 91–92, 103, 111–41; pottery, 97–104; prayer as, 163
creativity, 82–83, 85, 92, 98, 100–101, 116–32, 139, 148. *See also under* tradition
Crocker, Richard, 43, 57

Daniel, brother: on monastic vocation, 35; work period, 33–37
deep listening. *See* listening, deep
Desert Fathers and Mothers, 26, 89, 119
devotion, Marian. *See* Marian Devotion
DeWaal, Esther, 143–44
dialogue(s): in ethnography, 4, 10–13, 15–16, 20, 65, 75–76, 139–40, 163–64, 166n18; in liturgy, 84, 148–51; in monastic life, 3, 77, 85, 100, 108, 121, 127, 139–40; in musical performance, 71–72, 139–40
Divine Office (Liturgy of the Hours), 1, 2, 6, 11, 22–23, 44, 51, 54, 59, 61, 67, 77–79, 80, 83, 85, 87–88, 119–20, 124, 130, 139; order of, Rule of Benedict, 21, 53; order of, Weston Priory, 4, 67, 133–34
Dormition Abbey, 40, 82, 111, 154
Duffy, Eamon, 82

Dunne, John, 142
Dwyer, Kevin, 15–16

Elias, brother: on Gregorian chant, 66; on monastic vocation, 38–39, 152–54
ethnography, 21–42, 139; contemplative, 3–4, 13–16; *conversatio* in, 12–13; ethnographic knowledge, 31; ethnographic research and writing, 3, 17–19, 144; field notes, 93–94, 96–97, 108–10, 139, 143, 150; language in, 6–7, 31–32; listening in, 13–14, 19; memory in, 31; as *metanoia*, 20; performance in, 16–19; reflexivity in, 4, 9–16, 18–19; silence in, 3, 19; understanding the unfamiliar, 2, 8, 139, 144; as vocation, 3. *See also* contemplative ethnography; dialogues; reflexivity
epistemology. *See* way of knowing
exegesis, 79, 119–20, 172n6

Feuerbach, Ludwig, 16
fidelity, 12, 95, 97, 163
field notes. *See under* ethnography
field research. *See* contemplative ethnography; ethnography
Folk Mass, 117–19
folk music, 4, 43, 44, 84, 87, 93, 117–19, 126

Geertz, Clifford, 9, 16
gender, 48, 56, 70, 169n8 (chap. 3)
Gerleve Abbey, 39, 40, 80
Green, Arthur, 111, 124, 130
Guéranger, Prosper, 58–59, 81
guitar: as craft, 103–4, 163; in post-Vatican II liturgy, 51, 117–18; and spirituality, 160–61; at Weston Priory, 20, 21–22, 27, 28, 67–70, 74–75, 84–90, 114–18, 125–26, 130, 133, 136–38, 159–61, 162–63

habitus, 84, 120

Hammond, John (brother John): on craft, 91–92; on Gregorian chant, 43–46; on his monastic vocation, 43–46, 80; on language, 11–12, 82–85, 121–24; on liturgical reform, 122–24; on monastic profession, 76–77; on music as craft, 91–92; on performance, 122; on play, 124; on prayer, 1, 72, 73, 83–85; on singing, 61, 72, 73; on spirituality, 149, 151; on unity, 72, 73; on Vatican II, 82, 122–24; on Weston Priory music, 80–85
Hart, Kevin, 15
Hemming, Laurence, 122–24, 165n3
historical consciousness, 85, 120, 121, 130, 132
humility, 24, 91, 100–102
Husserl, Edmund, 16, 69–70

imago dei, 157
individual-communal dialectic, 104–8, 116, 137, 141, 157, 164
intersubjectivity, 14–15, 164, 166n18. *See also* space, interpersonal

John, brother. *See* Hammond, John
John the Baptist, 119–20

kitchen, social dimensions of, 61. *See also* monastery labor
Kohák, Erazim, 14–15

labor (work). *See* monastery labor
Lacoste, Jean-Yves, 157
language, 50–52, 59, 79, 111, 127, 130, 148; in ethnography, 7–8, 31–32, 48–49; in liturgical music, 44–46, 70, 83–85; in liturgy, 54–56, 81–85, 86–87, 121–24. *See also* vernacular
Latin America, 112–13
lectio divina, 105, 162
Leo, brother. *See* Rudloff, Leo
"Listen" (song), 111–16

listening, 4, 15, 18, 29, 74, 77, 114–16, 124, 140; with ear of the heart, 13–14, 19, 142–64; as liturgical theme, 23; deep, 15, 72, 116, 164; in ethnography, 13–14, 19, 162–64, 166n14; as monastic sensibility, 12–15, 29, 100, 135, 152, 156–57, 162–64
liturgical movement, 5, 39, 81, 121–24
liturgical music, 43–46, 51–52, 59, 65–67, 78–85, 139, 165n3; Alleluia, 21–22; call to prayer, 69, 162; language, 44–46, 82–85; Morning Vigil, 21–23; O Antiphons, 133–34; post-Vatican II, 117–21; spirituality, 89. *See also* chant; chant, Gregorian; guitar; psalmody
liturgy: authority in, 84, 116; Catholic, 81–84; common prayer as, 121–24; function of, 122–24; language in, 54–56, 81–89, 86–87; monastic, 22, 61, 70, 77–80, 85, 89, 157–58, 170n14; participation in, 122–23; study of, 52–53, 59, 165nn2–3; vernacular, 81–89, 116–19, 123–24. *See also* Divine Office; music, liturgical; Second Vatican Council
Liturgy of the Hours. *See* Divine Office
local, concept of: in liturgy, 83–85, 89, 116, 119–20; in monasticism, 39, 50, 52, 67, 73–74, 116, 121, 130, 132; in musical performance, 83–85, 89, 119–20, 141, 148; in social structures, 73–74
"Locusts and Wild Honey" (song), 117–21

Marian devotion, 56, 74, 169n8 (chap. 2)
Mark, brother: on baking, 91–97; on sung prayer, 73; on unity, 73
McGinn, Bernard, 15, 166n3
Merton, Thomas, 41, 137; on contemplation, 1; on Gregorian chant, 43; on writing and monastery life, 16–17

Michael, brother: on balance, 105, 128; on belief, 150-51; on composition, 128, 159–62; on craft, 91–92; on Divine Office (liturgy of the hours), 61, 77; on gender and language, 70; on liturgical music, 65–67; on monastic vocation, 123, 128; on performance, 127–28, 159–62; on play, 128; on sung prayer, 72; on tradition, 123–27

monachos, 2–3, 18

monastery labor (work), 32–37, 67, 91–110, 142–48, 156; animal husbandry, 33–37, 144–48; baking, 91–97; beekeeping, 36–37, 146–47; kitchen, 61–67, 91–97; pottery, 97–104; Rule of Benedict, 32

monastic life: balance in, 66–67, 96, 101–2, 104–10; contradictions in, 106–8; difficulties adjusting to, 5–6, 26, 29, 75, 109, 156–57; division of labor, 67; experience of time in, 85; history of, 78–79; humility in, 91, 100–102; rhythms of, 6, 37, 53, 85, 88, 110, 129, 132, 143; rituals in, 88, 97, 109; role of liturgy in, 72, 85; sources of, 134; vows, 76–77, 105, 152, 163. *See also* monasticism, cenobitic

monasticism, cenobitic, 2, 76, 78, 106, 152

Morning Vigil, 1–2, 4, 8, 21–27, 28–33, 67, 85, 111–16, 129–31, 142, 161–62

Morris, Brian, 16

music as craft. *See* craft, music as

"musical *metanoia*," 20, 158–64

musical performance. *See* performance, musical

musicianship, monastic, 161. *See also* musical *metanoia*

mystical turns, 152, 157–58, 164. *See also* coaffection

mysticism, Christian, 15, 93, 137, 155–58. *See also* spirituality, mystical

None (Divine Office prayer), 4, 21, 53, 67, 78–80, 86, 96

Norris, Kathleen, 156
novitiate, 76, 91–110

obedience, 76–77, 105, 153, 163
Okely, Judith, 31
ontology. *See* way of being

participant-observation, 5, 11
"Peace to You" (song), 74
performance, 52, 116, 127–28, 139–40; in ethnography, 16–19, 166n10; in liturgy, 72, 84, 119–20; memory in, 120–22. *See also* performance, musical
performance, musical, 3, 20, 59, 72, 119–20, 134, 137, 159; deep listening and, 15; as way of knowing, 13, 162–63. *See also* dialogues, in musical performance; local, concept of in musical performance; space, in musical performance
Peter, brother: on craft, 99–104; on creativity, 100; on historical consciousness, 85; on monastic profession, 102; on unity in prayer, 73
Philip, brother, 5–6, 111, 136–37; on silence, 142
play, 15, 18, 70, 99–100, 136, 124–30, 154–55
prayer: common prayer, 89, 121–24, 139; music as, 135, 161–64; sung prayer, 71–75, 88, 122–23. *See also* chant; chant, Gregorian; Divine Office; liturgical music; psalmody
presence, 1–4, 27, 29, 49–50, 57, 71; being present, 1–4; in ethnography, 1–2, 12–19, 109–10, 127, 143; in monastic life, 1–2, 74, 95, 97, 100; of God, 52–53, 61, 152, 156–57, 161
psalmody, 53, 67–74, 78–79, 169–70n9 (chap. 3)

refectory, 6, 11, 19, 61–63, 65, 67, 85; breakfast, 27–30; silence in, 27–30, 94–95, 152, 156, 158; Thanksgiving, 129–33
reflexivity, 4, 9–19, 166n10

reverse mission, 113
Rudloff, Leo (brother Leo), 50, 66, 80–82, 87, 111, 115–16, 123, 151, 153–54; founding of Weston Priory, 38–41
Rule of Benedict, 39–41, 51, 54, 58, 120, 122, 151; on balance, 66, 104; on community life, 106; on Compline, 52, 70, 110; on *conversatio*, 12; on craft, 91, 104, 106–7; on Divine Office (daily prayers), 21, 52–54, 65, 70, 152; on humility, 91; on labor (work), 32, 91, 97; on listening, 13–14, 115–16; on meals, food, 62; on silence, 2, 27–28; on singing, 52, 61
Ryle, Gilbert, 9

Saint Benedict. *See* Benedict, Saint
Saint-Benoît-du-Lac, 20, 45–60, 65–67, 70, 79–81, 121, 126; founding narrative, 50–51
Second Vatican Council (Vatican II), 5, 39, 51, 81–85, 121–24; active participation in liturgy, 117–18, 121–24; post-Vatican II liturgy, 86–90, 117–21, 124, 165n3; *Sacrosanctum Concilium* (Constitution on the Sacred Liturgy), 81–82
sensibility: Benedictine, 11, 116, 152; contemplative, 13–17, 75, 108; monastic, 54, 72, 74, 104–5, 135, 152, 157
silence, 49–50, 93–94, 124, 130; Grand Silence, 28–30, 32, 75, 94–95; in ethnography, 3, 15, 19; in monastic life, 2–3, 6, 12, 22–23, 26, 28–30, 60, 77, 105, 156, 158, 161; in monastic liturgy (prayer), 69, 89, 112
social structures: egalitarian, 73, 106–7, 148; gender and, 48; monastic hierarchy, 41, 66–67, 168n5 (chap. 1)
Solesmes: Abbey (Saint-Pierre-de-Solesmes), 45, 50, 57–60, 88–89; congregation, 80–81
space, interpersonal, 3–4; in ethnography, 8–10, 13–14, 18–19,

139–40; in liturgy, 72–73, 157–58; in musical performance, 72–73, 139–40; as way of knowing, 13–14
spirituality: listening as, 135; monastic, 3, 119–20, 135, 142–64; mystical, 116, 135, 142–64

tradition, 52, 92, 104, 107–8, 134, 140, 144, 148; as authority, 120; creating, 111–41, 162; creativity and, 116–21, 125, 127–30, 132; living, 85, 89–90; performing, 141

unity: as common voice, 85, 119–20; in liturgical music, 57, 71–74, 163; in monastery life, 37, 73–74, 107, 148, 152, 154; in prayer, 71–74, 163
Ulin, Robert, 16

Vatican II. *See* Second Vatican Council
vernacular, 20, 44, 52, 67, 82–89, 116–18; as common voice, 85, 89, 116, 123–24. *See also* liturgy, vernacular
Vespers, 4, 21, 50–53, 103–4, 108, 132–34, 149–51, 163
Vigil. *See* Morning Vigil

Watson, C. W., 9–10
way of being (way of life, form of life), 2, 8, 11–18, 20, 23, 28–29, 31, 37–41, 46, 48, 58–60, 74, 76–77, 80, 84–85, 88, 98, 104–8, 116, 120–21, 135, 143–48, 153, 155, 158, 160, 162–64
way of knowing, 3, 9, 14–15, 17, 19–20, 57, 143–48, 151, 162–63
"We Desire You" (song), 136–38
"We Gather" (song), 161–63
Weston Priory, history of, 37–42, 43–46. *See also* Weston Priory music
Weston Priory music, 4–5, 21–23, 43–46, 67–75; history of, 76–90
Wimmer, Boniface, 40–41
Winzen, Damasus, 39–40
Wisdom at Play (album), 125–26
"Wisdom at Play," (song), 125–26, 130, 159
World War II, 39, 41

www.ingramcontent.com/pod-product-compliance
Lightning Source LLC
Chambersburg PA
CBHW060952230426
43665CB00015B/2170